1994

OWEN THE POET

Dominic Hibberd

A boy, I guessed that the fullest, largest liveable life was that of a Poet.
(5 March 1915)

I was introduced as 'Mr Owen, Poet' or even 'Owen, the poet'.
(26 January 1918)

THE UNIVERSITY OF GEORGIA PRESS

Published in the United States of America in 1986 by
The University of Georgia Press
Athens, Georgia 30602

First published in Great Britain by
The Macmillan Press

Printed in Hong Kong

Library of Congress Cataloging in Publication Data

Hibberd, Dominic.
Owen the Poet.

Bibliography: p.
Includes index.
1. Owen, Wilfred, 1893–1918. 2. Poets, English—20th
century—Biography. 3. World War, 1914–1918—
Literature and the war. I. Title.
PR6029.W4Z66 1986   821'.912 [B]   86–1915
ISBN 0–8203–0858–7

Contents

List of Plates

Preface

This book is a study of what Wilfred Owen called his 'poethood'. It examines his origins and growth as a poet, his understanding of his poetic role, and the unity of his imaginative life, and it assesses his achievement. The publication of almost all his verse and letters, and the release of his surviving books and papers for research and quotation, have at last made it possible to consider his work as a whole. My subject is the poet and his work, rather than the man, so my principal source has been his manuscripts; but biography is included when his poetry can be illuminated by material not fully recorded elsewhere. The poet who emerges is not the impersonal voice of pity presented by the 1920 edition, nor the archetypal soldier poet of Blunden's memoir (1931), nor the champion of pacifism and social reconstruction that some modern critics have described; he is far from the unworldly idealist portrayed by Harold Owen and not quite the straightforward, innocent character shown in Jon Stallworthy's biography. Some commentators have come close to splitting Owen into two people, one before the trenches and one after, but Professor Stallworthy rightly gives him a single identity. There is an unbroken continuity from the lay assistant defying Revival in 1912, through the Aesthete admired by Tailhade in 1914 and the soldier in training and at war in 1916–17, to the poet of 1918. For that reason his early verse is worth more attention than critics have usually given it; unpromising though some of it may seem, it was the foundation for his mature work. His 1918 poetry, written in emotion deliberately 'recollected in tranquillity' as he contemplated 'the inwardness of war' in his cottage room at Ripon – perhaps the last Romantic undertaking in English poetry – deserves more recognition in the history of literature than it has so far received. By temperament and training he was exactly suited to becoming 'the poet of the war', and he has no rival for that title. For one year, beginning in October 1917, no one, soldier or civilian, wrote English poetry more significant than his.

Owen holds a transitional place between the nineteenth century and Modernism, inheriting the aspirations and moral urgency of the Romantics and Victorians but seeing the need for Modernist 'insensibility'. His poethood was shaped by Romantic dedication, Victorian energy, Evangelical fervour, the French and English Decadence, and Georgian innovation. By nature receptive and venerating, with a quick ear for voices, he became, as Murry said of him, 'the splendid borrower who lends a new significance to that which he takes', making original poetry out of material eagerly gathered from wherever he could find it. Passionately bookish but lacking the education that might have dampened his enthusiasm, he found himself in a period which brought culture into unusually violent contact with current events, so that he became a figure in history whom history books will always quote; but, just as the war grew out of the nineteenth-century culture which preceded it, so Owen's war poems were in embryo long before he ever guessed at the nightmare of the trenches. And they speak to our world still, as they were meant to do.

I have not attempted in this book to tackle the large and difficult question of Owen-as-spokesman and whether his view of the war was representative, realistic, useful or in the interests of stable peace. Some historians (John Terraine, for example) have suggested that it may not have been all of those things. The immense shift in general perceptions of the Great War that has developed since about 1930 has undoubtedly distorted the modern image of Owen, but perhaps all shades of opinion could agree that he has done as much as anyone to prevent the reading public from being persuaded ever again that death in battle is 'sweet and decorous'. *Poetry of the Great War: An Anthology*, edited by John Onions and myself (1986), gives some of the context of the war and its mass of verse in which – and against which – Owen's poems were written. I have not attempted here, either, to offer close 'evaluative' criticism of most of his poetry; critical studies by other hands are available in my *Casebook* (1981) and elsewhere, but the best close reading so far is that by Desmond Graham in *The Truth of War* (1984). I have tried not to repeat detailed research when it has already been published, referring instead to the notes and articles in which it first appeared. Over the years one's findings multiply and one's opinions alter; in cases of difference between this book and earlier publications of mine, I hope the book gets it right.

Quotations from Owen's verse are from *The Collected Poems and Fragments* (*CPF*), edited by Jon Stallworthy (1983), except that some passages from drafts which Owen never fully revised are my own readings from the originals, sometimes simplified to show what I take to be his intentions; a few phrases not in *CPF* are quoted from manuscript; and a few amendments to *CPF* are made, usually silently, as a result of recent checks against manuscripts. Owen's spelling is usually corrected. Words cancelled by him are in square brackets. See also Appendix B. Other sources are given in the Appendixes and Bibliography.

My principal debt is to Professor Stallworthy, not only for his labours as editor and biographer but also for his unstinted generosity in making manuscripts available and sharing his knowledge of Owen. It is in the nature of research that one has to record one's disagreements with other people's published conclusions more often than one's agreements, but despite the quibbles in my notes I accept far more than I doubt of his portrait of Owen and his text of the poems. I am also most grateful to Mr Leslie Gunston for his help and friendship and for so generously giving his Owen treasures to the collection at Oxford. Mr John Bell's editing of both the letters and Harold Owen's memoirs has been of inestimable value to Owen studies. I am indebted to the pioneering research of Professor Dennis Welland and the more recent work of Dr Sven Bäckman. Many people have kindly given me information, answered letters and sent me articles, including Mr Sydney Brock and other members of Dr Brock's family; Dr Philip Boardman; Dr Jennifer Breen; M Jean Loisy; Mrs Jean Mitchell and Mrs K. A. Jackson of North Queensferry; Mr F. J. Nicholson; Mr Martin Seymour-Smith; Mr M. M. Stuart; and Mr Simon Wormleighton. Professor Sir William Trethowan has been good enough to read my shellshock chapters. Dr Kathleen McKilligan, Dr Roger Pooley and Mr Tom Coulthard have read other chapters, and Mr James McLaverty and Mr John Onions have gallantly read and savaged the whole typescript; the book, though faulty still, is much the better for their wise advice. I have received tireless assistance from the staff of the English Faculty Library, Oxford, particularly from Miss Margaret Weedon, who established the Owen Collection there with the utmost skill and efficiency. Other librarians and archivists have been unfailingly helpful at the British Library (Manuscript Room and Newspaper Library); the Birmingham Reference Library (War Poetry Collection); King's College Library, Cambridge; the Imperial War Museum; the University Library, Keele (Sociological Society papers); the Brotherton Library, University of Leeds (Gosse Collection); the Berg Collection, New York Public Library (Marsh correspondence); the Bodleian Library, Oxford (Western manuscripts); the National Library of Scotland (Geddes papers); Sheffield Central Library (Carpenter Collection); the Shrewsbury Reference Library; and the Humanities Research Center, University of Texas at Austin. I am grateful to the British Academy for the grant that enabled me to visit Austin.

Acknowledgements are due to the following for permission to quote copyright material: the Owen Estate and Chatto & Windus Ltd, London, and W. W. Norton & Co. Inc., New York, for Wilfred Owen's poems, mainly from the *Collected Poems and Fragments*; the Owen Estate and Oxford University Press for Owen's letters, mainly from the *Collected Letters*, edited by Harold Owen and John Bell; Sir Rupert Hart-Davis for extracts from Siegfried Sassoon's unpublished letters; Mr George Sassoon and Viking Penguin Inc., New York, for Sassoon's published poems; Mr Robert Graves and the Brotherton Library, Leeds, for an extract from an unpublished 1917 letter; Mrs E. Scott Moncrieff for an extract from an unpublished letter by Charles Scott Moncrieff; the Rupert Brooke Estate for an unpublished passage from a 1907 letter; and the Harry Ransom Humanities Research Center, University of Texas at Austin, for extracts from various manuscripts.

I am grateful to Mr John Killham, Mr Leslie Gunston, Mr Sydney Brock and Mrs Gwen Hampshire for their help in obtaining photographs. Illustrations are reproduced by permission of John Killham (1), the Southampton Art Gallery (2), the Owen Estate (3, 4, 5, 15), Leslie Gunston (6, 7), Sydney Brock (8), the British Library (11, 14), the Royal National Institute for the Blind (12) and the Imperial War Museum (13).

1 The Origins of a Poethood

In the decade before the First World War the country town of Shrewsbury was remote from centres of culture, too far for a lower-middle-class schoolboy there to discover much about new developments in literature. It was still important to be earnest, at any rate in a piously Evangelical household. In school, poetry was still Romantic poetry (the respectable sort), its theory laid down by Wordsworth, its emotions and language exemplified in Tennyson and (rather to excess) in Keats. Wilfred Owen worked hard, writing neat essays on the standard authors. He later took pleasure in believing that his poetic vocation came from his native landscape, where he was a worshipper among the hills in Wordsworthian fashion as well as a properly Ruskinian botanist, geologist and archaeologist, but the beginnings of what he later called his 'poethood' had as much to do with books and religion as with nature. In his early years he was very bookish and devout, belonging entirely to the nineteenth century. His seriousness was as typical of that age as it is alien to ours; it is easy to laugh at him, but not very useful.

His artistic ambitions probably began to take shape while he was at school. He was certainly a keen student of literature, as can be seen from some 1907–8 exercise books[1] which show him working on the *Faerie Queene*, at least ten Shakespeare plays and many other texts that were to be of use to him later. His teacher seems to have had a particular interest in the Romantics, although she wrote 'Too strong!' against a 1908 comment that the eighteenth century had lacked 'imagination and moral nature'. She did not argue when he said in the same essay that Wordsworth and his followers, directly inspired by nature, had brought to literature 'a new sympathy with man especially the poor', a statement which gives a clue to the origins of what he described at the end of 1917 as his lifelong 'sympathy for the oppressed'.

1

Love of nature, belief in the imagination, and sympathy with suffering were characteristics which the would-be poet would have to encourage in himself. In his schoolboy thoughts about poetry and its function, Owen was a Wordsworthian, a position he never fully abandoned.

His only attempt to write a poem about the start of his poetic career seems to have been jotted down in the summer of 1914, while he was in Bagnères. The principal event for him in that momentous August was not the war but his being introduced to Laurent Tailhade, whose own commitment to poetry had begun long before in that part of France. Owen had already noticed that one of the local hills resembled one in Shropshire.[2] Going for a solitary walk under the moon and wondering what the war was going to mean for a poet, he took stock of his past; his memory went back to a Cheshire holiday ten years earlier, where 'at Broxton, by the Hill . . . was born / [Out of a dark and disobedient] moon so sweet and [so forlorn] . . . my [poethood]'.[3] There was probably some myth-making in this, but no doubt Broxton (Plate 1) had provided his first strong imaginative stimulus. He referred to its bluebells and heather in later letters. The hills of Cheshire and Shropshire, steep grassy ridges rising abruptly from the plain to flat tops covered in 'herb and heather', were always where his imagination felt most at home. His attic room in Shrewsbury looked towards Haughmond Hill and the Wrekin, and beyond them to Caer Caradoc and the Long Mynd, those 'landscapes whereupon my windows lean' which feature from time to time in his verse and letters and which seem to be reflected in the setting of 'Spring Offensive'.

Those 'blue remembered hills', as Housman had called them, were Welsh border country. Owen was Welsh by descent on both sides, a fact which he valued because he held the Victorian view that imagination and strong, often melancholy emotions were Celtic endowments. The elegiac strain and musical elaboration of his mature work are qualities typical not only of Tailhade's *ballades élégiaques* but also of ancient Welsh verse. Even during the action in which he won the Military Cross in 1918 he remembered those earlier soldier poets, 'my forefathers the agile Welshmen of the Mountains'. Doing some more myth-making while he was in France in 1914, he said his strength of feeling was a sign of an artistic temperament and suggested it was an inherited quality that could also be seen in his mother's brother (who had taken to drink) and an Owen aunt (who 'literally palpitates with physical sensation'). Welsh blood was even more worth having if it could be shown to be poisoned; he may have been reading about Baudelaire and other *poètes maudits* who had considered that a tainted ancestry and a capacity for exquisite 'physical sensation' were necessary attributes for a poet.[4]

Whether or not his poethood began at Broxton, there is no evidence that he wrote any serious verse much before April 1911, when, having left school and being 'in a ferment' of hopes and fears about his future, he fell predictably 'in love' with Keats.[5] Like many Victorians before him, he started his juvenilia by imitating Keats in a spate of poems, most of which can be paired with their originals: 'Before reading a Biography of Keats for the first time' ('On First Looking into Chapman's Homer'), 'Sonnet written at Teignmouth, on a Pilgrimage to Keats's House' ('Sonnet Written in the Cottage where Burns was Born'), 'On seeing a lock of Keats's Hair' ('On Seeing a Lock of Milton's Hair'), 'To Poesy' (a youthful declaration of faith like those in 'Sleep and Poetry' and *Endymion*), and others.[6] There are also several prose notes for sonnets that never got written, including this: 'Down by the outlet of the Teign, it is a fascinating sight to watch the brave current in its last moments quenching the breakers that incessantly fight to roll it up. It is like a new dating on his doom.'[7] The allusion to *The Fall of Hyperion* ('Thou hast dated on / Thy doom') shows the young devotee's interest in a poem which was eventually to be echoed in 'Strange Meeting'. The note is also an early example of his habit of sharing in or imitating the experiences of an admired poet. He marked personal details in Colvin's biography of Keats, particularly when they seemed to coincide with his own, noticing that Keats's mind was 'naturally unapt for dogma', that Keats and Hunt were given to 'luxuriating' over 'deliciousness', and that Reynolds came from Shrewsbury and 'lacked health and energy'. He involved himself similarly in the poems. *Endymion* and 'Lamia' kept his pencil especially busy as he underlined the rich vocabulary and marked the lush descriptions, including that of the sleeping Adonis. A bookmarker in *Endymion*, embroidered with the text 'Create in me a clean heart O God', seems to have prayed in vain among sensuous passages in which he evidently delighted, but perhaps guilt overcame him after reading 'Lamia' because four pages of erotic description have been carefully stuck together.[8]

However, too much has been made of Owen's passion for Keats. Critics give it prominence almost as a matter of routine, without paying enough attention to other influences. Mentions of Keats are common in Owen's letters until 1915 but after that they decrease and by 1918 disappear. Even in 1914 he looked back with some embarrassment on the days when he had supposed 'all Poetry' to be contained 'in J. Keats', blaming his ignorance on the narrowness of his life in Shrewsbury.[9] The pattern of his 1911 enthusiasm was repeated in other years: a biography, some pilgrimages, reverential study, and then compositions in the style of the new master. There had been a Coleridge pilgrimage in 1910 and there were probably several Shelley ones in 1912. But 1911 was the year for Keats. Owen explored Teignmouth for Keats associations in April, and in September went to Hampstead, where he presumably saw the lock of hair in the local library, gazed at the outside of Keats's house and walked over the heath.[10] He felt the '[dead's breath]' when he saw the lock, but on the heath heard the voices not only of Keats but also of other 'men long dead'.[11] The plural corresponds with his wish in 'To Poesy' to commune with the 'bards of old', a dream of speech with the dead that was to recur in his poetry until the conversation with the dead poet–soldier in 'Strange Meeting', that 'familiar compound ghost'[12] who embodies not just Keats but many of the poets Owen loved. By 1912 Keats was already losing his supremacy, Owen reluctantly admitting that Shelley was 'the brightest genius of his time, (yes, tho' *I* say it)'.[13]

His books, over three hundred of which are preserved as he left them in 1918, show the range – and limitations – of his interests at school and later.[14] Shakespeare, Scott, Keats and Dickens predominate, but he also worked on Milton, several eighteenth-century authors, and some Elizabethan and late-medieval poets. About two-thirds of his library can be classified as 'English literature', including biographies of at least twenty authors. (There was little demand for criticism in those days before the emergence of English as a major academic subject, so that books about poets tended to be 'lives' rather than critical studies.) There are also nearly fifty books in or about French, a high proportion for someone of Owen's respectable but ordinary educational background. The rest are mostly botany, history and classics. The imprints are often those of the popular 'libraries' of the time – Everyman's Library, the People's Books, the Home University Library, Penny Poets, – cheap editions aimed at the growing market of young people like himself who were keen on self-improvement.

Keats had seen the necessity for 'application study and thought'. Owen's earnest reading was accompanied by equally determined fieldwork in the local countryside, for as an admirer of Ruskin – 'my King *John* the Second' (1912) – he saw the arts and sciences as interrelated. Ruskin would have approved of his helping to found an 'Astronomical, Geological and Botanical Society' in 1907 and a field club in 1917. He seems to have called on Ruskin's biographer, W. G. Collingwood, in the Lake District in 1912, and afterwards, 'a little drunk on Ruskin', to have gone for another of his nocturnal rambles in the hills.[15] In the country or at his desk, he was storing up material for later writing, including his characteristic vocabulary ('fronds', 'granites', 'as quick as lilac shoots'). His approach to his studies was marked by awe and humility to a degree hard to imagine today, for his attitude was essentially religious and the central textbook in his early education was the Bible.

The first books in his library are Bibles. The largest is his mother's, who perhaps put it there. Brought up as a devout Evangelical herself, she reared him in her faith; he fully shared it at first, reading a Bible passage every day with the aid of Scripture Union notes and piously including texts and sermon topics in his early letters. This training was an all-pervasive influence on his approach to life and literature, its effects persisting long after he abandoned orthodoxy in 1912–13. The Evangelical movement was still strong and Owen would have been taught its simple, unchanging messages at prayer-meetings and Bible classes of the kind that he was later to conduct himef at Dunsden. An Evangelical bases his religion on a personal relationship with Christ, maintaining it by means of a daily period of private prayer and scripture-reading in which the Word of God is studied for promises and guidance. At the heart of Evangelical practice there is this literary activity, a discipline of intensive reading which is more imaginative than critical, a daily opening of the mind to a book. A high value is placed on the memorising of texts, so that the believer can hear God 'speaking' at any time and be aware of Christ as a living, ever-present companion. Mrs Owen was not a deeply spiritual woman but her faith was founded on this kind of devotion.[16]

Owen tackled literature in the way that he had been taught to read the Bible. Admiring poetry meant worshipping 'the bards of old', hearing them speak and making pilgrimages to places which their presence had made holy. He memorised texts, applying them to his own life in an effort to imitate the lives of the poets.'Turn [ye] to Adonais; his great spirit seek. / O hear him; he will speak!':[17] the biblical language ('Seek ye the Lord') is unmistakable. His repeated wish to know the poets of the past as companions parallels the Evangelical's desire to 'walk' with Jesus. As Evangelicalism tends to be more concerned with personal life and conduct than with abstract or social theory, so Owen was more attracted to authors' lives than to their ideas. Throughout his letters there are signs of his taking the behaviour of great writers as guides to his own: he and his sister must keep their letters, because Keats and his sister kept theirs; he ought to write home every day, like Ruskin; he was glad to visit the poor, because Shelley did.[18] Above all, he read poetry as scripture, looking for such guidance, exhortation and assurance as might be appropriate to one who wanted to set his feet on the path.

He was trained to read like this by his mother, whose methods can be glimpsed in the annotations in her Bible. From 1888 onwards she marked and often dated any verses that 'spoke' to her, including rules of conduct, calls to righteousness and the texts which Evangelicals prize as 'God's promises' (a term sourly echoed in the phrase 'death's promises' in 'S. I. W.'). Several of her marginal dates record a passage chosen for a New Year meditation, a custom which may lie behind her son's habit of reviewing the past year in late-December letters. In 1903 she pursued an especially serious course of Bible study with him, apparently in answer to some trouble that he was passing through. The carefully underlined verses include:

If we suffer, we shall also reign with him.
(2 Timothy 2:12, 'Wilfred   Sunday Feb. 8th 1903')

Satan hath desired to have you ... But I have prayed for thee.   (Luke 22:31–2, 'Wilfred')

As one whom his mother comforteth, so will I comfort you.   (Isaiah 66:13, 'Wilfred   Feb. 16th 03   Promise text').

Approaching his tenth birthday, Wilfred was being shown that passive endurance was the way to deal with unhappiness, suffering and temptation. He should rely on God to provide a divine version of the maternal comfort that was abundantly available at home. This religion of unquestioning 'self-sacrifice' (a term Mrs

Owen was 'inordinately fond of using'[19]) had many attractions for a boy who was naturally inclined to passivity, but it had to be resisted if he were ever to gain his independence. He was beginning to doubt it by 1911, if not earlier, and by 1913 had rejected it after a hard struggle, but its attractions remained. In 1917 he said at first that Christ was 'literally in no man's land' preaching 'Passivity at any price!', but that was not a view he was able to hold for long in the face of war experience. Mrs Owen had stopped marking her Bible by then. She had listed some texts in the back on his twenty-first birthday (March 1914) and slipped in a newspaper-cutting announcing his commission in 1916, but if she ever used the book after that she left no evidence. The greatest effort of her life was over. In a way she had failed, for her son had lost his faith and not become a clergyman despite her hopes and prayers. Nevertheless, she always believed that he had remained a Christian at heart; 'his Christian ideals . . . were really very deep – too deep to speak of', she wrote to Edmund Blunden after the war, as usual preferring emotional conviction to reasoned statement.[20] She was not altogether wrong, for although Owen may not have been a Christian poet he was certainly a religious one in a general sense.

His relationship with his mother was the closest of his life, but it caused him many difficulties. His literary interests must always have been a mystery to her, although she admired them, for her own reading scarcely extended beyond light novels and the pious, naïve verse of John Oxenham. It has been suggested that she read Keats to her son at Broxton, but that seems highly improbable (even in 1911 she had apparently not heard of the 'Ode to a Nightingale').[21] She thought all modern poetry was likely to be 'rubbish'.[22] Her simple, crudely punctuated letters to Blunden and others after the war show her to have been emotional, affectionate and good-hearted but not remotely intellectual or bookish. Owen's move away from Evangelicalism towards poetry was in part an escape from her into a world which she could not enter. It was not an easy move, for the bond between them was suffocatingly intense; there are connections between it and the many images of (s)mothering and drowning in his poems. Part of him longed for her because she provided rest and safety ('ease / For ever from the vain untravelled leagues'). She encouraged his dependence, sharing little jokes against his father and laughing him out of the few awkward friendships he tried to make with girls. She used her hypochondria – for one must suspect that her

incessant minor ailments were often more perceived than real –
as a means of exacting sympathetic enquiries, and in return she
encouraged his own similar tendencies so that she could nurse
him as much as possible. Her religion was another way of holding
him. As he freed himself, his health improved and so did his poetry.
He later thought that his first mature poem was 'Happiness', the
first draft of which laments that he is no longer 'a Mother's boy';
there is no mention at all of war in it, but it was written
immediately after his first tour of the trenches. If the completion
of his independence is recorded in that early 1917 sonnet, the
beginning of it seems to be hinted at in the words 'dark',
'disobedient' and 'secret' in his unfinished poem about the Broxton
holiday (and perhaps in Mrs Owen's anxious markings in her
Bible a year before Broxton, when she may have seen signs already
that her son was likely to go his own way). Many years later,
Harold Owen said that his brother had been nursed into poetry
at Broxton in sunlight and 'in the safety and understanding love
that my mother wrapped about him', but that seems to be merely
a pleasant fiction.[23] The fragment tells a quite different story of
a solitary walk in the dark, no doubt a forbidden excursion for
an eleven-year-old. Owen thought of his poethood as having been
'Born', 'Nursed' and 'Suckled' in secret solitude on the hills. It
was still a mother–son relationship, but the mother was nature
and Mrs Owen had to be disobeyed.

His inner life was hidden so that even his mother and brother
never perceived it. In his bedroom at Shrewsbury, there were
papers in a locked cupboard which his mother was never allowed
to see. Despite his complaints in 'To Poesy' and other early poems
that he was lonely, he was a Romantic and needed solitude.
Darkness was always strangely congenial, his verse and letters
often associating it with poetic inspiration.[24] One of his most
ambitious early poems, an ode on the ruined city of Uriconium
at the foot of the Wrekin, invites the reader to 'lift the gloomy
curtain of Time Past' in order to see through the 'riven ground'
the 'secret things that Hades hath', mostly traces of war. His
mature poems search the obscurity of his buried experience,
recording a journey through the riven ground into 'the sorrowful
dark of hell'. He found companionship there but that too was
secret.

2 The First Crisis: Religion

Owen began to emerge from his first Keatsian phase towards the end of 1911, under pressure of new influences and painful experience. 1912 was a crucial year, recorded in great detail in his letters because he was away from home for the first time and had much to tell. His verse was still unoriginal (he seems not to have experimented with sound-effects, for example, until he met Tailhade in 1914), but it records the formation of concerns and images that were to be developed in later poems. The commitment to literature which he had expressed in 'To Poesy' was now put to a strenuous test as it came into conflict with the demands of Evangelical orthodoxy, but by 1913 he had found his freedom to 'be a meteor, fast, eccentric, lone, lawless . . .'.[1]

When he left school in 1911 he wanted to try for a university scholarship and his mother wanted him to enter the Church, so it was arranged that he should become an unpaid assistant to the Vicar of Dunsden, near Reading, in return for tuition. Mrs Owen's sister, Emma Gunston, lived nearby, and her own vicar had been able to recommend Mr Wigan as having suitably Evangelical views.[2] After a brief period in which Owen was impressed by Wigan and the unaccustomed elegance of life in the Vicarage, frustration began to set in. There seems to have been little or no tuition and much tedious, formal conversation. Less than two months after his arrival, Owen spoke bitterly of 'the Wasted Hours', a phrase that reappears in a sketch for a poem about his pounding heartbeats;[3] his Dunsden troubles were already beginning to find their way out in physical symptoms and secret verse-writing. As a lay assistant, he was obliged to keep up a Christian front in public and to observe the kind of life that would be his if he were to take orders, so that his own faith came under strain. All literary activity was suspect. Although Wigan was a man of apparent culture, he thought books were an 'alternative to life, or an artificialized life'.[4] Owen found that the more he saw of theoretical Evangelicalism, as opposed to the

9

kindly, unthinking sort he had known at home, the more it seemed to deny everything he most valued. Even the beauties of language were potentially sinful because they were 'of this world' in their appeal to the senses.[5] He was in a dilemma familiar to many Victorians, caught between a sternly Pauline form of Christianity which condemned all pleasures of 'the flesh' and a concept of poetry that was still largely Keatsian.

Conscientiously, he tried his hand at hymn-writing, producing two hackneyed pieces which seem to be the only verse in which he ever expressed conventional religious sentiments, but his devotion to poetry could not be so easily diverted.[6] No doubt remembering Keats's belief that a long poem was a useful discipline, he composed two lengthy verse renderings of Hans Andersen stories, one of them quite un-Christian and the other, 'The Little Mermaid', full of Keatsian descriptions which sometimes foreshadow the war poems in language ('bugles floated in far citadels') and in details of pain and horror. He knew from Colvin that Keats had also trained himself by joining Shelley and Leigh Hunt in writing poems on chosen subjects. Since his cousin, Leslie Gunston, was beginning to share his interest in 'Books and their Makers', they set themselves the task of each composing on 'The Swift', the swifts flying round the Vicarage being convenient symbols of an enviable liberty and aspiration. There were to be more poems on agreed subjects in later years.[7]

But these were only poetic exercises. Poetry seemed to make far higher demands, and they were apparently irreconcilable with those of religion. In an effort to resolve the issue, Owen turned to his third main interest, the earth sciences, doing his earnest but unscholarly best to tackle the Victorian debate between science and religion. He was soon 'reading, analysing, collecting, sifting, and classifying Evidence' and 'grappling as I never did before with the problem of Evolution'. He read a statement of the Christian answer to Darwinism but contemptuously wrote 'Shallow!' against its discussion of art.[8] His conclusion was probably summed up in a comment he had marked in Keats's letters, 'nothing in this world is proveable'; when he met these words again in W. M. Rossetti's life of Keats, he added, 'at least *proved* W. O.'.[9] Proof certainly seemed lacking for personal immortality, an essential belief of traditional Evangelicalism: 'Science has looked,' one Dunsden poem begins, 'and sees no life but this'. 'The Dread of Falling into Naught' (18 September 1912) is a typical piece from this period, concealing under its affected, Tennysonian rhetoric a genuine ache at human mortality that was to find clearer expression less than six years later in war elegies such as 'Futility'.

However, the crisis was not brought to a head by his own questionings, as might seem the case from existing biographical accounts, but by challenges which were put to him. When he first arrived in the parish, he found that the Vicar had 'the hope of a Revival in the place much on his mind, during these times'.[10] That was ominous. When the phenomenon of Revival sweeps through an Evangelical church at national or local level, believers gain a deeper faith, while doubters and backsliders find strength to make the full sacrifice of their lives to Christ. 'We yearn for times of Revival', said the *Christian* on 25 July 1912, beginning its lengthy reports of the annual Keswick Convention but perhaps not speaking for Owen, who attended the Convention for two or three weeks that summer. He heard the famous preachers of the day repeat their now all too familiar messages. 'The secret of Keswick', said Dr Griffith Thomas, 'is handing over your individuality to Christ.' Some people heard the appeal ('no day was without its trophy of grace') but the *Christian* said gloomily on 1 August that for some the Convention was 'a dark, hidden tragedy, secret sin strangling the soul'. Owen returned to Dunsden in considerable distress but hid his feelings as well as he could.[11] He might have got away with it, but the even pace of parish life was quickening, building up to a fine village drama in November–December. Whether in answer to the Vicar's prayers or as a result of the soul-winning zeal of Clyde Black, a new lay assistant, Revival came at last.[12]

Parishioners began to be converted or converted anew at meeting after meeting. Black was busy 'cornering' people and asking them to accept Christ. The excitement in the Vicarage must have been immense, making it impossible for Owen to keep his opinions to himself or to escape the general expectation that he would join Black in doing the Lord's work. Privately he composed one of his harshest poems ('Unto what pinnacles', dated 6 November), a fierce denunciation of 'good men' who commit 'soul-suicide' in their quest for holiness, becoming obsessed with their own spiritual lives:

And their sole mission is to drag, entice
And push mankind to those same cloudy crags
Where they first breathed the madness-giving air
That made them feel as angels, that are less than men.

The unvarnished, angry style is similar to that of Shelley's tirades against religion in *Queen Mab*, a poem which Owen may well have been reading. His exasperation at the activity around him and at his own bewildered conscience may have been one cause of a Vicarage 'furor' in December in which he was in some way involved.[13] A Christmas present of a new book about Mrs Browning 'from his friend Clyde Black' was perhaps a peace-offering to show that Black, too, liked poetry, provided it was Christian. But the Vicar was stern: if Owen was still considering ordination, he must recognise that it meant complete obedience to God's will and a renunciation of all wordly pleasures, including 'verse-making'.[14]

Owen's letters do not record what happened to the Revival but the outcome of his own crisis was no longer in doubt, although discussions with Wigan continued into 1913. He left the Vicarage on 7 February, not long before his twentieth birthday. One of his manuscripts leaves a vivid record of his state of mind.[15] On one side there is a scrawled first draft of 'The Unreturning' – a sonnet about the finality of death – together with quotations from Keats and a few clumsy lines about romance. 'The Unreturning' did not reach its final version for some years, but without this early draft one would never have guessed that such a forceful poem could have been started as early as 1913. 1913 it must be, however, for on the other side there is a scrappy outline for a letter:

To Vicar – solely on the ground of affection

I was a boy when I first came to you and [boyishly] held you in the [doubtful] mischievous esteem that a boy has for his Headmaster. It is also true that I was an old man when I left, that is like [an   ol   ] I have a senile & a stupefaction for

The Christian life is – affords no imagination, physical sensation, aesthetic philosophy –
There is but *one* dimension in the X^n relg the strait line [upwards] to the Zenith – whereas I cannot conceive of less than 3
But all these considerations are Nothing to the conviction that the philosophy of the whole system as a religion is but a religion and therefore one Interpretation of Life & Scheme of Living among a hundred – and that not the [best] most convenient.

That is all that survives of what was perhaps Owen's only attempt to write down a full statement of his objections to 'the Christian life' (a favourite Evangelical phrase). His mention of 'imagination, physical sensation, aesthetic philosophy' suggests that his 1912 reading had included some recent Aesthetic work, a field he was to explore more thoroughly in the next few years.

Owen's letters from Dunsden are a possibly unique record of a young man's struggle with religion, respectability and growing-up in provincial England before the Great War, but their importance for a study of his poethood is that a knowledge of what happened at Dunsden contributes to an understanding of the later poems. The public role to which he aspired in 1918 was that of an evangelising preacher against hypocrisy, false creeds, oppression and lack of pity. His anger against Wigan, Black and the Keswick speakers in 1912 prepared him for his later indignation at the support which the churches gave to the war, and at the way in which individuals were treated as cannon fodder to be 'dragged, enticed and pushed' into fighting. No longer convinced by promises of salvation and immortality, he grieved over the loss of hope and life which war inflicted in this world, scorning the glib pieties of civilians who said that men killed in battle were saved by God 'even before they fell'.[16] Like the Victorian writers who broke away from Evangelicalism he retained a set of Christian standards, referring his reader to them by means of biblical language and allusion, but he did not recover his early faith; the Christian views which he expressed in some of his 1917 letters would not have satisfied Wigan. He gained much at Dunsden but also lost much, and the loss was permanent. And, in his secret inner life, the visions, torments and delights of his peculiar imagination began to manifest themselves in images which were to reappear later as images of war.

There were other factors in Owen's loss of faith than difficulties over doctrine and personal evangelism. If Wigan was an example, 'the Christian life' did not seem to include much concern for social inequality, nor much allowance for the strong feelings of early manhood. The lay assistant was expected to visit the sick, so that he soon became aware of the contrast between the comforts of the Vicarage and the stark poverty of some of the villagers. He was also expected to teach the local children in Sunday school and choir practices, and the pleasure which he derived from observing youthful beauty was disturbingly inconsistent with the attitudes that he was supposed to be inculcating. As the strain grew, his health suffered and terrors filled his dreams.

Having concluded before he went to Dunsden that the poets he most admired had brought into poetry 'a new sympathy with man especially the poor', he was struck by a comment in a history of literature that the ideals of the French Revolution had 'inspired the British School of revolt and reconstruction in Burns, Shelley, Byron, Wordsworth, Coleridge and Tennyson, till its fires have died down in our own day'. 'Have they!' Owen exclaimed when he read this in April 1912.

> They may have in the bosoms of the muses, but not in my breast. I am increasingly liberalising and liberating my thought, spite of the Vicar's strong Conservatism . . . . From what I hear straight from the tight-pursed lips of wolfish ploughmen in their cottages, I might say there is material ready for another revolution . . . . Am I for or against upheaval? I know not; I am not happy in these thoughts; yet they press upon me.

In the same paragraph he mentions Tennyson and Dickens.[17] Literary history and poetic ambition played a large part in the 'liberalising and liberating' of his opinions. He became especially interested in Shelley, among the poets of 'revolt and reconstruction', noting in a verse letter about the literary associations of the Dunsden area that Shelley had written poetry, music that could still be heard, among 'beechen solitudes' on the nearby Thames. The 'music' which he heard must have been that of *The Revolt of Islam*, for he discovered in January 1912 from a biography of Shelley that *The Revolt* had been composed in a boat 'under the beech-groves' not far away.[18] This poem was to remain in his mind for the rest of his life, providing him with the theme and title of 'Strange Meeting' in 1918. Shelley's passionate defence of freedom against tyranny would have strengthened the lay assistant's rebellion in 1912, just as his advocacy of non-violent resistance affected the young subaltern's attitude to war only a few years later.

Another, much less predictable influence on Owen's thinking at Dunsden and later began in October 1911 when he happened to buy a book of new poems by 'a modern aspirant (unknown to me) . . . . I am idly-busy in trying to discover the talent of our own days, and the requirements of the public'. This book was undoubtedly *Before Dawn: Poems and Impressions* by Harold Monro. Owen read it carefully and could still quote from it two months later.[19] It was thus at this early stage in his career that he encountered Monro's work and not, as might otherwise be supposed, in 1915, when his letters first record a conversation with Monro in person. *Before Dawn* was a chance find but an important one, for Monro was soon to become proprietor of the Poetry Bookshop and publisher of *Georgian Poetry*. There is a clear line of development from that random purchase in 1911 to the proud claim six years later: 'I am held peer by the Georgians'.

Just as Owen had imitated Keats and Shelley, so he imitated Monro, drafting a satirical verse portrait (perhaps of Wigan) on the back of a respectable hymn he had been writing.[20] Critics generally assume that he learned to write satire from Sassoon in 1917, but it is time that Monro's 'Impressions' had their due. In fact Monro's influence can be seen even in some of Owen's 'Sassoonish' 1917 work. One of the 'Impressions', for example, is a description of a rich man dining in a London club who picks up the evening paper and begins

> to read it and to carve
> A shilling strawberry. 'Twas about the strike –
> A hundred, in the cause, had sworn to starve.
> He put it down, and muttered: 'Let them starve!'

This ending may be compared not only with the last lines of 'The Dead-Beat' but also with those of another 1917 piece, an early sketch for 'The Sentry', in which Owen attempted to cap a grim record of a trench experience with a picture of civilians in a club:

> turning down his cards.
> The Evening news was [brought into] the Clubbers
> They glanced at Haig's dispatch between the rubbers
> [Nothing! – Advanced   A paltry]
> said: 'Only fifty yards?'[21]

He would have been interested to see that the revolutionary fires which had burned in Romantic poetry were still alight in the work of the first modern 'aspirant' he had so far encountered, and that Monro was hostile to clergymen and religion (some

sceptical lines by Monro are unmistakably echoed in the 1913
version of 'The Unreturning').[22]

Before Dawn lays stress on another theme which was increasingly
alive to Owen at Dunsden, the value of 'physical sensation' and
beauty. Monro's creed is a fervent humanism, symbolised by the
titan of the coming dawn who will be man himself, beautiful in
body as in soul, liberated from sexual as well as social restraints
and able to lead a full physical life. Like other young writers of
the period, including D. H. Lawrence, Monro had been strongly
influenced by the progressive views of Edward Carpenter,[23] whose
advocacy of sexual liberation and fulfilment is implicit in such
Before Dawn poems as 'The Virgin':

> I
> Am made of flesh, and I have tingling nerves:
> My blood is always hot, and I desire
> The touch of gentle hands upon my face
> To cool it, as the moonlight cools the earth.

Owen's verse was to echo this passage several times in the next
few years. His own 'tingling nerves' were troubling him. In
November, with the Revival gathering strength around him, he
gave his mother a glimpse of his new 'aesthetic philosophy':

> *my* philosophy teaches that those mortals who have nerves
> exquisitely responsive to painful sensation, have a perfect right
> to use them . . . *to respond equally keenly to enjoyment.* I know I
> have a tingling capacity for pleasure . . . and if such be the
> operation of a tense nerve, then must I content me with nerves'
> foolish ado when things offend and lacerate them. . . . I am
> willing to pay this price, to purchase the delight to the full . . . .[24]

Like his fragmentary letter to the Vicar, this suggests he had been
thinking about the principles on which his poethood should be
based. Perhaps he had already looked into some literature of the
French Decadence; at any rate, he seems to be aware that sensitive
nerves were important in artistic theory. Late Romanticism held
that the exclusive goal of art was beauty, and that since beauty
could only be apprehended through physical sensation it was
necessary for the artist to have 'exquisitely' responsive nerves, to
observe their workings closely and to react with as much intensity
to pain as to pleasure.

It would be easy but inaccurate to dismiss Owen's many references to his nervous condition and general health in 1912 as signs of nothing more than adolescent hypochondria. He told his mother at intervals that he was suffering from weak sight, insomnia, indigestion, giddy fits, palpitations, and – towards the end of the year – painful breathing. Some of these afflictions, even the eye trouble, may have been caused by nothing more than Vicarage meals; the only picture of him in spectacles is his cartoon of himself undergoing a dizzy 'vertigo' in the dining-room after a heavy lunch (Plate 3). However, the attack occurred in mid November, when the Revival was beginning. Similarly his breathing-difficulty, which culminated in a severe attack of 'congestion of the lungs' after he left Dunsden, was both a genuine symptom and an expression of psychological stress; perhaps the *Christian* had been right in saying that some people had felt 'strangled' at Keswick, and Owen may not have been exaggerating when he said in December that his nerves were in a 'shocking state' and his chest 'continually "too full"'. Just as if one had been over-long in a putrid atmosphere, and had got to the advanced stage of being painfully conscious of it.'[25] His physical troubles represented not only mental distress but also resistance to external pressure (even the vertigo saved him from attending a religious meeting), and they were encouraging proof that he had a poet's temperament. He recognised their psychological origins with lively interest, showing something of that inner resilience that was to keep him sane during his shellshock in 1917.

His collapses at the Vicarage were often rather comical but his illness afterwards seems to have been serious, although little is recorded about it because he was at home and wrote no letters. Looking back on it later, as he often did, he said it had been accompanied by 'phantasies', 'horrors' or 'phantasms'.[26] These seem to have been nightmares or even hallucinations, an acute form of the vivid and unpleasant dreams from which he suffered throughout his life. Their content was probably not unlike that of a 'horror' which haunted his first months at the Vicarage, as recorded in the 'supposed Confessions of a Secondrate Sensitive Mind in Dejection', an absurdly literary piece which nevertheless records in metaphor a real experience:

> think not, if your life-blood still is warm,
> That ye have looked upon Despondency.
> Ye have but seen her in another's eye,

As Perseus fearfully beheld the form
Of Gorgon, mirrored in the stilly well.
There may ye guess the beauty of that Head,
The pallor and the mystery – but the Dread
Ye feel not, nor the horror, nor the spell.

But, face to face, she fixed on me her stare:
Woe, woe, my blood has never moved since then;
Down-dragged like corpse in sucking, slimy fen,
I sank to feel the breath of that Despair.
With autumn mists, and hand in hand with Night,
She came to me. But at the break of day,
Went not again, but stayed, and yet doth stay.
'— O Horror, doth not Pain take note of light
And darkness, – doth he not hold off betimes,
And yield his victim for an hour to Sleep?
Then why dost thou, O Curst, the long night steep
In bloodiness and stains of shadowy crimes?'

The violence of these nocturnal ordeals ('bloodiness and stains of shadowy crimes') implies that they were sado-masochistic 'phantasies', comparable in kind if not in degree with his shellshock nightmares in 1917. The poem goes on to say that Despondency will never leave him and that he will eventually be transported to hell. There was a kind of truth in this, for the image of the deathly face always obsessed him, emerging in his 1917–18 dreams and in the poems inspired by them such as 'Dulce et Decorum Est', 'The Sentry' and 'Strange Meeting'. The face was a projection of his own imagination and unspoken urges, arousing guilt, fear and helplessness, but even in its first appearance in his verse he was able to give it a literary form. The allusion to Perseus (who also first appears in his verse here) and the Gorgon's head may be based on a Pre-Raphaelite source such as Burne-Jones's painting *The Baleful Head* (Plate 2), or D. G. Rossetti's poem 'Aspecta Medusa', but the more general image of a fatally beautiful face with eyes that turn men to stone is recurrent throughout Romanticism (it will be discussed under 'Perseus' in the next chapter).[27]

That he continued to be susceptible to 'horrors' in 1912 is evident from his curiously strong reaction to Borrow's descriptions in *Lavengro* of daylight 'fits of the horrors' and from his bookish but attentive account of a near-faint after a fall from his bicycle:

sudden twilight seemed to fall upon the world, an horror of
great darkness closed around me – strange noises and a
sensation of swimming under water overtook me, and in fact
I fell into a regular syncope. I did not fall down however, nor
yet lose all consciousness; but the semi-blindness, and the chill
were frightful.

The language in this bit of self-dramatising is lifted from Genesis,
Pilgrim's Progress, and Clarence's dream in *Richard III*, but it
points to several images in Owen's later poems, including 'sudden
evening' ('Conscious'), 'Suddenly night crushed out the day' (the
final version of 'The Unreturning'), or that submarine imagery
in 'Dulce et Decorum Est' and 'The Sentry' which marks two
rare references to his war dreams. Another Dunsden poem,
'Written on a June Night. (1911)' (apparently written in 1912,
despite the title), again uses imagery of burning eyes and violent
crime in describing summer sleeplessness. Owen seems to have
been accurate in later telling his mother that his nights had been
'terrible to be borne' (and in implying that his sufferings had
been a result of suppressed sexual feelings for which he had never
been prepared by his parents).[28]

There is persistent imagery in all this of passivity, of smothering,
drowning, petrifaction – a nightmare parallel to the maternal
affection of his 'idle, protected, loving, wholesome, hidden,
intimate, sequestered' home life.[29] When he wrote about beauty,
even in 1917 work such as 'The Fates' and 'My Shy Hand', he
often gave it qualities of smoothness, embracing, pillowing,
sheltering, sleep, languor, timelessness and escape from action.
He wrote some verse on his nineteenth birthday about the pleasure
of recovering from pain (another bout of indigestion at the
Vicarage), saying that he preferred 'the placid plains' of convalesc-
ence and being mothered to the exposed heights of health in 'the
dangerous air where actual Bliss doth thrill'.[30] After Dunsden he
collapsed at home, his 'congestion of the lungs' corresponding not
only to the pressure of recent events but also to Mrs Owen's
anxious nursing, but he managed to get on the move again after
a few months because there was no hope of becoming a poet on
those plains. His instinct was to seek shelter and reversion to
childhood, but in his first 'mature' poem ('Happiness', 1917) he
recognised that the old happiness of childhood was unreturning
because he had gone beyond 'the scope / Of mother-arms'. In
'Spring Offensive', his last poem, the soldiers push past the

'sorrowing arms' of brambles, advance up the hill and at the top
meet the 'even rapture of bullets' as grown men facing experience
in the 'dangerous air'.[31] That much at least could be achieved,
but beyond it there seemed to be passivity again, the tormented
helplessness of death which Despondency's visitations had
foreshadowed since 1911 or even earlier. Beauty, the poet's goal,
had two personifications: in one she was a protector and healer,
a bringer of rest, whose eyes were the 'secret gate' by which her
devotee could escape from time, as in 'The Fates'; in the other
she was a 'phantasm' whose terrible stare also brought timelessness
but no rest ('no rest for thee, O Slave of mine', she promises in
the 'Confessions'), a state suffered by the 'encumbered', groaning
sleepers in 'Strange Meeting'. For Owen, even in 1912 before he
knew anything of war, the second personification was the true
one; his imagination allowed him no choice. Painfully discovering
his own nature in the muddle of adolescence, he began to see
that what he might have to say as a poet would not be quite the
same as anything that other poets had said, comforting though
their words had once been. The 'pressure of Problems' was forcing
him to voice his own 'dim reveries', the frightened 'croonings of
a motherless child, in gloom', but perhaps his own verse might
one day bring comfort to someone in need.[32]

Although one cause of his distress in 1912 was religion, another
seems to have been sexual difficulties. There is an erotic element
implicit in much of what he wrote at that time, often suggesting
a deep-seated disorientation. He was still devoted to Keats, saying
even in 1913 that 'I fear domestic criticism when I am in love
with a real live woman. What now I am in love with a youth,
and a dead 'un'!'[33] Reading W. M. Rossetti's biography in 1912,
he was overcome by its account of Keats's death: 'Rossetti guided
my groping hand right into the wound, and I touched, for one
moment the incandescent Heart of Keats.'[34] The language is that
of religious ecstasy, with its allusion to St Thomas, but the
emotion seems to be partly sexual. These statements suggest the
extent of Owen's confusion; his mother ('domestic criticism'),
Keats, the dead, a youth, a woman ('I fear . . . '), sado-masochism,
religion - love seems to have many objects. The fear of criticism
from home was a particularly severe hindrance to his sorting
himself out. Looking back in 1918 on his younger days, he urged
his mother not to deny his youngest brother 'the thing he craves,
as I was denied; for I was denied, and the appeal which, if you
watched, you must have seen in my eyes, you ignored . . . . And

my nights were terrible to be borne.'[35] He was not so clear-
sighted in 1912 but gave in to his mother's unspoken demands:
'Oh how do I stand (yes and sit, lie, kneel and walk, too,) in
need of some tangible caress from you. . . . my affections are
physical as well as abstract – intensely so – and confound 'em for
that, it shouldn't be so.'[36] In the absence of his mother he
developed a streak of narcissism which was to remain with him,
but his feelings also attached themselves to the parish children.

The lay assistant was expected to take an interest in the local
youngsters, but Owen was reckless in his friendships with them.
He was moved by the innocence and suffering of childhood,
finding 'the blanch of sickness, and the dark-cirqued eye' strangely
beautiful.[37] In 'Impromptu' he implores a little girl to comfort
him, since he is 'in pain for human sin' and 'heart-ease and rest'
can no longer be had from 'Mother and Brethren, Teachers, Holy
Guides':

> Oh, now, unless my face hath set too granite-hard
> And hurt thy tender hands to stroke it o'er,
>
> Unless the fires that ever rage behind my eyes,
> Hot-sear thy lips in pressing kisses there,
>
> I crave thee, place thy two soft hands upon my cheeks,
> So shall long-treasured tears be loosed at last.

This image of a youth guilty of some unnamed sin, with the stony
fixedness of a statue but incessantly burning eyes, was to recur
again and again in later poems. One source is Monro's virgin,
with her longing for gentle hands to cool her hot face, and another
is the legend of Medusa, for Owen had looked on the face of
Despondency and felt himself turned to stone, 'too granite-hard'
to be restored by a girl of any age.

The child who is the subject of a number of these Dunsden
poems was probably Milly Montague, his favourite among the
small girls who came to infants' meetings, but his closest friendship
was with a thirteen-year-old boy, Vivian Rampton, about whom
little is recorded except that he had 'melancholy brown eyes' and
was intelligent, fond of music and books, and within a year or
two of secondary school. Owen had Rampton to a secret tea at

the Vicarage, probably gave him piano lessons at his home, and on at least one occasion 'secretly met with Vivian . . . and went a delicious ramble; lay in hawthorn glades . . . . He read to me, and I told him tales.' He kept all this hidden from the Vicar, apparently regarding Rampton as a private discovery whose intellectual abilities he could encourage without getting tied up with religion. When Revival came, did Black 'corner' the boy and try to convert him (as he had certainly cornered Milly's brother)? Owen would have been furious, insisting that his protégé should be left alone, and the secret would have been out. The Vicar would have been far from pleased to find that his senior lay assistant had been conducting this clandestine friendship for many months and was now even refusing to help save the boy's soul. That seems a possible explanation for a mysterious passage in a January 1913 letter which refers to a recent 'furor' which has 'now abated in the Vicarage, thank Mnemosyne; but I hope that I, who "discovered" him something over a year ago, may' – and here the paper has been cut away in one of Harold Owen's most thorough attempts at censorship. Rampton was to haunt later poems. The friendship probably began when Owen first went to Dunsden, in which case it would have lasted for a year and three months, a span roughly corresponding to 'something over a year' in the letter, and 'a year', 'two years' and 'two short years', three inconsistent phrases in a later fragment about a friendship. In this sketch for part of an autobiographical poem that never got written, Owen remembers how his unnamed friend had undergone the 'inalterable change from boy to man' during the year (or two) that they knew each other, and how 'many of my thoughts were given to him / And many of his hours were given to me'. Then, very hesitantly, he asks whether it would have been better if he had not seen the boy's face, heard his voice or touched his hand.[38] He wrote this in Bagnères in 1914, at the same time as his piece about the birth of his poethood at Broxton; even allowing for myth-making, both fragments are about crucial stages in his growth as a poet. The memory of Rampton persisted, becoming an idealised figure with deep, sad eyes, a hand that could sometimes be touched and a beauty that was for ever unattainable. The relationship was perhaps Owen's first love affair, although he may well have been much less aware of its sexual implications at the time than Wigan probably was. Rampton is present in many poems after 1913, but if he appears anywhere in Dunsden verse it is perhaps only as the brown-eyed child in 'The Two Reflections', a sonnet evidently based on recollections of summertime rambles among the pines and beeches of the Chilterns in 1912.[39]

When Owen finally reached the point of deciding whether or not to become 'a religious devotee', the Vicar stipulated that he would have to give up 'verse-making' and friendships with village children ('all my pretty chickens / At one fell swoop?').[40] Whether he remained at Dunsden or left, the relationship with Rampton was over. The 'melancholy brown eyes' and shy hand of his young friend were to become symbols of pain and loss as well as of love. He worked out a kind of solution in 1913. Two sonnets which belong stylistically to 1916–17 are relevant here. In 'To the Bitter Sweet-Heart: A Dream', Eros takes the poet by the hand, promising to 'fill with Yours my other hand'; but in the end the god takes the other hand himself and the human lover is not found again. In other words, the idea of love is compensation for a lost relationship (which included hand contact). In the sequel sonnet, 'To Eros', the poet has been abandoned by the god, despite sacrificing 'fair fame', 'Old peaceful lives; frail flowers; firm friends; and Christ'.[41] Sacrificing Christ must refer to Dunsden, while 'fair fame' may represent Owen's good name in the Vicarage. Breaking the relationship was made tolerable at the time by Owen's imagining that he would dedicate himself to the spirit of love through poetry, an ideal stated in another sonnet, 'Stunned by their life's explosion into love', in which most men are said to be forced by that 'explosion' into lust or the 'bitter chastity' of religion without seeing that poetry could slake their thirst. It was not until later that he realised how unsatisfactory a solution this was. Eros left him, caring nothing for the sacrifices of a worshipper who had tried to know Love in solitude.

If this reconstruction of the Vicarage 'furor' is accurate, it sums up the nature of the Dunsden crisis. Rampton stood for Owen's private world of music, nature, books, strong feeling, mystery and delight, as well as of guilt and sin; the Vicarage represented the smothering prison of piety, respectability, self-denial and sham. Evangelicalism taught that anyone who had heard the Gospel and rejected it was certain to be damned. Hell fire was still a reality, a terror to many Victorian and Edwardian children and perfectly credible to Owen, with his nights steeped at times in 'bloodiness and stains of shadowy crimes'. 'I can believe in Hell', he wrote in autumn 1912, despite his doubts about heaven. Wigan's sermons were 'horrifyingly dismal'.[42] Owen was doubly damned, having rejected the Christian message and touched a boy's hand. The 'fires that ever rage behind my eyes' were burning dreams, a foretaste of eternal torment. He may have been disgusted at himself, for there are several strong expressions of disgust against humanity in general in the Dunsden poems. That phase passed, but he never quite shook off the fear that his secret desires and his break from religion were sins which would not be forgiven, so that his poetry from 1912 onwards returns obsessively to images of guilt, fire, hell and everlasting pain.

One of the most promising (or at any rate least unpromising) of his 1912-13 poems in which these concerns emerge is 'Deep under turfy grass and heavy clay', in which the funeral of a mother and child prompts a protest against the folly of having children:

> So I rebelled, scorning and mocking such
> As had the ignorant callousness to wed
> On altar steps long frozen by the touch
> Of stretcher after stretcher of our dead.
> Love's blindness is too terrible, I said:
> I will go counsel men, and show what bin
> The harvest of their homes is gathered in.

The first four lines here are perhaps the earliest in which Owen's imagination can be felt as authentic and original, showing the beginnings of his later technical control. The rhyming of 'wed' and 'dead' stresses the dual function of the altar steps, while the word 'touch' at the climax of the stanza is applied to the coldness of death rather than the warmth of marriage. The sensation of chill continues in alliteration into the repeated 'stretcher' of the next line, as generations of coffin-bearers rest their burdens gratingly on stone that seems to have drawn its coldness from the dead. Stretchers more usually carry living people, a meaning which reinforces the unexpected significance of 'touch'; life and death are closer than is realised by those who wed on the altar steps. In the next stanza the grass and clay in the churchyard are seen to be half-burying the wreaths, making the village children wonder 'what might mean / Rich-odoured flowers so whelmed in fetid earth'. The rich flowers and rotting earth take up the contrast between warm life and chilling death; like the dead mother and child, the flowers have grown out of clay and are returning to it. The poet's rebellion is overcome for the moment by the sight of a child 'whose pale brows / Wore beauty like our mother Eve's', but in later years his protest was redoubled when he asked, 'Was it for this the clay grew tall?' ('Futility'), or showed that soldiers understood the deathly significance of the flowers given to them by women ('The Send-Off'). The pale brows of the child made him accept the mortality of beauty, as Eve had made Adam eat the bitter fruit, but five years later the 'pallor of girls' brows' ('Anthem for Doomed Youth') became an emblem of death, like the pallor of Medusa, for the girls had been responsible for sending their men off to war. The child at the Dunsden graveside was to grow into a *femme fatale* in later work.

Owen's religious background left him with the urge to 'go counsel men'. The poet, able to explore farther than other people, had the task of reporting back on what he had seen. This role is expressed in 'O World of many worlds' in the ornate metaphor of the poet as meteor, pursuing a 'lawless' way through space. There the meteor will meet other poets, whose combined light will rival the sun's (as the soldiers challenge the sun in 'Spring Offensive'). He will warn 'the earth of wider ways unknown' (as in 'Storm'), not following the crowd's 'fixed' course ('the march of this retreating world'). Such ideas would have appalled the Vicar, who may have liked to quote St Jude's denunciation of 'filthy dreamers' who creep secretly into the Church and defile 'the flesh', 'wandering stars, to whom is reserved the blackness of darkness for ever'. Owen incorporated this text into his poem, declaring his poetic manifesto in defiance of the biblical orthodoxy which had tried so hard to deny him his freedom.[43]

In discussing the dangers of poetic dreams which might defile the flesh, Wigan may have pointed to St Paul's assertion that 'they that are Christ's have crucified the flesh with the affections and the lusts'. Owen worked this into the closing lines of an extraordinary poem, 'The time was aeon', introducing St Paul in person as a 'small Jew' leading a crowd of (no doubt Evangelical) 'railers'.[44] The poem presents a vision, not a dream but a 'true resumption of experienced things' (here as elsewhere Owen insists that he deals in experience, not mere dreams), in which the world's ugliness is made lovely by a spirit with an evil name, 'the Flesh':

150, 465

It bore the naked likeness of a { maid } { boy }
Flawlessly moulded, fine exceedingly, . . .
His outline changed, from beauty unto beauty,

As change the contours of slim, sleeping clouds.
His skin, too, glowed, pale scarlet; like the clouds
Lit from the eastern underworld; which thing
Bewondered me the more. But I remember
The statue of his body standing so
Against the huge disorder of the place
Resembled a strong music; . . .

Then watched I how there ran towards that way
A multitude of railers, hot with hate
And maddened by the voice of a small Jew
Who cried [with a loud voice]: saying 'Away!
Away with him!' and 'Crucify him! Him,
[With] the affections and the lusts thereof.'

Like the text from St Jude, the Pauline statement is turned back
upon its author, so that crucifying the flesh becomes a crime
similar to crucifying Christ. In this remarkable contradiction of
Evangelical belief, Owen seems to be taking his cue from the
opening poem in Harold Monro's *Before Dawn* ('Two Visions'),
in which the baseness of contemporary life is contrasted with the
beauty of the coming dawn of freedom. Monro describes the
'Titan of the dawn – Humanity':

His visionary eyes looked out afar
    Beyond the transient semblances of death.
No sound of supplication came to mar

The rhythm of his calmly-taken breath.
    No ripple of a thin or faint delight
Moved round his crimson lips; and underneath

His bright skin aureoled by the rose twilight
    Rolled the vast torrent of majestic thews.
Master of his strong passion . . . .

The homosexual quality of this description was probably not
accidental, since Monro's current guru, Edward Carpenter, was
almost the only person at the time who was prepared to write
publicly in defence of 'Uranian' or homosexual love. Like many
young men of the time, including Sassoon and Graves, Owen owed

his eventual freedom in part to Carpenter's liberalising and liberating views. He may have been completely unaware of both Carpenter and the implications of Monro's poem when he wrote 'The time was aeon', but he certainly first imagined 'the Flesh' as male, adding the alternative 'maid' only as an afterthought. The Vicar's challenge may have forced him towards such honesty.

The 'statue' of the Flesh, with its 'pale scarlet' dawn colour and constantly changing silhouette, is one of a series of similar figures in Owen's poetry. Representing his desires as both man and poet, its various manifestations are often associated with pain and its triumph is never complete. Its earliest appearance is in a passage which he added to 'The Little Mermaid' in September 1912. The mermaid finds on the sea bed

> a marble statue, – some boy-king's,
> Or youthful hero's. Its cold face in vain
> She gazed at, kissed, and tried with sighs to thaw
> For still the wide eyes stared, and nothing saw.
>
> Thereby she set a weeping willow-tree
> To droop and mourn. Full dolefully it clung
> About the form, and moved continually,
> As if it sighed; as if it sometimes wrung
> Convulsive fingers in sad reverie.
> And ever o'er the light blue sand it hung
> A purple shade, which hour by hour the same,
> Burnt softly on, like lambent sulphur-flame.

Despite the traces here of 'Isabella' and *Endymion*, the imagery in the description can now, I hope, be recognised as Owen's own. It contains elements from his Dunsden dreams, experiences and poems, worked into an impersonal pattern. The statue is of a boy with sad eyes. The 'wide eyes' gaze for ever and see nothing, like Moneta's in *The Fall of Hyperion*. Flame burns unchanging, colouring the stone flesh purple, while the convulsive fingers of the shadow make an ever-changing outline. The stony face – for the image is of Owen as well as of Rampton – cannot be softened by a girl's caresses. The submarine setting is a smothering underworld from which there seems to be no release. The material for 'Mental Cases' and 'Strange Meeting' is already beginning to take shape.

Owen had made his rebellion and chosen his course through darkness. He left Dunsden behind him, with the friends and enemies which he had made there. He had found some of the subject matter of his future poetry; now he had to strengthen his 'aesthetic philosophy', develop his own style and establish his freedom, tasks which might be more easily accomplished abroad than at home.

3 Aesthete in France

TAILHADE AND OTHERS

By mid September 1913, Owen was established as a teacher in the Berlitz School of Languages in Bordeaux. He began his two years in France by telling his new acquaintances that he was the son of a knight, a ruse which made him acceptable in higher social levels than had been open to him at home;[1] it was in France that he acquired the social and literary graces which were to make him a welcome member of the circle round Robert Ross, Oscar Wilde's champion, in 1918. The sickly lay assistant of 1912, his languors and ardours derived from Tennyson, Keats and Shelley, was replaced by a dapper, sun-tanned Aesthete, with a *chic* little moustache and a lively knowledge of recent French culture. His dedication to poetry grew stronger than ever, warmed by the southern sun and Laurent Tailhade's encouragement. Owen's debt to Tailhade and French literature has been generally overlooked (partly because fewer poems and letters survive from 1913–15 than from any other period of his adult life); unlike most British poets of his generation, he encountered late Romanticism in France rather than at home. Whereas much of the early verse of Sassoon or Rupert Brooke is modelled on Swinburne, Wilde and the poets of English nineties, Owen's writing shows little trace of Swinburne until 1916 or of Wilde until 1917–18. Although he seems to have been familiar with some English Pre-Raphaelite work, his knowledge of Decadent literature came from French originals, not from imitators such as Wilde. He went to France already interested, as is shown by his reference to 'imagination, physical sensation, aesthetic philosophy' in his 1913 letter to Wigan, as well as by his fondness for purple, the chosen colour of the Aesthetes, and by his sense of belonging to a secret order of poets.[2] He made his first attempt at writing verse in the French style ('The Imbecile') as soon as he reached Bordeaux.

The dominant creed in French art was still that known broadly as Aestheticism,[3] the late-Romantic belief that the artist's sole aim was to hunt and capture beauty. The first French Aesthetes, Gautier ('L'art pour l'art') and Baudelaire in the mid century, and the novelists Flaubert and Huysmans, had led the withdrawal from bourgeois reality into an autonomous, imaginative world where art was supreme. In the eighties, a group of young Aesthetes in Paris declared themselves 'Decadents', maintaining that civilisation had reached a state of ripeness indistinguishable from decay, a cultural autumn. Modern man, with his morbid sensibility and exhaustive knowledge, had grown beyond ideals and morals; left only with his senses and their objects, his highest activity was to develop sensation to its utmost refinements in the pursuit of beauty. Thus the Decadents had at least one idea in common with their contemporaries, the Impressionists and the Naturalists, that the function of art was to explore and embody physical sensation. Art had nothing to do with morality; the work of art concentrated sensation into a perfect form, and the form was all that mattered. When an anarchist threw a bomb into the French parliament in 1893, one of the leading Decadents, Laurent Tailhade, had remarked in a notorious phrase, 'Qu'importent les victimes si le geste est beau?' In meeting Tailhade in 1914, Owen was meeting a poet who had been at the centre of Parisian artistic society in its most famous period. Like Owen, Tailhade had been destined for a career in the Church but had broken away in order to devote himself to art for art's sake. He was famous for his satires against middle-class respectability and for his elegant lyrics. He had been a close friend of Verlaine, a regular attender at Mallarmé's *mardis* (where he had met Wilde), an anarchist sympathiser, a dabbler in the occult and a celebrated dandy. No one could have told Owen more about French literature of the later nineteenth century.[4]

The relevance of Aesthetic, and more particularly Decadent, conventions to Owen the future war poet is not difficult to see. For example, Aestheticism's search for exquisite sensation and its rejection of orthodox moral constraints led to *ennui* and disgust at contemporary society (that was one reason why Brooke and others welcomed war in 1914). Artists were attracted not only to strange cults and religious mysteries but also to violence. There is a strong sado-masochistic element in the literature of the period, in Flaubert's *Salammbô*, for example, or the heady, pagan verse of Swinburne. Women became *femmes fatales*, as in Rossetti's portraits, their brows white with pain and their lips red with the

blood of lovers. Blood flowed freely. One very common image
was that of a bleeding sunset to denote catastrophe, killing or
erotic passion; there are sunsets of this kind in Baudelaire,
Flaubert, d'Annunzio, Wilde, Hardy and even late Dickens.[5]
The image can be associated with the larger one of the last sunset,
the dusk of the nations in which civilisation would finally perish.[6]
The great collapse would bring a moment of strange, sweet
sensation and then darkness. Meanwhile, an outburst of violence
would at least reduce the boredom of living. Swinburne
complained that the world had grown 'grey' from Christ's breath.[7]
'The earth has grown too grey and peaceful', exclaims a character
in a 1905 novel which Owen read in 1917. 'We need colour –
good red splashes of it – good wholesome bloodshed.'[8] Brooke,
who was an assiduously Decadent poet in his early years, wrote
from Antwerp in 1907 to a friend with similar tastes, 'I am going
to drag my tired body out . . . in the faint hope of finding a riot.
The sight of fire and street-fighting and men hurt might soothe
my seared soul.' In the same letter, he describes the sunset: 'In
England of an evening the sun-god used to be crucified in beautiful
agony on the red places of the west: here only a suppurating sore
is opened afresh . . . .'[9] That is an elegant pose, but Owen's image
of the bleeding sun in 'Mental Cases' is in the same tradition:

> Sunlight seems a blood-smear; night comes blood-black;
> Dawn breaks open like a wound that bleeds afresh.

The purpose is different; the imagery and language are the same.
   The blood and pain which pervade Decadent art are usually
associated with passive suffering and (preferably illicit) sexual
pleasure (even 'Mental Cases' is a version of an earlier erotic
poem). Artists thought of themselves as passive victims, often
comparing themselves to the original Decadents in ancient Rome,
refining their perception of beauty even as the barbarians broke
down the gates (a subject for several paintings). 'I love this word
decadence,' Verlaine wrote in a well-known passage,

> all shimmering in purple and gold. It suggests the subtle
> thoughts of ultimate civilisation, a high literary culture, a soul
> capable of intense pleasures. It throws off bursts of fire and the
> sparkle of precious stones. It is redolent of . . . the consuming
> in flames of races exhausted by their capacity for sensation, as
> the trump of an invading enemy sounds.[10]

In political terms the barbarians were the Prussians, who had marched through Paris in triumph in 1870 and might do so again. There were many prophecies of international disaster. Death was strangely attractive as the most intense of all experiences, and martyrdom was a subject of obsessive interest. Self-sacrifice might have a religious value or it might be futile; as Tailhade would have said, what mattered was that the gesture should be beautiful. St Sebastian, for example, the naked youth passively receiving the arrows, was a recurrent image of what Wilde called 'all the pathetic uselessness of martyrdom, all its wasted beauty'.[11] And the martyr smiles (as in Owen's 'Has your soul sipped') with a secret joy known only to the few. In their pursuit of sensation beyond morals, the Decadents were fascinated by the links between pain and ecstasy, and by all forms of sexual deviance. The hermaphrodite became a frequent image of tormented desire and strange, ambiguous beauty ('Perseus', the long poem which Owen planned in France, was to have included such a figure). Many poets, including Tailhade, wrote about dangerously beautiful boys, either as classical figures such as Antinous or as tempters on the modern streets. If such subjects outraged public opinion, so much the better; one of the artist's duties was to shock the middle classes (*épater le bourgeois*), especially the older generation.

All this produced a strong sense of exclusiveness. There was a special vocabulary – 'strange', 'sweet', 'mystery', 'smile', 'secret', 'exquisite', for example, all words which Owen used – and range of symbols. The near-occult mystery enshrouding French poetry of the period was particularly apparent in Symbolism, a mode of writing derived from Gautier and Baudelaire and developed by Mallarmé and his followers, in which the symbol became an expression of mystic truth beyond all rational statement, to be apprehended only through the artistic consciousness. By meditating on a rose, a waterlily, a jewel, a colour, the artist emptied his mind of everything that was not art and entered the secret world of pure form, pure language. Symbolism was concerned with language alone, with the perfection of words as music – 'de la musique avant toute chose', Verlaine insisted, because music was the supreme example of an art form fully separated from daily reality. But in the hands of lesser writers, among whom Tailhade and Wilde may be included, the symbols which Mallarmé wrote about with barely intelligible abstruseness became repetitive material for charming but shallow lyrics, so that any young hopeful could adopt both the manner of Symbolism and Mallarmé's (and Tailhade's) ambition to 'purify the dialect of the tribe'.

Later chapters will discuss the effects of French Aestheticism and its English counterpart on Owen's thinking and writing in 1916–18. A few examples here may help to prepare the ground. Dreaming of a book of his own sonnets in 1917, he decided to call it 'Sonatas in Silence' and to have it bound in purple and gold.[12] The quotations given above from Verlaine put these details into place. Music – or, even better, silent music – was the art to which poetry should aspire. Calling a poem a sonata – or rhapsody, impromptu, nocturne, all fashionable titles which Owen duly toyed with – suggested Chopin, who was with Wagner the cult composer of the Decadence. Purple was the cult colour. The Mermaid's willow tree (1912) had cast a 'purple shade', and in the Verlaine-like sonnet 'Purple' (1916) the colour's associations with melancholy and passion are fully, if crudely, set out. The purple wound in 'Disabled' (1917) illustrates the Decadent element in Owen's mature poetry, the colour still carrying its poetic significance and thereby giving new meaning to the bloodthirstiness of war.[13] When he was in the trenches he enjoyed the company of a Captain Sorrell, 'an aesthete' who challenged him to write sonnets. He described Sorrell as 'not virtuous according to English standards' but 'one of the few young men who live up to my principle: that Amusement is never an excuse for "immorality", but that Passion may be so'.[14] It was only in such occasional comments that Owen recorded his Aesthetic creed, but a reader who keeps it in mind can see not only the force of his remark from the trenches, 'extra for me there is the universal pervasion of *Ugliness*',[15] but also the radical change of approach implicit in his 1918 manifesto: 'Above all I am not concerned with Poetry'. Even in 1918, despite that move away from art for art's sake, poems such as 'The Kind Ghosts' and 'Greater Love' show him still writing in the Decadent tradition; and all his war poems, like Sassoon's, had *épater le bourgeois* as a principal motive. That Decadent scorn for middle-class respectability also helped to free his sexual nature and reinforced his sense of being mysteriously set apart ('I had mystery . . . To miss the march of this retreating world'), an isolation that was to be crucial to his 1918 work.

It was in France, too, that he learned the importance of

technique. The French poets, with their high esteem for formal elegance, were bold experimenters with sound-effects; a 'Sonnet' by Tailhade includes the lines

> O Lune pâle qui délie,
> Liliale en le soir berceur,
> Ta lueur d'opâle appâlie
> A la douceur d'une alme soeur.

Sequences such as 'pâle ... -ale ... opâle appâlie ... al-' were the kind of patterning that Owen was to use in his later poems. The first traces of his famous pararhyme ('mode meed mood') appear on Bordeaux manuscripts;[16] it is one of the ironies of literature that a device invented for musical effect in Decadent love lyrics should have become a means of expressing the harsh realities of war experience.

1914 was perhaps the happiest year of his life. It started badly, with illness reminiscent of Dunsden troubles, but there was no one to fuss over him and no point in languishing. Free at last from home and piety, he could no longer avoid mature relationships. In his letters home, he gently rebuked his mother for having kept him ignorant of sex; nevertheless, he assured her that all women, 'without exception, *annoy* me, and the mercenaries . . . I utterly detest'. If Mrs Owen had no 'revelations to make to me, at 14, I shall have no confessions now I am 21. / At least none such as must make me blush and weep and you grow pale.'[17] In April, a friend took him to visit the Poitou family in the country; he was shaken by the beauty of the daughter, Henriette, and by finding himself 'like an Egyptian piece of Statuary' in her presence. Walking with her in the woods may have reminded him of Rampton; at any rate, in his letters from France spring flowers and woodlands became recurrent symbols for physical and psychological states. The Poitous saw him off at the station, giving him masses of lilac, 'and the odour was carried by the inblowing breeze into my brain, to be an everlasting memory. Then those faces and those places fell away from me.' Back in his lodgings, he wrote '50 lines of poetry in as many minutes! (thing not attempted for "years")'.[18] The Henriette episode seems to be referred to in 'The One Remains', in which the poet seeks perfect beauty 'once for ever, in one face' and remembers

> the secret traces
> Left in my heart, of countenances seen,
> And lost as soon as seen, – but which mine eye
> Remembers as my old home, or the lie
> Of landscapes whereupon my windows lean.

The phrasing suggests that this sonnet was written in France, not only with nostalgia for Shrewsbury but also with a sharper 'everlasting memory' of 'those faces and those places' seen on the Poitou visit. He was troubled at his inability to respond to women; in August, he said he was 'too old to be in love' and in November he complained that he lacked 'any touch of tenderness. I ache in soul, as my bones might ache after a night spent on a cold, stone floor.'[19] Imagery of stone, statuary and age persisted from his Dunsden verse. Then came a change.

In July, one of his pupils, a Mme Léger,[20] invited him to join her as tutor on a family holiday near Bagnères-de-Bigorre at the foot of the Pyrenees. Owen's two months there were to be a milestone in his poetic career. He arrived on 30 July, on the eve of war, delighted to be in fine country. The Légers had rented a villa in the secluded valley of La Gailleste. This was the '[fair] house, secret, ['mid] hills' of the first draft of 'The Sleeping Beauty', and the 'Beauty' was Albine (Nénette), the Légers' only daughter, who immediately adored and captivated Owen although she was too young, as the sonnet records (with regret or perhaps relief), to be kissed 'to the world of Consciousness'. Mme Léger was an elegant, successful businesswoman, her husband a talented man of the theatre. Owen was always to remember his stay with these intelligent, cultured people as a time of 'amazing pleasure'; he described it three years later in 'From my Diary, July 1914', tactfully changing the date to commemorate the last month of peace. The poem incorporates memories of his bathes in a mountain stream, his helping M Léger to get in the hay crop because the farmhands had been mobilised, and the excitement of conducting two flirtations at once, one with Nénette and one, more seriously, with her mother. Quite how seriously is difficult to guess, but Madame was certainly in earnest, telling her tutor flatteringly that she did not love her husband 'excessively' but that she liked handsome people.[21] Then she asked Owen to go with her on her forthcoming business trip to Canada. In the event, she embarked alone and he remained on friendly terms with M Léger, calling on him at least twice in Bordeaux, but Mrs Owen was alarmed in England and even M Léger's old friend Tailhade avoided mentioning Owen to him in 1915 for fear of being indiscreet.[22] It was all a welcome change from the stuffiness of Dunsden and Shrewsbury, anyhow, despite the distant background of war. When news of the war came, Owen made the thoroughly Aesthetic gesture of playing Chopin's *Marche funèbre*, suffering 'torture' because Nénette forced him to repeat it but also delight because of her expression. Through the window he could see a hill 'exactly like' one at home.[23] Pleasure and pain, Romantic music, the beauty of a child's face and of the Shropshire landscape thus mingled in the first 'physical sensation' of war.

At the end of August, Laurent Tailhade came to Bagnères to deliver some public lectures at the Casino. M Léger gave supporting recitations, while Owen and Madame sat rather close together in the audience (Plate 4). Over the next few weeks, the two poets saw a good deal of each other, Tailhade becoming very much attached to the young Englishman. They were photographed together in the garden, Tailhade affectionately showing him a book (Plate 5). The picture marks a significant moment in Owen's poethood, as the first famous author he has ever met introduces him to French literature – for the book is almost certainly the copy of Flaubert's *La Tentation de Saint-Antoine* which Tailhade gave him in September.[24] The old poet may not have had any spare copies of his own books to hand and had in any case ceased to publish verse, but he must have lent him one of his two volumes of collected poems because Owen soon started a translation of a *ballade élégiaque* from it.[25] Later on, Tailhade presented him with both volumes, inscribing a copy of the lyrical *Poèmes élégiaques* (1907) for him when they met again in Paris in May 1915, 'en souvenir de nos belles causeries et des beaux soirs à La Gailleste', and at some stage sending him the satirical *Poèmes aristophanesques*.[26]

Since Tailhade was a master of the *causerie*, it was probably his conversation rather than his poetry that fascinated Owen at first. Two principal topics must have been war and literature. Dennis Welland (1960) has suggested parallels between Owen's war poems and Tailhade's essays, *Pour la paix* and *Lettre aux conscrits*, but subsequent critics have echoed this to such an extent that

Tailhade's importance in Owen's life has come to be imagined as exclusively that of a pacifist. Certainly *Lettre aux conscrits* (1903) is a powerful appeal, burning with the anarchist fury that had earned its author a prison sentence in 1901. He urges conscripts never to kill, arguing that war is a conspiracy by the rich, the old and the aristocracy. The conscript is warned that he will be ordered to kill young workers like himself:

> Ils ont, là-bas, des compagnes, leur mère et des amis dont les yeux se mouillèrent au départ. Ils aiment, eux aussi, la clarté du soleil et le parfum des bois. Ils portent dans leurs veines le sang pourpré de la jeunesse. Ils s'avancent, comme toi, pleins de la vie, à la conquête du bonheur. Ne tue pas!

This appeal may be distantly echoed in 'Strange Meeting' ('Whatever hope is yours, / Was my life also'). Another passage suggests some of the imagery in 'Spring Offensive' and 'The Kind Ghosts':

> L'offrande à Moloch du printemps sacré, de vos vingt ans, ô jeunes hommes! laisse indifférentes et soumises, crédules, peut-être, à la hideuse fiction du patriotisme, celles mêmes dont les entrailles vous ont portés.

Nevertheless, it is as well to be cautious in claiming Tailhade as a source of Owen's later loathing of war. As a veteran duellist, the old poet was not opposed to all fighting. The two essays had been written in protest at a French alliance with Tsarism for foreign wars, but an invasion of France herself, directed at his beloved Paris by the same Prussian war-machine that had invaded it in his youth, seem to have produced a different reaction; he was 'shouldering a rifle' by November, which made Owen wonder uncomfortably whether he ought not to be doing the same thing himself. Tailhade's first comments on the war may have been more *élégiaques* than *aristophanesques*, nearer the mood of the *Marche funèbre* than of *Lettre aux conscrits*. He claimed in his 1914 volume of essays that 'La douleur s'affirme comme le principe de toute poésie', a statement reminiscent of Wilde's *De Profundis*, Verlaine's poems and other Decadent works. An essay on masochism, though deploring 'la folie algolagnique', refers at length to works he deeply admired, including the *Tentation*.[27] One of his *ballades élégiaques*, 'Les fleurs d'Ophélie', which Owen liked and probably translated, contains imagery of a distinctly masochistic, Decadent and warlike nature:

> Amour! Amour! et sur leurs fronts que tu courbas
> Fais ruisseler la pourpre extatique des roses,
> Pareille au sang joyeux versé dans les combats.

He perhaps discoursed at the villa about youth's noble sacrifice, the melancholy beauty of death and the purple 'sang joyeux' that was being spilt. It was that strain, at any rate, which was to be paramount in Owen's writing until 1917. But anger and satire were expressed, albeit in an Aesthetic way that is hardly to the modern taste:

> While it is true that the guns will effect a little useful weeding, I am furious with chagrin to think that the Minds which were to have excelled the civilisation of ten thousand years, are being annihilated – and bodies, the products of aeons of Natural Selection, melted down to pay for political statues.[28]

Owen made these Darwinist remarks soon after a conversation with Tailhade in the privacy of the latter's hotel room. The older man found him interesting as a poet, being always ready to encourage the efforts of the select few who were 'tourmentés, à l'égal de lui-même, par le pur amour de l'art et de la beauté',[29] but this hardly explains the warmth of his affection. 'He received me like a lover', Owen reported. 'To use an expression of the Rev. H. Wigan's, he quite slobbered over me. I know not how many times he squeezed my hand; and, sitting me down on a sofa, pressed my head against his shoulder.' At about the same time, he said that Tailhade 'calls my eyes "So very lovely!!!" etc and my neck "The neck of a statue!!!! etc" – because he is a poet, and unconsciously appreciates in me, *not* the appearance of beauty but the Spirit and temperament of beauty, Tailhade says he is going to write a Sonnet on me'. Mrs Owen was sufficiently convinced by her son's assurances to feel able to quote this passage (the punctuation is probably hers) to Blunden in 1930, but the original letter was subsequently 'lost'.[30] There are a great many sonnets to beautiful youths by Decadent poets, and they are by no means always concerned only with the 'Spirit' of beauty, as Owen may have been well aware. To judge from various poems and anecdotes, Tailhade was not unused to treating young men as lovers. He taught Owen more things than pacifism, if indeed he taught him pacifism at all.

Owen discovered that expressions of passion between men (including hand contact) were not only permissible but also a subject for poetry. In 'Maundy Thursday', he describes how he kissed the warm hand of the acolyte instead of the 'very dead' crucifix; as in 'The time was aeon', the flesh is set against religion, but the irony and witty sexual suggestion of the sonnet is far from the Monro-inspired portentousness of the earlier poem. 'Maundy Thursday' is perhaps Owen's best effort in Tailhade's *aristophanes-que* vein (a style which took a while to master, because the sonnet is clearly a memory of Easter 1915).[31] Tailhade's high regard for formal elegance may explain why there is a deftness in Owen's sonnets from 1915 onwards that is lacking in his earlier work. But in 1914 Tailhade's example aroused an altogether deeper memory of a hand, recorded in a much less polished piece of verse; on the back of his translation from the *ballade élégiaque* Owen roughed out the lines about a boy which have been referred to in the previous chapter (see above, p.22). At about the same time, he wrote his fragmentary record of the birth of his 'poethood', reminded of the Broxton landscape by the hills at Bagnères where Tailhade's own poethood had begun. These manuscripts suggest the depth to which he was influenced by the French poet in 1914, showing him not only translating Tailhade's verse but also, perhaps even on his new friend's advice, exploring the roots of his own poetic imagination by recollecting two symbolic first encounters, one with love and the other with nature.[32]

It seems clear that Tailhade encouraged Owen to start reading intensively, although the clues are sparse. French literature was suspect in England, so that Owen did not say too much about it in his letters home and some of what he did say was later destroyed. On 7 September, 'son vieil ami' gave him the *Tentation* and Renan's *Souvenirs d'enfance et de jeunesse* (an account of yet another writer who broke away from religion in his youth). After returning to Bordeaux with the Légers later in the month, Owen met another poet, Carlos Larronde, who gave him a book of his poems with the hope that 'ces vers lui en feront aimer d'autres – plus beaux – des Poètes que j'aime'. On the thirtieth, he said he was 'studying French literature' and in October he was still busy with 'my interesting books'.[33] A few of those books can be identified.

In his copy of Vigny's *Chatterton*, he marked the sentence, 'En

toi, la rêverie continuelle a tué l'action', and in Renan he marked
a comment that the Celts know how to plunge their hands into
a man's entrails and bring out secrets of the infinite. What he
always thought of as his Celtic strain would have been fascinated
by *La Tentation de Saint-Antoine*, in which Flaubert meticulously
describes the saint's visions of strange and dreadful beings. Owen
read the book with care, underlining frequently. Tailhade had
also marked it, writing 'crétin!' against a criticism by the editor
of the novel's 'grands défauts'. Evidently agreeing with Tailhade,
Owen went on to read at least two more of Flaubert's novels,
Madame Bovary and *Salammbô*. 'Flaubert has my vote for novel-
writing!', he exclaimed to Gunston in July 1915, and he told his
mother that he was reading *Salammbô* 'with more interest than
the Communiqués'.[34] This book is a minutely detailed, gruesome
story of a war in ancient Carthage, told in Flaubert's exquisitely
finished prose. George Steiner has said that 'its scarcely governed
ache for savagery' stems from Flaubert's frustration in the society
of his time and that 'this frenetic yet congealed narrative of blood-
lust, barbaric warfare and orgiastic pain, takes us to the heart'
of the question of war and violence in our century.[35] That Owen
was reading *Salammbô*, and at the same time recording that he
was now keen to enlist (but in the Italian cavalry 'for reasons
both aesthetic and practical')[36] is, one might say, appropriate.
The current of nineteenth-century culture drove him, as it drove
a continent, towards war.

   The most obvious result of his first readings of Flaubert is the
curious poem beginning 'Long ages past'.[37] The only manuscript
is dated 31 October 1914, which has led some of its few
commentators to draw what seems to be the groundless conclusion
that it is about the war. It is in fact a rhapsody about a lover
(presumably imaginary), written as thoroughly in the Decadent
style as Owen could manage. Conventional details include
references to the ancient world, human sacrifice, jewels, music,
frenzy, opium, the Gorgon's head, 'wild desire', 'pain' and
'bitter pleasure'. Flaubert's descriptions are full of such material,
providing the model for later works such as Wilde's *Salomé*. True
to form, Owen's subject has the red lips of a vampire and the
pallor of a *femme fatale*, but the gender is left ambiguous, as is
often the case in Decadent poems of this kind; initiates could be
left to assume that the subject was a boy if they wished, but the
attributes of the fatal lover could belong to either sex:

Thou slewest women and thy pining lovers,
And on thy lips the stain of crimson blood,
And on thy brow the pallor of their death.

The 'pale brows' of the child in 'Deep under turfy grass' and the 'pallor' of Despondency–Medusa in the 'Supposed Confessions' were similarly marks of fatal beauty, and the echo of 'Long ages past' in 'Anthem for Doomed Youth' (1917), where dead soldiers are commemorated by the 'pallor of girls' brows', implies that wartime girls have the same deadly quality. The image of the bloodstained mouth also recurs in the war poems, as will be seen. Such images have their origins in the Decadence and, as later chapters will suggest, in those dreams of 'bloodiness and stains of shadowy crimes' which had plagued Owen's nights at least since 1911.

He is likely to have read a good deal of French verse as well as prose during the winter of 1914–15; there are several relevant books in his library, including a few marked anthologies, and a 1914 transcription of Verlaine's sonnet 'Mon rêve familier'.[38] Verlaine's dream of an unknown, unreached lover, with a gaze like that of statues and a calm, grave voice like the loved voices of the dead, left traces in 'The Unreturning', 'Autumnal', 'On a Dream' and other sonnets which Owen probably composed or redrafted in Bordeaux. His first exemplars in the form had been Keats and Shakespeare, but most of his sonnets can be associated with his two years in France, where Verlaine was an obvious model to follow (no doubt Tailhade recommended him); the erotic melancholy and quasi-Symbolist imagery of these poems clearly show the influence of the master and of his sometime disciple Tailhade. In the end, Owen abandoned the form altogether after 'Hospital Barge' (December 1917), but between 1914 and early 1917 it was his favourite. When he wanted to impress a new literary friend, such as Monro or Sassoon, it was his sonnets that he produced, since they were the only finished poems he had to show for his labours on larger projects such as 'Perseus'. A number of them seem to have been quarried out of 'Perseus' material, a process which had it origins in his 1911 practice of shaping sonnets out of prose drafts. While few of them are work of real distinction, they were at least a useful discipline which was to bear fruit later in the organisation of such war poems as 'Conscious' and 'Inspection', both of which were developed from quatrains into what are in effect sixteen-line sonnets, or 'Dulce et Decorum Est, which begins with a block of eight lines, then one of six, or the long stanzas or verse paragraphs of 'Spring Offensive' and other 1918 poems.

By February 1915 he felt ready to start some writing of his own, having sated his appetite for novels and everything else, except 'pure strong Poetry', which was in short supply now that he had read all that he could find. 'All that novelists have to tell has been told me, and by the best of them. I have even found out more. And that *more* which I had not been told I feel I ought to tell.' The stress on realism here suggests that he had been reading Zola, a writer whom Tailhade had known and revered. The experiences which Owen had in mind for writing may have been those of Dunsden, for the phrase 'In Dunsden' is just legible in the manuscript of another February letter before the sentence, 'I have made soundings in deep waters, and I have looked out from many observation-towers: and I found the deep waters terrible, and nearly lost my breath there.' Nevertheless there were also observations and adventures in 1914–15, some of them hinted at in letters and verse but in the end never 'told' in full. It is impossible to know now whether Owen in 1915 really had any '*more*' to tell than the novelists or whether he was merely being self-important, but his feeling of having escaped drowning ('congestion of the lungs'?) and having come back from the dead with new things to tell was to be reflected in the 'Perseus' fragments, with their mysterious tales from the underworld, and eventually in the 'truth untold' of 'Strange Meeting'. The voice of the future war poet reporting from hell is also heard in a detailed description of war wounds, this time not borrowed from Flaubert but seen in a French hospital in September 1914: 'I deliberately tell you all this to educate you to the actualities of the war.' Owen's later urge to 'educate' his readers owes something to his study of French novelists, just as his delight in beauty, form and 'physical sensation' derives in part from his knowledge of French poets. Much of his debt to French literature of the later nineteenth century stemmed from his friendship with Tailhade, and its results began to emerge in the strange fragments of 'Perseus'.[39]

'PERSEUS'

'Perseus', the most ambitious and irrecoverable of all Owen's poetic endeavours, was begun in France and became a central expression of his poethood. It survives only as a few scribbled leaves, understandably ignored by critics as incoherent 'juvenilia', fragments of raw, unfinished verse which seem hopelessly devoid of literary merit despite some odd parallels with the famous poems of 1917–18. But through all this chaotic material Owen seems to be feeling his way towards a myth of his own life and identity, giving it shape in a pattern that is strangely close to that of his war poetry, so that the 'Perseus' manuscripts, crude stuff in themselves, are a key to his eventual achievement.

When he left the Léger household in the autumn of 1914, he took up freelance teaching in Bordeaux for some months, corresponding occasionally with Tailhade, who had returned to Paris, and becoming something of a man about town. Rumour has always had it that it was in this period that his first sexual encounters occurred;[40] certainly, his involuntary coolness towards Henriette and Mme Léger, as well as Tailhade's demonstrativeness and the liberty of a great French city, would have given him all the clues he needed. He described several youths with incautious admiration in his letters, while the homosexual element in his verse became conspicuous in 1915. Whatever the case, he enjoyed his freedom, despite repeated assurances to his mother that he would like to return home. In December 1914 he accepted a post at Mérignac on the outskirts of the city as tutor to some Anglo-French boys. The local woods and moors in the spring provided imagery for his 1915 work. He said little in his letters about his poetry but referred mysteriously to 'certain writings' which he wanted to finish. In response to British recruiting-propaganda (there was little in France because conscription was in force from the start) and parental worries about his future, he felt more strongly than ever that his career had long been chosen. 'A boy, I guessed that the fullest, largest liveable life was that of a Poet. I *know* it now . . . .' Universities and the Church had lost their attraction. 'There is *one* title I prize, one clear call audible, one Sphere where I may influence for Truth, one workshop whence I may send forth Beauty, one mode of living entirely congenial to me' (March). He quoted Keats, adding that 'as trees in Spring produce a new ring of tissue, so does every poet put forth a fresh, and lasting outlay of stuff at the same season' (April). The purple heather on the moors in August reminded him of Broxton. As for enlisting, he maintained at first that a poet was more useful to his country alive than dead but later he began to think that military life might be good for his writing.[41] These statements of literary ambition, fired by his recent explorations of French literature, were accompanied by work on the new vehicle for 'Truth' and 'Beauty', a long poem or verse drama under the title of 'Perseus'.

A full account of Owen's plans for 'Perseus' can never be given, since much of the poem has perished or was never written down. He was probably unsure about them himself, for he kept returning to the manuscripts with additions and alterations. The earliest drafts may date from 1914, at least three belong to 1915, one to 1917, and even in 1918 he was still intending to finish the project. In the account which follows I have given each fragment a number (P1, P2, etc.) for ease of reference and have omitted many small details, in an attempt to disentangle what is left of an undertaking that occupied him intermittently over several years.[42]

The longest fragment, P1 (*CPF*, 467–70), consists of a little more than fifty lines of blank verse monologue, scribbled hurriedly on a large double sheet. It is marked 'For Perseus' and has a few added mentions of Pluto and Persephone, but there are no references to classical myth in the main body of the verse except two to Eros, who also appears in several of Owen's sonnets. The original speaker of the monologue seems to have been Owen himself, not some classical character. It is possible, in fact, that this is the '50 lines of poetry' which he poured out 'in as many minutes' after meeting Henriette in April 1914; there is certainly no other fragment surviving among his papers that fits this description. By 1915 he seems to have decided that he could make the material presentable by incorporating it into a long work on Perseus, its vaguely mythical quality making it suitable for such treatment. The subject of Perseus was probably selected in consultation with Gunston, for the two cousins had apparently agreed to compete once more, each choosing a classical hero associated with flying, just as they had agreed to write on 'The Swift', another flying subject, in 1914. In the summer of 1915 Gunston wrote ninety lines on Icarus, his own subject, churning them out at a line a minute, a speed his cousin had no doubt recommended as a way of getting started.[43] But P1 was never altered much, so that it has nothing to do with the Perseus legends though plenty to do with Owen's 'Perseus'.

P1 opens with a heavily cancelled line, 'What have I done, O God, what have I done?' If this and what follows are part of Owen's response to his helplessness in the presence of Henriette, when he had felt like 'an Egyptian piece of Statuary', the fragment

shows him starting very soon after the event to turn experience
into something like myth. The speaker describes a night when
Eros descended to him with a sound of fire, heralding the
perfection of love: 'I knew the thing was come at last'. But then,
mysteriously, this first and last chance is lost (Owen's wording
loses all coherence at this point) because the speaker pauses to
'renounce the world', using biblical language reminiscent of a
lapsed Evangelical's training and guilt:

> Let not the sun drop sweetness on me more
> Nor let the moon be comforting by night . . .

The speaker turns away 'great friends' and 'all youth', for he has
'touched the god; [and] touch me not'.

> On all that had been sweet to me, I laughed.
> I trampled on the flowers I so much loved
>   . . .
> [And the dear books I blotted out and tore]
> Let music [be my terror] a jar [to all] my peace
> I would no more remember my old home
> Nor the old days or people or the places
> And turned adrift even my helpless hopes
> And bade the flame of this love burn them down.[44]

There are echoes here of 'The One Remains' ('my old home')
and of the Henriette excursion ('those faces and those places'),
while the last lines contain a rough version of the burnt offering
in 'To Eros':

> In that I loved you, Love, I worshipped you.
> In that I worshipped well, I sacrificed.
> All of most worth I bound and burnt and slew:
> Old peaceful lives; frail flowers; firms friends; and Christ.[45]

It is evident that the two sonnets 'To the Bitter Sweet-Heart: A
Dream' and 'To Eros' maintain the sequence of P1; like other
sonnets, they may have been quarried from draft work for the
long poem. The autobiographical content seems clear: when
Owen left Dunsden, he left religion ('Christ'), children ('all
youth'), the old people he visited in the parish ('Old peaceful
lives'), botanical studies at Reading ('flowers'), musical activities,

and his hopes for a degree ('the dear books'?). Then he left Shrewsbury ('my old home'), family and friends. The reasons for the sacrifice can only be guessed at but it was made to Eros, the treacherous god of love. 'What have I done, O God . . ?' The question seems to be answered: 'I have touched the god', thereby losing the power to respond to an ordinary lover. Was Owen remembering touching a boy's hand in a hawthorn glade in 1912? Poets have agonised over smaller matters.

There is considerable confusion over genders in P1. The speaker could be of either sex, but the voice is so personal that one assumes it to be the poet's own. The speaker's lover was originally male, either Eros or a human equivalent, but Owen later made some half-hearted attempts, as in 'The time was aeon', to change this representative of beauty into a female figure, in this case the goddess Persephone. He also tried to turn the speaker into Persephone's husband, Pluto, who was to have been shown miserable and alone in hell, lamenting his queen's annual absence in the upper world. This would have disguised the homosexual and personal implications of the original draft, while perhaps allowing Owen secretly to imagine Pluto as himself alone in the city, and Persephone as Henriette, goddess of the spring woods. Since several of the 'Perseus' fragments refer to the seasons, it may be that he intended to base his scheme on the seasonal cycle, a structure which he used for rather too many of his shorter poems, but there does not seem to be any ancient Perseus legend which allows for this or for a descent into the underworld. He would have had to have taken as many liberties with classical myth as Keats had done in writing about Endymion or Hyperion. Whatever his plan, he never got round to amending P1 consistently, and the lover remains neither Persephone nor Henriette but Eros or an idealised youth, with cloudy brows and snowy feet:

> Between the summits of his shining shoulders
> Are there not valleys for my rest for ever
> Is not the flower of all flesh opened me?
> Shall I not have enough of joy [with him]?

The sexual confusions of P1 and other poems end in disaster. Although the poet accepts Eros in 'To the Bitter Sweet-Heart' as a substitute for his partner and reaches the happy valleys ('My face fell deeply in his shoulder'), in 'To Eros' he is deserted by the god. Similarly, P1 ends with 'my love' rejecting the speaker, who finds himself suddenly corpse-like, with a skull smile and empty eye sockets.

> I entered hell's low sorrowful secrecy
> My arms were wrenched with inexplicable weakness
> Methought my heart would loosen out of me
> Most like it was what men tell of the first
> Terrific minute of the hour of death . . . .

After this death-like agony, he meets a 'haggled crone', Age, who promises to be his new lover in hell. An excessive devotion to young male beauty seems to have brought painful retribution.

Some of the leading images in Owen's later poems can be seen in all this, including the skull smile and descent alive into hell ('Mental Cases', 'Strange Meeting'), the rejection of the sun's blessing ('Spring Offensive'), the climax of agonised death and the prohibition of touch ('Greater Love'), the figure of Beauty that offers 'rest for ever' (or 'ease / For ever' in 'My Shy Hand'), imagery of the male body as cloud and mountains ('The Wrestlers'), and the unreachable glory of youth. Material from or similar to P1 occurs frequently in Owen's verse from 1915 onwards, as will be seen.

P2 (*CPF*, 465–6) consists of some unfinished rhymed stanzas headed 'The cultivated Rose (From the Greek)'. Since the marginal note 'Danae speaks' is the only link with the Perseus story, this fragment also seems to have begun as an independent piece. Like P1, it seems impossible to date with any certainty, but the subject is a little like that of 'Long ages past' (October 1914), being a beautiful youth racked with desire. He has eyes dark 'with gloom of death and hell', a mouth red 'like fresh, uncovered blood' and beauty 'Dangerously exquisite, from toe to throat; / Contused with sap of life like a bursting bud':

> As shakes a high-trilled note
> His fingers ever trembled, with his eyes
> While hot thoughts ever loosened from his hair
> Perfume; and pearls of the fierce, vast desire.

The fragment ends with an attempt to explain this figure as a hermaphrodite tortured in the hell of unquenchable lust, but this and the title may have been afterthoughts designed to conceal any personal elements in the poem by placing it even more thoroughly within Decadent convention.[46] The core of P2 remains one of Owen's obsessive images, a boy in the grip of helpless sexual frustration, a hellish parallel to the triumphant 'Flesh' in 'The time was aeon'. The Rose's ever-trembling fingers are like those of the Mermaid's willow-tree, while several of his characteristics reappear in 'Purgatorial passions', a 1916 fragment about sufferers in hell which was to be used for 'Mental Cases'. His tormented eyes come from the most persistent of Owen's nightmares, that of the staring face. The Rose is thus an embodiment of Owen's personal difficulties and of the sort of figure that he found desirable; here as elsewhere the poet and his object seem one and the same.

P3 (*CPF*, 464) is one of a group of three fragments apparently written in the spring of 1915. By this stage Owen has decided on Perseus as a subject from the start, for Danae and Perseus are both mentioned in the verse. According to the Greek myth, Danae was the daughter of a king who locked her up in a tower to keep her away from men, a vain precaution because Zeus himself fell in love with her and entered the prison in the form of a shower of gold or, in versions by William Morris and others, a shaft of sunlight. Owen made a few notes for this event and its result: 'And then the whole sky fell / In vortices of flashings and showering gold', and 'Of all this sprang the infant Perseus. / Fair from the moment of his birth'.[47] However, most of this brief fragment is about Danae, alone in her cell, suffering from desire too intense to be satisfied by any human and watching 'trembling' human lovers who seem to be compared to trees in a storm ('Shook and were bowed before embracing winds'). The similarity between her torments and those of the Rose in P2 and the speaker in P1 suggests that Owen is beginning to adapt existing material to fit the Perseus legend, giving Danae the sufferings of those two characters and Zeus the fiery descent which had been attributed to Eros in P1. The imagery here was to remain in his poetry even as far as his last poem, 'Spring Offensive', where climactic fire again falls from 'the whole sky'. There is a particularly clear parallel between P3 and the mysterious sonnet 'Storm' (1916), in which someone (Eros? a youth?) is like destructive lightning fire:

> His face was charged with beauty as a cloud
>   With glimmering lightning. When it shadowed me,

> I *shook*, and was uneasy *as a tree*
> That draws the brilliant danger, *tremulous, bowed.*

(My italics.) If 'Storm' is compared with the Danae legend it becomes a little more intelligible than it has been until now, although such a reading still leaves questions to be answered. In both the sonnet and the fragment, the descent of fire is a sexual assault which results in the birth of beauty; stated in those general terms, the metaphor can be seen to represent the descent of inspiration on the poet and the resulting birth of the truth and beauty of poetry. Owen may have had some idea at this stage of developing 'Perseus'into that archetypal Romantic poem, a myth about the nature and origins of poetry itself.

P4 (*CPF*, 449–50) is another spring 1915 manuscript. I take it to be further work for 'Perseus', since it includes phrases about the sunlit air being 'thick with gold' or 'fire'. Furthermore, one of Perseus's flying-exploits was the rescue of Andromeda from a sea beast, and this folio refers to wartime Germany as a 'vast Beast / Whose throat is iron and whose teeth are steel'. There are also lines about the arrogant, shameless 'Emperor' (Kaiser), 'our' (French?) ministers smiling 'ministerially', and a Zeppelin ('horrible absurdity') over the Thames, all of which show that Owen took the popular Franco-British view of Germany in 1915. So 'Perseus' briefly and unpredictably emerges as a poem about the war. One of Owen's 1916 letters gives some clues as to what he had in mind; it discusses his short-lived ambition to become a pilot in the Royal Flying Corps and to battle against 'Zeppelin, the giant dragon', wearing the wings of Hermes as his badge and being in the same fellowship as 'Perseus and Icarus, whom I loved'.[48] The modern Perseus-pilot, born of Zeus (sunlight) and endowed with the power of Hermes, the winged messenger of the gods, would rescue Andromeda–France from the German dragon.

This romantic–heroic view of the war matched Owen's thoughts about enlisting in 1915. His Mérignac letters refer several times to 'the power of the midday sun'; taking pleasure in every 'nature-shock' from sun and wind was a 'sure sign of being Right with Nature'. He was conscious of being much fitter than he had been at Dunsden, where he had been supposed to have had a weak heart. 'This aft. I ran, with the boys, almost a mile – significant!' – he was strong enough for war. France was strong enough, too: the grapes were ripening in the sun and 'the muscle of France keeps resisted, – while her heart scarcely beats faster – The

Emperor yet frowns imperially; and our ministers yet wear a
ministerial smile' (August 1915, quoting from P4).[49] His exulting
runs in the hot sun were preparation for what he described in
1917 as the 'extraordinary exultation' of advancing across No
Man's Land under fire.[50] That 1917 advance was actually at
walking pace, but when the experience was reworked for 'Spring
Offensive' in 1918 his imagination returned to running, moors
and trees; the men in the poem stand like trees, then race across
a moor in sunlight until 'the whole sky' burns against them, the
final 'nature-shock' in his poetry.

P5 (*CPF*, 448), the third spring 1915 manuscript, contains a
few draft images which were probably more work for 'Perseus'.
A gloomy winter forest is contrasted with a summer landscape.
Like the trees in P3, the forest has a psychological connotation,
seeming like the 'horrors of an obscene mind . . . afraid of self'.

P6 (*CPF*, 470) is a monologue marked 'Speech for King' and
'Perseus'. It contains some familiar material about frustration
and finding ideal love but it is remarkably late, being written on
a type of paper which Owen used at Craiglockhart in 1917.
Overleaf is the line, 'O piteous mistake: O wrong wrong word'.[51]

These six fragments, and a few others which may have been
intended for 'Perseus', reveal little about the shape that Owen
planned for his project. Perhaps he had in mind a Romantic epic
or drama, like *Endymion* or *Atalanta in Calydon*, but he seems to
have begun P1 and P2 as separate poems, only later deciding
that he might be able to incorporate them into his new project.
How he imagined he could include Danae, Perseus, Pluto,
Persephone and Eros in a poem about the Great War, heaven
knows; P6, the 1917 fragment, makes no reference to the war, so
by then he had perhaps abandoned that aspect of the scheme.[52]
Nevertheless, whatever the formal plan for 'Perseus' was, the
fragments and some of the poems related to them do seem to
contain a shadowy but insistent pattern, a secret myth which he
seems to have been making out of his own experiences. It is in
this pattern that the importance of 'Perseus' lies for any study of
his poethood, since it can be related to some of his most successful
1918 work as the following outline may indicate.

The pattern starts with the hope for an ideally beautiful but
human and usually female lover ('The One Remains', 'On a
Dream', 'Mon rêve familier', P6). If the ideal is found, she is
sexually unawakened and the poet cannot or will not 'kiss her to
the world of Consciousness' ('The Sleeping Beauty', Henriette,

several poems about Dunsden children). Frustrated desire grows 'vast' and is seen in symptoms such as severe trembling (Danae, the Rose).

Then Eros or Zeus descends in sunlight, fire or lightning (P1, P3, 'Storm', 'Spring Offensive'). This is the moment of awakening, when the poet has the opportunity of sexual fulfilment and of generating beauty–poetry. There is a parallel here with the sun at Mérignac, a fiery challenge to enlist which Owen met with answering excitement, believing that enlisting might benefit his poetry. At this point the poet sees a beautiful youth of ambiguous status: a living statue, whose shifting outline sometimes makes him appear androgynous; a god, with human flesh; a spiritual symbol of 'physical sensation', embodying the beauties of music, landscape, seasons, jewels (the Mermaid's statue, 'The time was aeon', 'Long ages past', P1, 'My Shy Hand', 'Spells and Incantation').

The poet now sacrifices to Eros, initially hoping that he will be able to love his earthly lover more fully ('To the Bitter Sweet-Heart'). Other loves – friends, family, reputation, creed – are offered up (P1, 'A Palinode', 'To Eros'). 'I have touched the god': hand contact seems the crucial action (the 1914 fragment about touching a boy's hand, and much hand imagery in other poems).

The new relationship suddenly collapses, the poet being rejected and/or abandoned by the lover or the god (P1, 'A Palinode', 'To Eros'). Something he has said or done seems to be a cause of this disaster ('What have I done, O God . . . ?', 'O wrong, wrong word'). The sun ceases to 'drop sweetness' on him and is angry ('Reunion', 'Spring Offensive') or withdraws its power or light (P1, 'Futility', 'Exposure' and the numerous 1917–18 poems set in darkness).

The abandoned devotee finds himself entering hell–Hades, alive but like a corpse, with sensations of paralysis, drowning, being turned into stone ('Supposed Confessions' and other Dunsden poems, P1, 'Dulce et Decorum Est', 'The Sentry', 'Mental Cases', 'Strange Meeting', 'Spring Offensive').

He meets some of the inmates of hell, who show him his own possible fate (the Rose, Age, 'Purgatorial passions', 'Mental Cases', 'Strange Meeting'). These descriptions have plenty of literary parallels, of which Dante's *Inferno* is the most obvious (Owen owned a copy of the Cary translation). Lewis Morris's *The Epic of Hades* and Harold Monro's 'The Swamp' (in *Before*

Dawn) are other examples which he certainly knew.

Those seem to be the main stages in the obsessive sequence which underlies 'Perseus' and many of Owen's subsequent poems. It had little to do with Perseus originally, but the Perseus story itself had several features which Owen would have found attractive once the subject had been agreed upon with Gunston. First, many comments in his letters show that he was fascinated by flying, both as a modern skill and as an image of poetic creation. References to the 'physical sensations' of flying, falling and drowning (the fate of Icarus) can be found throughout his verse. Secondly, traditional representations of the Greek myths, including some in his schoolbooks, allowed for descriptions of the male nude. Mr Gunston still has a little bronze figure of Hermes which Owen seems to have bought in Bordeaux (Plate 6).[53] Beauty is often represented in Owen's verse as a naked statuesque figure (Tailhade had even told him that he had the beauty of a statue himself). Thirdly, the most celebrated object in the Perseus legends is the head of Medusa the Gorgon, with its terrible stare that turned men into statues. He had used that image already in 'Long ages past' and in the 'Supposed Confessions', where Despondency–Medusa is blamed for his adolescent 'horrors'.

The Gorgon's head has two different forms in artistic tradition: the original, archaic image is of a devilish face with glaring eyes and lips drawn back in a death grin, but in later representations the face becomes one of agonised loveliness. The archaic version has been associated by many psychiatrists with the terrifying faces that are a common feature of dreams. It is the face given to shellshock nightmares by a cartoonist in the Craiglockhart Hospital magazine in 1917 (Plate 10). Dr William Brown, who was in charge of the Casualty Clearing Station where Owen was a patient, recorded a case of shellshock in which the victim was rigid and trembling continually, especially in the arms ('My arms were wrenched with inexplicable weakness'): 'his face wore a fixed stare of horror, with starting eyes, dilated nostrils, the mouth slightly open . . . . This was the petrifaction of fright, such as the Greeks knew and portrayed in the Gorgon myth.'[54] The 'fixed eyes' of the dead poet in 'Strange Meeting' or the tormented faces of the damned madmen in 'Mental Cases' are combinations of artistic convention, dream and wartime experience. The later, beautiful version of Medusa was known to Owen through nineteenth-century literature and painting. As Frank Kermode (1957) has shown, 'the face' is a pervasive image in Romantic

art, notably in *The Fall of Hyperion*, where Keats is frozen into a
timeless agony by the eyes and deathly beauty of Moneta,
reaching his poetic vision through this torment. To see and bow
down before the face of death-in-life is the poet's privilege and
the reward for his suffering. More generally, staring faces and
fixed eyes are frequently encountered in Gothic novels and
other Romantic narratives. Mario Praz (1970) has studied the
psychological significance of 'the face', beginning with Shelley's
poem on Medusa's head and showing how this image of fatal
beauty developed into that of Fatal Woman. The *femme fatale* (of
whom Salammbô is one of the first examples) is, according to
Praz, a sado-masochistic, Decadent symbol by which the male
artist allows himself to be tortured and consumed. Death and
erotic beauty are inseparably linked, sometimes barely distinguish-
able; the male's role is one of passive suffering (hence the frequency
of the hermaphrodite as a symbol). Much of this would have
made immediate sense to Owen by 1915. He never got as far as
writing about the Gorgon for 'Perseus', but her paralysing stare
and beautiful or terrible face were to be manifested in some of
the most forceful images in his poetry.

I have tried to outline some of the reasons why the verse that
Owen wrote and might have written on his chosen title of 'Perseus'
is worth more attention than critics have so far given it. As a
work of art, the finished piece would probably have been old-
fashioned and cumbersome, so that one need not regret his failure
to complete it, but as an expression of the principal drives in his
imaginative life it remains a fascinating if enigmatic key to the
rest of his poems, especially to those which describe his later
visions of the underworld. It is the connecting link between his
Dunsden torments, his explorations of life and literature in France,
his trench experiences and his 1917–18 war poems.

The rest of the 'certain writings' which he wanted to finish at
Mérignac are mostly not known. He redrafted 'The Swift' and
'The time was aeon', both relevant to 'Perseus', and composed
or copied out afresh two little poems, 'Nocturne' and 'A Contempl-
ation', which show something of the social conscience which
critics have tried to find in his early verse. 'Impromptu', a lyric
about a child's hand and eyes, is worth noticing for its evidence
of a new interest in sound-effects of the kind used by the French
poets ('And kiss across it, as the sea the sand').[55] Material
probably intended for verse can be seen in several letters, for
instance in a description of yet another springtime ramble with

a child, this time a small boy who was heir to a large estate:

> Into his woods we go in the hot afternoons; into the woods we
> go; and the floor of the coppice surges with verdure; the
> meadows heave with new grass as the sea with a great tide;
> the violets are not shy as in England but push openly and
> thickly; the anemones are dense like weeds, and the primroses
> like the yellow sands of the sea. And there the nightingale ever
> sings; but I had rather she did not, for she sings a minor key.
> And the idyll becomes an ode-elegiac.[56]

(Or a *ballade élégiaque?*) Owen expresses his own concealed
excitement and the energy of the growing boy in characteristic
imagery of promiscuous flowers and foliage. With passages such
as this in mind one can make some sense of the 'Perseus' drafts
and of that curious sequence of three 1914 fragments: the Tailhade
ballad (which is about going into 'virginal' April woods), the
lines about touching a boy's hand, and the attempt at a poem
about the birth of Owen's poethood at Broxton.

He returned to England in May 1915 for a month on, of all
things, a trade mission for a scent-manufacturer. On the way, he
paused for a night or possibly more in Paris, where he was given
a taste of Parisian social life by Tailhade. He spend his last two
evenings in England in the East End of London, wandering
through the Jewish quarter in Whitechapel. 'I never saw so much
beauty, in two hours.'[57] The 'beauty' seems to be explained in a
1917 poem, 'Lines to a Beauty seen in Limehouse' (also entitled
'A Vision in Whitechapel'), a Decadent portrait of a godlike
youth whom he had admired but not dared to approach. He may
well have walked from Whitechapel on that 1915 evening through
the dock areas of Limehouse and Shadwell (seeing a Zeppelin
over the river) and emerged at Tower Bridge, 'sonorous under
rapid wheels'. The Cockney youth and the places associated with
him were to be material for several later poems, including
'Disabled' (1917).

Traces of these experiences and of 'Perseus' are evident in 'A
Palinode', a riddling poem apparently written in October 1915.
By then Owen had left Bordeaux for good after a busy summer
and was joining the British Army.

4 Preparing for War

The modern notion that the Great War came as a complete break in continuity, a shattering surprise to Europe, is a product of post-war mythology rather than of history. The same notion dictates that critics should be astonished at the phrase 'stunning guns' in Owen's 'Little Mermaid' (1912) because it seems to foreshadow his war poems, or that they should accept Sassoon's suggestion that 'Exposure' was written a month after its author came out of the trenches, as though front-line experience alone had created Owen's mature style. The world which Owen grew up in was rife with military activity and prophecies of coming disaster. There had been either a war or a war scare nearly every year since 1895. As a child, he had been photographed in uniform with a home-made rifle and had played what a friend later remembered as battles of 'attrition' with toy soldiers. Large-scale Army exercises were reported at length in the newspapers while he was at Dunsden. A bishop said at Keswick in 1912 that the 'growth of armaments still remains a standing threat to our peace and that of the world'.[1] In art and philosophy, as in many of the political groupings of both right and left, there had been a hunger for action and violence. Rupert Brooke was true to his antecedents as a young Decadent and Socialist when he greeted the war as a glorious chance not only for martyrdom but also for radical social change. If Owen was never as enthusiastic, that was more because of his Evangelical, conservative background and his absence from England during the war fever of 1914 than because he was out of sympathy with Brooke's feelings. Joining the Army in 1915 did not significantly alter his poetic direction, for his training in Romanticism had attuned his imagination to war and given him a language and imagery with which to tackle its strange conditions. What changed his style was not experience of the trenches but meeting Sassoon, yet even that had been prepared for by his meetings with Harold Monro at the Poetry Bookshop in 1915–16. If there is one theme in his 1916 verse, it is that of growing-up, a process which involves both change and continuity.

It has been usual to argue that Owen tried to get rid of the Romantic elements in his war poetry and that what remains of them is there only for the purpose of bitter contrast. This seems too simple. He went into war equipped in two ways by Romanticism. On the one hand, the humanitarian values of Shelley, Wordsworth and others gave him a standard by which to judge his eventual knowledge of the trenches; thus measured, war seemed an evil opposed to everything literature stood for. So his 1917–18 poems contain many deliberate allusions to the early Romantics. On the other hand, the later Romantics' obsession with pain, martyrdom and physical sensation made war a profoundly interesting experience. It is no coincidence that Owen seems to have started reading Swinburne in earnest in 1916. When he returned to the front in 1918, knowing that he would kill and probably be killed, he took volumes of both Shelley and Swinburne with him, but after he had been in action he sent the Shelley back to Shrewsbury, keeping only Swinburne's *Poems and Ballads*, the one book of poetry still in his kit at his death. It was Swinburne's gloomy underworld, not Shelley's bright heaven, that seemed his home at last, but he never ceased to be a disciple of Romanticism.

Owen is interesting not only for the intrinsic worth of his late poetry but also as a representative figure of his time. Like the men in 'Exposure', many of the war generation believed that they had been born to die in war. The culture and fashions of their youth had predisposed them to such thoughts. Of the innumerable prophetic parallels between late Romanticism and the war, one bizarre example may be enough here: Max Beerbohm's parody of Decadent conventions, *Zuleika Dobson* (1911). In this urbane and entertaining novel, the undergraduates of Oxford drown themselves *en masse* for love of the heroine, a *femme fatale*. Only the poorest specimens are left alive and the dons dine in silent halls. In 1914, three years later, the President of Magdalen said of the real Oxford that 'emptiness, silence reigns everywhere . . . . The remnant of undergraduates, the invalid, the crippled, the neutrals, make absolutely no show at all.'[2] The only men who could live and die in the waste land of the trenches were of necessity fit and young; they left behind them the old men, who praised their valour without understanding their suffering, and womenfolk, like those in 'Disabled' and 'The Send-Off', who encouraged them to go. The attitude of the early volunteers themselves was often one of sacrificial joy as they turned from the world like 'swimmers into cleanness leaping', a famous simile from one of Brooke's sonnets that was, as it happened, drawn from river bathing at Cambridge. As Beerbohm's young idealists leap into the river at Oxford, an old don falls in by mistake:

> He whimpered as he sought foot-hold in the slime. It was ill to be down in that abominable sink of death.
> Abominable, yes, to them who discerned there death only; but sacramental and sweet enough to the men who were dying there for love. Any face that rose was smiling.[3]

This was to become a standard language for war poetry. Although 'love' was reinterpreted as love of country or even more commonly as the 'greater love' of Christ's saying before the Crucifixion ('Greater love hath no man than this, that a man lay down his life for his friends'), the term did not altogether lose its sexual meaning. Dying for love in war was seen as sweet, decorous and sacramental,[4] a sacrifice comparable to that of the Mass yet described in terms that were sometimes as much erotic as religious. Civilian war poems of this kind eventually irritated the soldier poets, who responded by stressing the exclusiveness of martyrdom: death in battle had a beauty unintelligible to old men and beyond the beauty of women. Only a soldier could understand a soldier's smile. The best-known poems in this idiom are Owen's 'Greater Love' and 'Apologia pro Poemate Meo', which several reviewers of the 1920 edition of his poems, including experienced soldiers such as Blunden, singled out as the truest and most beautiful in the book. The attitudes of the generation of 1914 were rooted in Romanticism, which is one reason why Owen can be seen as, in John Middleton Murry's phrase, 'the poet of the war'.[5]

Owen's early responses to the crisis were characteristic of the period, with little trace of either originality or scepticism. His sonnet '1914', perhaps written in that year, sees the late nineteenth century as a European autumn, as the Decadents had seen it, and the war as an inevitable winter during which young men's blood would be the 'seed' for a new spring. Like other people, he was not blind to the probability of heavy casualties. British heroics in 1914–15 are misleading to a modern observer if they all seem to be ways of suppressing reality rather of coping with it. Before he enlisted, Owen read *Salammbô* and the *Song of Roland*, visited

a medieval battlefield (scene of a major English defeat by the
French), dreamed of joining the Italian cavalry and began turning
'Perseus' into a war allegory, but what made him finally decide
to volunteer was the simple conviction that Germany had to be
resisted and that calls for reinforcements could not be ignored
after the Gallipoli losses. He had seen war wounds by then and
knew what he was risking, but there seemed no alternative in the
face of what virtually everyone in France and Britain saw as
ruthless German aggression. P4 (1915) describes the Kaiser as
shameless and 'arrogant', a view repeated in the 'Artillery' sonnet
(early 1917?), where one of 'our' guns is urged to hurl 'Huge
imprecations' at enemy 'Arrogance', and even in preliminary
work for 'Anthem for Doomed Youth', where 'our' guns are said
to utter 'deep cursing', 'deliberate fury' and 'majestic insults'.[6]
Owen's political understanding of the war was as unquestioning
as most people's until he met Sassoon in 1917.

His emotional attitude begins to emerge in December 1914
when he described soldiers as 'the thousand redeemers by whose
blood my life is being redeemed', an image no doubt picked up
from the newspapers he was receiving from home. Reading the
casualty lists was like reading Severn's account of Keats's death
or Christ's prophecy over Jerusalem.[7] This sentimental, religious–
poetic note continued into 'The Ballad of Peace and War',
subtitled '1914', which was to be his longest-running war poem.
The first drafts date from 1915, if not 1914; another was mentioned
in 1916; three more seem to have been written at Craiglockhart
in 1917, by which stage it was the 'Ballad of Kings and Christs';
and the last version, 'The Women and the Slain', may even be
1918 work.[8] All these drafts describe soldiers as modern King
Arthurs and Christs, at first very confidently but by 1917 with
some hesitation. In the end 'The Women and the Slain' attributes
these heroic statements exclusively to women, who are flatly
contradicted by dead soldiers. The ballad shows how Owen's
views changed but also how he retained a weakness for popular
wartime imagery; even though he decided in 1917 that the poem
was based on false values, he could not bring himself to scrap it
but instead turned it upside down by ascribing its idealism to
ignorant women. Metaphors of Arthur and Christ for soldiers
were perhaps the most common of all wartime images, turning
up somewhere in the work of most 1914–18 poets and extensively
used in pictures and memorials. Owen drew on both, identifying
Tommies as Arthurs even in December 1917 in 'Hospital Barge'

and as Christs later still in 'Greater Love'. The soldier–Christ image implied that a soldier who died in battle was earning salvation for himself and his country, an attractive consolation, but the idea was irreconcilable with Protestant doctrine, as the *Christian* sternly pointed out in 1914, because it denied the unique value of Christ's death.[9] Its occurrence in Owen's war poems is sometimes mistakenly seen as proof that his faith had revived, but the image was more sentimental than Christian; it was suspect, too, because it lent itself to exploitation by propagandists in support of the war. He came to recognise it in 1917 as 'a distorted view to hold in a general way'[10] but even so he went on to give it elaborate expression in 'Greater Love'. The war only deepened his original belief that front-line soldiers were heroes and martyrs, beautiful in death.

The first drafts of his 'Ballad of Peace and War' contain several other themes which were widespread in contemporary verse. The third stanza declares with no hint of irony that it is 'sweet' and 'meet' to die for brothers – the 'old lie' that he was later to denounce so savagely in 'Dulce et Decorum Est'. Ensuing stanzas develop a more interesting idea, touched on in '1914', that men were dying to ensure the return of spring: the 'Sun is sweet on rose and wheat', the 'soil is safe' and 'children's cheeks are ruddy'

> Because the good lads' limbs lie cold,
> And their brave cheeks are bloody.

This was to be hinted at again in 'Exposure' (1918), where there is a distinct echo of the ballad ('Nor ever suns smile true on child, or field, or fruit'). Owen may have been aware of *The Golden Bough*, J. G. Frazer's recent study of pagan vegetation rites in which kings or gods (or, as it might be, Arthurs or Christs) were sacrificed in winter to guarantee a fertile spring. The hope that society might be born anew out of destruction kept many soldiers going, but Owen finally rejected it in 1918, writing its elegy in 'Strange Meeting' and 'Exposure'.

Most of the ideas in the few poems which he wrote directly about the war before 1917 were expressed better by other writers. The most striking effect of his getting into uniform was not any advance in his thoughts about public events but the experience of working as a man with men. His growing-up was almost finished at last. Excitement is evident even in the handwriting of his breathless letters in the winter of 1915–16. His 1916 verse

revolves around themes of social and sexual maturity with such
strange ambiguity that love and war seem indistinguishable. New
images from parade ground and firing-range are used for both
subjects alike. For example, in April he heard a drum-and-fife
band:

> A thrilling affair. The sound . . . has finally dazzled me with
> Military Glory.
>   The fifers are worthy to rank with the demented violins that
> make Queen's Hall to spin round as a top, and with the
> Cathedral Choir that pierces thro' the heights of heaven.
> Sweetly sing the fifes as it were great charmed birds in Arabian
> forests. And the drums pulse fearfully-voluptuously, as great
> hearts in death.[11]

The language of late Victorian lyricism is being adapted to a
military subject, and Owen is accumulating a store of poetic
material: 'great hearts in death' reappears as 'hearts' made great
with shot' in 'Greater Love', 'demented violins' as 'demented
choirs' in 'Anthem for Doomed Youth', while other phrases turn
up in work for 'The End', 'Music', 'An Imperial Elegy' and other
1916 poems of love and war.

Some of the excitement may not have come from Army life, since
his postings to various training-camps gave him opportunities to
meet civilians. There were spring rambles again, this time with
some Boy Scouts whose 'affection – which has come up swiftly as
the February flowers – seems without bounds and without
restraint',[12] and there were visits to London. The manuscript of
'To——' is marked 'May 10 1916 London', an unusually
precise dating; he revived a pre-war habit on that day by visiting
the annual Academy Exhibition, presumably with an old friend.[13]
The metaphor in the octave of Eros running between the two
boys on the beach may well have come from a painting, since
Academicians were fond of such scenes, but an actual relationship
seems to lie behind the poem. Eros is soon to awaken the pair
from childish affection to adult love. But the last line, 'The sea
is rising . . . and the world is sand', sounds as much like a reference
to the war as a lament for lost innocence.

Another sonnet, written later in the year, begins with an octave
that is entirely about the lost 'heaven' of childhood; not until the
sestet of 'A New Heaven' does one discover that this is a war
poem:

Let's die back to those hearths we died for. Thus
Shall we be gods there. Death shall be no sev'rance.
In dull dim [chancels, flower new shrines for] us.
For us, rough knees of boys shall ache with rev'rence;
For girls' breasts are the clear white Acropole
[Where our own mothers' tears shall heal us whole.][14]

Death in battle is proposed as a way of regaining childhood happiness. This remained a possible consolation even in September 1917, when Owen rephrased the idea in the sestet of 'Anthem for Doomed Youth', but neither 'A New Heaven' nor 'Anthem' expresses his maturity as a poet or soldier. In soldiering as in love there was no way back to childhood and maternal affection. His 1918 poems were to explore the implications of a world in which the doors of home were closed for ever. The soldiers in 'Exposure' go back in dream to 'those hearths we died for' but they see only the 'innocent mice' rejoicing by the embers while women and children sleep in forgetfulness, so they return to their dying in the winter night. Owen battled for years with his ache for home until accepting, in what he regarded as his first 'mature' poem, that he could never again be 'Harboured in heaven' as 'a Mother's boy'.[15] In his more truthful moments in 1916 and earlier he knew he had forfeited 'heaven', both at home and in the next world. Somehow his destiny seemed to be darkness and torment, either in the 'low sorrowful secrecy' of the underworld of guilt and desire (P1) or in the 'perishing great darkness' of war ('1914'). 'The sea is rising': drowning and underwater imagery are recurrent in his poems of nightmare. More positively, 'O World of many worlds' had foreseen that 'blackness of darkness' was the realm of meteor-poets, so that the darkness and pain of maturity were to be welcomed. 'The Poet in Pain', an undated sonnet, suggests a purpose for the suffering that seemed an inevitable accompaniment of poetic creation:

Some men sing songs of Pain and scarcely guess
Their import, for they never knew her stress.
And there be other souls that ever lie
Begnawed by seven devils, silent. Aye,
Whose hearts have wept out blood, who not once spake
Of tears. If therefore my remorseless ache
Be needful to proof-test upon my flesh
The thoughts I think, and in words bleeding-fresh

> Teach me for speechless sufferers to plain,
> I would not quench it. Rather by my part
> To write of health with shaking hands, bone-pale,
> Of pleasure, having hell in every vein,
> Than chant of care from out a careless heart,
> [And mock with musics man's eternal wail.][16]

Pain was a way of proving truth on the pulses and of learning
how to be a spokesman for 'speechless sufferers', an idea expressed
first in 'On my Songs' (1913) and eventually in Owen's famous
statement in 1918 that he wanted to 'plead' for his voiceless
soldiers. There is a similar continuity from his Dunsden poems
about the endurance of human suffering to the phrases 'man's
eternal wail' in 'The Poet in Pain' and 'whatever moans in man'
in 'Insensibility' (1918). The poet could only bring health and
light to others if he shared in their misery to the utmost. Owen
hoped in 1917 that his best poems would 'light the darkness of
the world'.[17] The consistency of metaphor in his statements of
poetic intention is a further illustration of the unity of his early
and late work. 'The Poet in Pain' was probably written in wartime
but it may refer to the pain either of love or of war, for his
imaginative responses to both were strangely similar.

   Most of the poems which he managed to finish during his
fourteen months of training in England were sonnets, drawing
some of their style from his reading in France but owing their
existence mainly to a new partnership with Gunston and a friend,
Olwen Joergens. The trio agreed to write sonnets on at least ten
chosen subjects.[18] Six of Gunston's sonnets are in the book which
he published in November 1917, two by Joergens survive in
manuscript and four more by her are mentioned in Owen's letters.
The subjects, with the dates of Owen's contributions, are as
follows: 'Purple' (September 1916), 'Music' (final draft dated
'Oct 1916–17'), 'The End' (probably late 1916), 'Golden Hair'
and 'Happiness' (both February 1917), 'Sunrise' (May 1917),
'How Do I Love Thee?' (not later than summer 1917), 'Fate'
(Owen's 'The Fates' was written early in July 1917), 'Beauty'
('My Shy Hand' was first drafted on 'Aug 29–30, 1917' as 'Sonnet
to Beauty') and 'Attar of Roses'. If Owen wrote on this last
subject, his completed sonnet has not survived.

   The two cousins may have hoped to submit their work to the
Little Books of Georgian Verse series which had been launched
in June 1915 by the publisher Erskine Macdonald, with support

from the editor of the *Poetry Review*, Galloway Kyle. A slim volume of Joergens's poems appeared in the series in April 1916. Kyle, an enthusiastic discoverer of youthful 'talent', used to encourage aspirants to send work to Macdonald, who would then consider their manuscripts on condition that they bought four Little Books and subscribed to the *Review*. Anything that Macdonald published was duly puffed by Kyle in the *Review*. Gunston, who apparently subscribed to the magazine, sent his cousin at least one Little Book and three more are still in Owen's library. Among Owen's papers there is what seems to be a plan for a contribution to the series, to have been entitled 'Certain Sonnets of Wilfred Owen' or 'With Lightning and with Music' (a phrase from *Adonais*) or, inaccurately but with an eye on the nature of the series, 'Minor Poems – in Minor Keys – By a Minor'. An accompanying note declares that his sonnets have simplicity, unity of idea and 'a solemn dignity in the treatment'. Recovering from shellshock in 1917 and meeting someone who claimed to know Macdonald, he sketched out what was probably to have been another Little Book, this time entitled 'Sonnets in Silence' or, preferably, 'Sonatas in Silence'. It was as well that none of this got anywhere, because 'Macdonald' was an unscrupulous publisher of amateur verse, making profits out of his unsuspecting authors; in fact, a court case in 1922 revealed that the name was nothing more than an alias for Galloway Kyle, who had played a double role throughout the war of helpful critic and demanding publisher. One of the few people who suspected Kyle of deception was Harold Monro, who advised Owen against the Little Books in 1916. Nevertheless Owen continued to hope that his sonnets might get into print; it may have been as late as early 1918 that he fair-copied most of them and arranged twenty in a numbered sequence.[19]

Some of the workings for his 1916 sonnets show him starting out with a set subject and an idea to illustrate it, but some are less straightforward. 'The End' was a title which caused particular trouble; he tried it out on what eventually became 'To Eros' and on an unfinished piece that was designed to end a book, before attaching it to some notes he was making for a poem about a sunset. He said that the sonnet which emerged was 'intentionally' in Joergens's style but could have said more accurately that it was in Swinburne's, a poet whom Gunston frequently imitated. Owen's manuscript begins with a stanza from Swinburne's 'Laus Veneris' about man's mortality:

> And lo, between the sundawn and the sun,
> His day's work and his night's work are undone;
>   And lo, between the nightfall and the light,
> He is not, and none knoweth of such an one.

Then comes Owen's first attempts at a quatrain:

> There [blew] a blast of sunlight from the east
> A flourish of high clouds; and [men marched hot]
> A mighty noise of drumming rolled, and ceased.
> The bronze west blew retreat; [and they were] not.

Work for further lines includes:

> The fire of day fell blazing from its fount
> Cascaded thro' the leafage; ricoched
> Across the rippling pool.

> The light so smote the forehead of the earth
> She lay in daze as dead.

> The touch of heat was like a too bold lover's [touch]
> Full of offence

> Aloof lone foxgloves in their ferny glooms

> The Pond, like an eternal July night
> [Wetted and cooled and hid his body white]
> [Closed on the youth with cold and dim] delight
> Wetted his body with a dark

> The same pond [which] was a [London] Paris July night[20]

Most of this harks back to France: bathing at Bagnères, the sun at Mérignac ('This kind of blazing heat stuns one pleasantly, like strong music', August 1915[21]), visits to London and Paris (May and June 1915), the rape of Danae in 'Perseus'. However, the metaphors of military music and gunnery belong to 1916, and the fragment is typical of 1916 work both in its echoes from earlier periods and in its oddness. It was to have been something more than a description of evening, for the youth sinking into a 'Paris night' seems to be a captive of love. Hence the link with 'Laus

Veneris', which is about the soldier poet Tannhäuser, the prisoner of Venus in the Mountain of Love.[22] Swinburne dwells on the knight's agonies of unsated desire, which are much the same as those of the Cultivated Rose; the youth sinking into the pond may have been doomed to similar torment.

However, Owen scrapped all of this Swinburnian fantasy except the first four lines. These he added to further lines from a quite different fragment about mortality to form the octave of the final sonnet, completing the poem with a newly composed sestet:

> After the blast of lightning from the east,
>   The flourish of loud clouds, the Chariot Throne;
> After the drums of time have rolled and ceased,
>   And by the bronze west long retreat is blown,
> Shall Life renew these bodies? Of a truth,
>   All death will he annul, all tears assuage?
> Or fill these void veins full again with youth,
>   And wash, with an immortal water, age?
>
> When I do ask white Age, he saith not so:
>   'My head hangs weighed with snow.'
> And when I hearken to the Earth, she saith:
>   'My fiery heart shrinks, aching. It is death.
> Mine ancient scars shall not be glorified,
>   Nor my titanic tears, the seas, be dried.'

The summer day in the first draft has become the Last Day, ending with the last sunset of the Decadents when not one but all youth dies and the great darkness begins. The sonnet may be read as a comment on war, but one could hardly call it a war poem. Its conclusions go back to Owen's loss of belief in immortality as he watched the Dunsden children, its imagery to the 'thrilling' military band and the stunning sunlight at Mérignac. One of the least personal and most memorable of his sonnets, 'The End' owes such force as it has to its being founded on a number of personal but significant experiences. The invisible presence of actual experience in the later poems is similarly a source of their strength.

He was as yet uneasy about using his own experience in verse, feeing the typically late-Romantic need to conceal it under symbols and large statements. Although he read Rupert Brooke

in 1916, probably for the first time, he seems to have had
reservations about that poet's Georgian egocentricity, for in the
only draft of 'An Imperial Elegy' (1916) he contradicted Brooke's
most celebrated phrase: 'Not one corner of a foreign field / But a
span as wide as Europe . . . I looked and saw'. There was not one
grave at the front but a trench of death right across the continent.
'And I heard a voice crying / This is the Path of Glory.' This
unpromising piece was never finished but its grand language
shows how Owen felt about the war while he was in training.
This time the style really is that of Joergens, who was prone to
similar prophetic vagueness (the 'Elegy' manuscript actually
quotes two lines from her book).[23] The opening lines refer once
again to the drum-and-fife band and the draft is subtitled 'Libretto
for *Marche Funèbre*', the tune he had played to Nénette in August
1914. He may even have been strumming the march with one
hand and writing with the other, since the words are scattered
about the page in unusual confusion. The confusion increases
when one finds over the page not more of the 'Elegy' but (echoing
a change in Chopin's sonata?) an outline for a lyric comparing
a beautiful body to jewels and seasons ('diamonds like the
diamond dawns of spring', and so on).[24] These comparisons were
rescued for use in 'Spells and Incantation' in 1917 but for the
time being Owen scratched them out and began a fresh sheet.

And again there is a startling change of subject:

[Purgatorial passions]

Their teeth leered wicked like the teeth of skulls
Their necks were bowed like moping foxgloves all
Aloof, lone foxgloves in their ferny glooms
And like that melancholy flower's their mouths
        Bitterly and wide
Hung drooping and stroke on stroke of pain
Has gouged blue chasms round their eyes [. . .]
[Pain weltered] from their feet and from their palms.
Eternal terrors fingered in their hair.
Their crimson eyeballs twinged and twitched
The Wrong that wrung their fingers like a rack.
The awful falsehood of the smile of skulls
Their hideousness of set, hilarious teeth
And the attention of their empty eyes.

On the back of this second sheet there are some notes for a
description of an infernal landscape:

It was an evening
    Yet less an evening than a stagnant dawn,
    . . .
[Wherein the sun] for ever smouldering [blood]
    [He found not Cybele
He saw not Proserpine, for he was lost,
    As all their ways [were] lost Who wandered there]

I thought 'My heart has failed,
As I desired, in sleep. And this is Hell.[25]

Much of this material was used again in 1918:

Who are these? Why sit they here in twilight?
Wherefore rock they, purgatorial shadows,
Drooping tongues from jaws that slob their relish,
Baring teeth that leer like skulls' teeth wicked?
Stroke on stroke of pain, – but what slow panic,
Gouged these chasms round their fretted sockets?
Ever from their hair and through their hands' palms
Misery swelters. Surely we have perished
Sleeping, and walk hell; but who these hellish?

That is the first stanza of 'Mental Cases'. In the other stanzas, the shellshocked soldiers are further described: they 'helpless wander', 'their eyeballs shrink tormented', 'Sunlight seems a blood-smear', 'their heads wear this hilarious, hideous, / Awful falseness of set-smiling corpses', 'their hands are plucking at each other'. 'Purgatorial passions' has been thought of as an early draft of 'Mental Cases', but it does not seem to refer to war. It seems more like work for 'Perseus' (although its association with 'An Imperial Elegy' makes that hypothesis an awkward one to prove). The image of the foxgloves, borrowed from the first draft of 'The End', suggests a gloomy setting but not a wartime one. Cybele and Proserpine, goddesses of the underworld, seem irrelevant to the hell of the trenches. Owen is thinking of the caverns wandered in by Endymion (who did see Cybele) and the hells in *fin de siècle* works such as the *City of Dreadful Night*, where bleeding and stationary suns were standard properties. The damned sufferers, racked by 'passions' and a 'Wrong' which they themselves have presumably committed, are in the same state as the sinful Tannhäuser, tormented in the prison of the Venusburg (Swinburne describes him as trembling and feverish), or the

Cultivated Rose. The 'Wrong' is lust not war-making, and its victims now watch the bleeding last sun of the Decadence in an eternal agony of 'physical sensation'. The 'blue chasms' round their eyes are the same as the purple marks 'round a youth's eyes, strained with love looks' in preliminary work for 'Purple'.[26] More broadly, the adjective 'purgatorial', which survives into 'Mental Cases', suggests Dante.[27] The inmates of Dante's hell are there as a consequence of their own sins; the transfer of guilt in 'Mental Cases' to 'us who smote them, brother . . . us who dealt them war' is not implied in 'Purgatorial passions'.

The similarities between this fragment and 'Perseus' are evident. The Cultivated Rose had eyes dark 'with gloom of death and hell', ever-trembling fingers and a sweating scalp, as he writhed in the 'everlasting fire not quenchable' of lust. The speaker of P1 had sought Persephone (Proserpine) in 'hell's low sorrowful secrecy', finding himself smiling 'the wide bright smile of skulls', looking through empty eye sockets and suffering 'inexplicable weakness'. Earlier verse had described the ever-changing outline of 'the Flesh' and the Mermaid's statue standing in the 'purple shade' of the willow tree's 'Convulsive fingers'. In a series of poems from 1912 to 1918, Owen returned to his vision of hell, a place incorporating elements of the Inferno, the Venusburg and the subterranean and submarine regions explored by Endymion. Its inhabitants are versions of himself paralysed and drowning under the gaze of Despondency–Medusa at Dunsden, but their eyes are nightmare versions of the 'melancholy' eyes of Rampton. Like the hermaphrodite, each of these figures seems to be two persons in one. Most of Owen's mature poems have their origins in his earlier verse, not because he liked (as he certainly did) to make use of images and turns of phrase that had pleased him in the past, but because the development from love poetry (if one may call it that) to war poetry was an expression of his whole self, including his knowledge of literature. He took the twilight of the Decadence out of dream and fantasy and related it to history, too grandly in 'The End' but with grimly controlled accuracy in 'Mental Cases' and 'Strange Meeting'; at the same time, his private 'horrors' were fulfilled in his 1918 poems as he looked on his face of death-in-life, the staring eyes and skull-like smiles of war's victims. It was only after he had been in the trenches, repeating in vastly magnified form the crisis he had suffered at Dunsden, that he was able to transform his pre-war self into the poet of 1918; in 1916, although he was in the Army, his verse derived from Dunsden and Bordeaux. Nevertheless the speed with which he moved from 'An Imperial Elegy' to a fragmentary love poem to a description of hell indicates both his peculiar suitability for his future role as a war poet and the usefulness of the literary tradition in which he had trained himself. Late Romanticism had always associated love and horror, so that an image such as the staring face, which had originally been a way of interpreting his own fears and craving for beauty, could develop easily into a metaphor for the 'truth untold' of war.

Owen needed advice. His 1916 verse was moving too far towards generalisation, partly because he was imitating Olwen Joergens. Its tone is sombre, elegiac, with 'a solemn dignity in the treatment', tending as always towards the biblical and hymn-like; its view is wide, sometimes aerial, prophetic (like Isaiah, he hears 'a voice crying'). The best of this was to serve him well in such poems as 'The Show' and 'Insensibility' but the worst was no better than the sort of thing that could be found in any Little Book of Georgian Verse. He was fortunate in getting some help from Harold Monro, whom he met in October 1915 and several times thereafter. Monro's Poetry Bookshop had become widely known as a centre for all serious readers and writers of poetry in London; it stocked a large range of books (except titles published by 'Erskine Macdonald') and callers were welome to browse. Owen attended several of the famous poetry readings, bought Monro's latest book, *Children of Love*, and became a familiar visitor. He was impressed by the war poems in *Children of Love*, for Monro was one of the few poets who had always regarded the war with sad scepticism, writing about it in a cool, modern style far from the nebulosities of Joergens or the naïve heroics of the 'Ballad of Peace and War'. In March 1916 Owen stayed in one of the rooms at the shop which were available to needy poets, and apprehensively asked Monro to read his sonnets. Monro had received dozens of similar requests but showed his usual kindness and shrewd judgement:

last night at eleven o'clock, when I had strewn about my goods preparatory to sorting and packing, up comes Monro to my room, with my MSS! So we sit down, and I have the time of my life. For he was 'very struck' with these sonnets. He went over the things in detail and he told me what was fresh and clever, and what was second-hand and banal; and what Keatsian, and what 'modern'.

He summed up their value as far above that of the Little Books of Georgian Verse.[28]

By 'modern' Monro meant something nearer 'Georgian' than 'Modernist', although he would not have used either of those terms. He had considerable doubts about the advanced work of Ezra Pound and the Imagists but was both a contributor to and the publisher of *Georgian Poetry*, the anthology edited by Edward Marsh which had caused a mild sensation with its first two volumes (1912 and 1915). Monro was friendly with most of the younger contributors and had known their original leader, Rupert Brooke. As an example of freshness, cleverness and modernity, Brooke was the obvious choice. Owen bought a May 1916 reprint of Brooke's poems, slipping into it a photograph from a magazine captioned 'A "Corner of a foreign field that is for ever England": Rupert Brooke's grave on Skyros'. There is little sign of Georgian influence in any of his 1916 verse but in the longer term Brooke's clear, anti-Victorian language would have appealed to him, especially in 1917 after he had received advice from two more Georgians, Sassoon and Robert Graves, both of whom were contributors to the third *Georgian Poetry* (1917). Graves's *Over the Brazier* (1916) was published by the Bookshop, where Owen may well have seen it. Monro gave him access to new work that was to be invaluable to him in 1917–18 and may have drawn his attention to several established writers whom he had hitherto neglected (Yeats, Housman and Tagore, for instance, are mentioned in 1916 letters for the first time). But at the end of the year Owen's reading and writing came to a sudden halt. On 30 December he returned to France, not a tutor this time but as an Army officer prepared for active service.

5 The Second Crisis: Shellshock

CASUALTY

As the strain of events at Dunsden had led to Owen's nervous collapse in 1913, so his trench duty in 1917 ended in 'neurasthenia' or shellshock. He had never guessed at the horrors of the trenches but they were not entirely unfamiliar; waking and sleeping, his mind translated them into images he had known before. There is no need here to give more than a brief outline of his front-line experience since his own letters tell the story vividly, as they were meant to do, and Professor Stallworthy has filled in most of the gaps, but his shellshock and its treatment are worth more attention than they have so far received from his commentators. He reached the war zone in the first week of January, keeping his mother informed of his whereabouts by means of a simple code[1] and assuring her, echoing Sydney Carton, that 'I cannot do a better thing or be in a righter place.'[2] But soon, somewhere near Beaumont Hamel, he found himself obliged to hold a flooded dug-out in No Man's Land where he endured the events described in 'The Sentry'; as his futile match burned out in the darkness, leaving him with the mental picture of his sentry's 'huge-bulged' eyes, his training as an officer and as a poet came to an end. He had finally reached maturity, and the fixed, sightless eyes of nightmare had stared at him 'face to face' at last, a dream made real.

The disciple of beauty found the trenches hard to bear, but his preaching instincts were aroused:

> extra for me there is the universal pervasion of *Ugliness*. Hideous landscapes, vile noises, foul language . . . everything *unnatural*, broken, blasted; the distortion of the dead, whose unburiable

71

bodies sit outside the dug-outs all day, all night, the most
execrable sights on earth. In poetry we call them the most
glorious.[3]

Some literary parallels were still appropriate though, however
inadequate: 'Gehenna', 'Hades', 'seventh hell', 'inferno', 'the
Slough of Despond', 'Sodom and Gomorrah', 'the eternal place
of gnashing of teeth'.[4] He longed for 'an inoffensive sky, that does
not shriek all night with flights of shells', adding that he was
writing down unpleasant details 'for the sake of future reminders'.[5]
This anticipation of the offensive sky in 'Spring Offensive' and
the 'shrieking air' in 'The Sentry' is one of so many passages in
his trench letters used eventually for poetry that it seems clear he
did indeed turn back to these records when he came to write
poems months later, but at the time his motive for accurate
reporting was simply that he wanted to tell the truth to people
at home. Many soldiers chose not to do that on the grounds that
it would cause useless distress, but Owen had no such qualms. 'I
must not disguise from you the fact that we are at one of the
worst parts of the Line', he wrote from Beaumont Hamel, and
then, 'I can see no excuse for deceiving you . . . I have suffered
seventh hell.'[6] His family were used to being 'educated' in this
way: 'Why am I telling you these dreadful things? . . . to let them
educate you, as they are educating me, in the Book of Life'
(1911); 'I must not conceal from you my malady' (1913); 'I
deliberately tell you all this to educate you to the actualities of
the war' (1914); 'that *more* which I had not been told I feel I
ought to tell' (1915).[7] Just as he had been unable to contain his
indignation at Dunsden, so he insisted now that his letters should
be typed out and circulated as a small contribution to waking up
the nation. 'The people of England . . . must agitate. But they
are not yet agitated even.'[8] He particularly wanted his reports to
be read by the Gunston brothers, Leslie, who was medically unfit
for military service but prone to patriotic sentiments, and Gordon,
whom Owen considered to be what the newspapers would have
called a 'shirker'.[9]

In the light of this strong response to front-line conditions, it
may seem surprising that Owen wrote no poems aimed at the
civilian conscience for more than six months after he first saw the
trenches, but all the evidence suggests that such was the case.
'Exposure' was once believed to have been written in February
1917 but in fact it was not even started until December, while

'At a Calvary' and 'Le Christianisme', two short pieces formerly ascribed to early 1917, seem likely to belong to the end of the year. There were several reasons for his not writing any significant war poems before Craiglockhart. First, he lacked a theoretical basis for protest. Many of his early 1917 comments were the standard 'grouses' of front-line troops which he was picking up for the first time. Soldiers grumbled endlessly about such topics as the supposedly fit men who had avoided conscription or the ignorant complacency of civilians, especially journalists.[10] Justified though such complaints may have been, they were not a foundation for original poetry, nor did they imply any weakening of the general belief that only war could end the war. Protests against 'shirkers' were protests in support of the war effort, not against it. The intellectual arguments against further fighting were being hammered out mostly by civilians, but Owen knew little or nothing of them until the summer. A second reason for his not working on serious verse until then was simply that conditions were not right. He always needed solitude, quiet and even secrecy, valuing his privacy at Shrewsbury and Dunsden and even renting a room outside camp in 1918 so that he could work undisturbed. Apart from his literary friends, few people who knew him were ever aware that he wrote poetry. Thirdly, the horrors of trench service began to take effect well before his shellshock was diagnosed, so that reflecting deeply on immediate experiences would have been an intolerable ordeal.

What kept him going as a verse-writer in the first half of 1917 was his partnership with his cousin, with whom he remained on the friendliest terms, and Olwen Joergens. Several sonnets resulted but no war poems; he seems to have kept war in one mental compartment and poetry in another, registering surprise when an artillery officer gave him 'a book of Poems to read as if it were the natural thing to do!!' Sent behind the lines for the whole of February, perhaps because his superiors had already seen signs of the strain he had undergone, he was soon 'settling down to a little verse once more, and tonight I want to do Leslie's subject "Golden Hair" and O.A.J.'s "Happiness" ' – extraordinary subjects, it might seem, for a poet who had just spend a month on the Somme. But, despite the fact that he signed both sonnets 'Adolescens' when he rewrote them in the summer, 'Leslie's subject' proved to be a fruitful one. Later, in August, it was from the first draft of 'Happiness' that he quoted what he had come to think of as his first mature lines:

Tennyson, it seems was always a great child.
So should I have been, but for Beaumont Hamel.
(Not before January 1917 did I write the *only lines* of mine
that carry the stamp of maturity: these

> But the old happiness is unreturning.
> Boys have no grief so grievous as youth's yearning;
> Boys have no sadness sadder than our hope.

The theme of growing-up which had been prominent in his 1916
verse is here brought to a conclusion. He had just been reading
A. C. Benson's *Tennyson*, which records Coventry Patmore as
having said that 'Tennnyson is like a great child, simple and very
much self-absorbed.'[11] Owen's comment has frequently been
quoted as a judgement on Tennyson's poetry, but in the context
of Patmore's remark it should be seen more accurately as a
characteristic response to a piece of biographical information, for
Owen had not lost his habit of comparing his own life with those
of 'the bards of old'. Beaumont Hamel seemed in retrospect to
have ended his self-absorption and forced him at last into
maturity.

Even in 'Happiness', however, there is no mention of war. The
old happiness of childhood has been lost because the poet has
gone 'past the scope / Of mother-arms', laughing 'too often since
with Joy' and committing 'sick and sorrowful wrongs'. 'You must
not conclude that I have misbehaved in any way from the tone
of the poem (though you might infer it if you knew the tone of
this Town)', Owen hastily assured his mother from Abbeville in
February, implying that the 'sick' (or in a later revision 'strange')
'wrongs' were sins of the flesh rather than acts of violence in war.
The language is of the evasive, mysterious kind that had been
used by the Decadents when they had confessed to 'strange' (but
unspecified) sins. Another draft concludes that we who have
'played with human passions for our toys, / Know that men suffer
chiefly by their joys'. The 'passions' here are those of 'Purgatorial
passions', that 1916 portrait of smiling sufferers in torment for an
unexplained 'Wrong'. In the final version of 'Happiness' the
maternal arms become, memorably, 'the wide arms of trees', a
metaphor which moves Owen's poetry away from private state-
ment towards the impersonal strength of 'Spring Offensive',
where the embrace of maternal nature was to be represented in
the more specific image of clinging bramble shoots. The break

from his mother had become a break from nature too ('Let not the sun drop sweetness on me more').[12] Everything in war was '*unnatural*, broken, blasted'; the Mérignac sun had been trying to destroy him after all. As that transition developed in his imagination under stress of experience in 1917–18, so also did the evolution of his erotic verse into war poetry. His poethood grew fast but it maintained its continuity from his original 'dark' and 'disobedient' escape from his mother at Broxton in 1904.

Within a few weeks of returning to the trenches in March he was in a Casualty Clearing Station (CCS) with concussion, having fallen into a ruined cellar. A letter describing this incident was seen by Blunden but has since been lost, so that not much is known about what happened. One significant detail in another letter has been overlooked, however: 'I lost count of days in that cellar, & even missed the passing of night & daylight, because my only light was a candle.'[13] The poet of the underworld had been trapped in a dark hole underground for twenty-four hours or more. The dreadfulness of the experience may be guessed at, coming as it did not only after his peacetime horrors of paralysis and drowning but also after his fifty hours in the dug-out, when the roof had threatened to collapse under shellfire and he had been tempted to let himself drown in the slowly rising floodwater. It was not safe to think or feel deeply. He managed to find a cheap exercise book in which to draft sonnets while he was in hospital, completing 'With an Identity Disc', a piece that has some wit and charm but little substance.

'My long rest has shaken my nerve', he admitted on 4 April, back in action after about a fortnight in the CCS. The enemy was retreating to the Hindenburg Line and the Allies were taking the bait; Owen's battalion moved beyond the trenches to fight in a relatively undamaged landscape, advancing in the open to attack Savy Wood on 14 April. He got through the barrage unscathed, feeling an 'exultation' which he was always to remember, but his accounts of events after that are confused and incomplete. It seems that his unit was left fighting without relief for twelve days; his nerve finally broke when a shell just missed him on a railway embankment, after which he spent several days sheltering 'in a hole just big enough to lie in' near a brother officer who had been blown to pieces some weeks earlier. He never said why he remained in the hole for so long. He may have been pinned down by enemy fire or he may have been helpless with shock, perhaps even unconscious for a while because he later spoke of 'coming-to after the Embankment-Shell-Shock'. Whatever the case, he can have been little use to the men he was supposed to be leading. In the end he returned to base safely but was obviously in a bad state. Perhaps word got round; at any rate a week later the Colonel spoke sharply to him, ordering him to report to the Medical Officer. Neurasthenia was diagnosed and Owen found himself back in the CCS.[14]

It is now generally forgotten that the circumstances of Owen's shellshock were a matter for some debate soon after the war. In 1920 Charles Scott Moncrieff said in print that Owen had been officially recorded as having suffered a loss of morale under shell-fire, a remark that was taken up by several reviewers of the newly published poems. Sassoon drew Mrs Owen's attention to the spreading report, remarking acidly that Scott Moncrieff's 'very objectionable' article had been written 'entirely for his own advertisement'. Edith Sitwell, no doubt with Sassoon's encouragement, published a counter-attack, quoting Mrs Owen as saying that 'Wilfred was *not* sent home on account of any loss of morale.' The anxiety of Owen's supporters that he should not be presented as a coward helps to explain the insistence on his courage that often appears in early criticisms of his poetry, a insistence which is still sometimes repeated although the argument which caused it has long since faded from view. Scott Moncrieff is unlikely to have been lying, since he worked in the War Office in 1918 and almost certainly saw Owen's file. He replied to Edith Sitwell's protest but did not substantially alter his point. His evidence seems to be reinforced by the less reliable testimony of Robert Graves, who met Owen in 1917 and said in the first (1929) edition of *Goodbye to All That* that Owen 'had had a bad time . . . in France; and, further, it had preyed on his mind that he had been accused of cowardice by his commanding officer. He was in a very shaky condition.' When Blunden came to write his memoir of Owen in 1930 he drafted a denial of this 'callous mis-statement', quoting Sassoon as remembering that 'The "cowardice" was only an indefinite idea which worried O', but the Owen family asked him to omit all reference to Graves and the cowardice question. Blunden therefore deleted the passage, also omitting part of a letter which he had received from Mrs Gray, a friend of Owen's in 1917. Mrs Gray told him that Owen had 'grieved deeply' over his failure to live up to his own standards.

Nevertheless in his most despondent moods he could never be said to have experienced despair. His courage was too

indomitable for that, and he never laid down his arms, – even
in the grip of his painful delusion, the belief in his commanding
officer's regarding him as a coward.

Blunden dropped the words after the dash, although they shed
some light on what precedes them. Owen was under no delusion.
The reprimand may have been no more than an angry exclama-
tion from an exhausted man, but it was given and it would have
been a severe blow in an age when most people did not clearly
recognise the distinction between cowardice and involuntary
nervous collapse. Valuing the esteem of his fellow soldiers and
usually remarkably happy in their company, Owen would have
felt himself disgraced. The importance of the incident lies not in
whatever truth there may have been in the accusation, since the
notion of 'cowardice' on those battlefields has now rightly become
meaningless, but in its effect on Owen's subsequent poems and
actions. It helps to explain his return to the front in 1918 and
the heavy weight of guilt that loads his finest writing.[15]

As Wigan had perhaps contributed to his illness in 1913, so
the Colonel's words seem to have precipitated the neurasthenia
which had been threatening since March. Owen did not break
down completely, any more than he had done in 1913, but he
must have been seriously ill. The senior psychiatrist at the CCS,
William Brown, reckoned to send seventy per cent of patients
back to the trenches after about a fortnight,[16] but Owen was in
hospital for six months and unfit for active service for another
nine. The visible symptoms were probably not much more
than the usual sweating, especially from palms and scalp, and
uncontrollable shaking. He may have experienced those before,
since they figure in 'The cultivated Rose' and 'Purgatorial
passions'. Other common symptoms which would have been
familiar to him were a rapid pulse and a sense of suffocation,
both of which he had often mentioned in his verse. More severe
cases of shellshock were marked by temporary paralysis, acute
depression and terrifying dreams. He had described himself as
paralysed by the stare of Despondency in 1911–12, and it seems
possible that he suffered actual paralysis in that 'hole just big
enough to lie in' on the railway embankment, the third and
perhaps the worst of his near-burials at the front. Mrs Gray
remembered his 'despondent moods' at Craiglockhart, so that
depression was probably another of his symptoms, but his letters
and poems show that the most painful and enduring effects of his
illness were violent nightmares, predictably enough. Even before

the 'horrors', 'phantasies' or 'phantasms' of his post-Dunsden illness, Despondency had steeped his nights in 'bloodiness and stains of shadowy crimes'. It was well known among psychiatrists that any weakness that a patient had suffered from before the war was likely to emerge in a more acute form in shellshock.[17]

Although the doctors no doubt forced Owen to remember and describe the events at Savy Wood, since full recall was considered to be an essential step on the road to health, such memories were not yet material for poetry. He began drafting sonnets again in his notebook but none of them refers to war.[18] One at least is on a set subject, 'Sunrise', and some fragments in the book may be attempts at 'Nocturne' and 'A Wind in the Night', subjects which Mr Gunston remembers as having been selected by the trio of poets. There are attempts at Tailhadesque sound-patterns ('Waned . . . wanner . . . was . . . wan . . . worn', for example, within three lines in 'Sunrise') and the usual imagery of jewels, flowers, seasons and times of day, exercises revealed by some flippantly archaic spelling in 'Sunrise' to be self-conscious literary diversions. One of the drafts introduces violence but only as Decadent metaphor: the fire of love having been 'quenched by mine own blood in spurts', the poet seeks for 'Beauty the eternal' in the 'sweet wound' left in his flesh by the flames. A phrase in the same sketch, '[Fastening of feeling] fingers on my wrist', is a connecting link between the hands that had been laid on Owen's arm 'in the night, along the Bordeaux streets' and the erotic menace of the snow in 'Exposure' ('Pale flakes with fingering stealth come feeling for our faces'), illustrating once again the continuity from his Bordeaux experience into his 1917–18 poems, and the sexual unease that underlies some of his most successful late imagery.[19] But there was a long way to go before work such as 'Exposure' could even be imagined. He went on making notes for sonnets, struggling to shut out what he had been through. Perhaps there would be enough for a Little Book of Georgian Verse – 'Sonatas in Silence', purple and gold, with type 'like Before Dawn' . . . but he had forgotten Monro's advice.

Shellshock continued to affect his verse for some months. He was sent home by stages, arriving at Craiglockhart War Hospital for Neurasthenic Officers, just outside Edinburgh, on 26 June.[20] He was soon telling his cousin that a new ballad was 'going strong' but it was not a serious poem. He called its heroine Yolande (she was originally Mildred), a name probably borrowed from Swinburne, whom he seems to have been reading again.[21] He also wrote two more sonnets on agreed subjects, 'The Fates'

and 'How Do I Love Thee?', the former setting out what he told
Gunston was 'almost my Gospel', the Aesthetic creed that the
only way to escape 'the march of lifetime' was to gaze into the
eyes of Beauty. Neither sonnet was among his best, but as his
health began its slow return he tried some more original writing.
His early Craiglockhart manuscripts contain not only his first
attempts at pararhymed verse but also two of the strangest
statements he ever made of his private imaginings, 'Lines to a
Beauty seen in Limehouse' and 'Has your soul sipped'. Whether
as a result of shellshock and its aftermath or because the doctors
had made him look into his inner mind, two of his most indelible
memories emerged with peculiar explicitness; both mental pictures
were of smiling youths, one a handsome boy he had seen in the
East End and the other a soldier whose death he had witnessed,
and both were to appear several times in later poetry.

The 'Beauty' of Limehouse, presumably remembered from
Owen's walk there in 1915 or perhaps a more recent visit, is
compared to a carved and painted idol receiving human sacrifices:

> I watched thy lips
> Vermilion like a gods; [dyed bright] with dips
> [In my] own blood in dreams that woke me faint.

But the 'half-god' ignores the poet, who knows that the boy is
not bound like himself by social convention but is free to 'take
thy pleasures with thy kind, / Where love is easy, where I cannot
go'. The poem was not worth finishing but it recorded a strongly
felt experience: seeing a beautiful youth in a working-class district,
Owen had come up against the social and psychological obstacles
which prevented him from offering more than an admiring glance,
despite dreams of making himself a blood sacrifice at the boy's
'smooth, smooth naked knees'. The fragment revives imagery of
sculpture, stoniness, incense, eyes and fingers from earlier letters
and verse, including 'Perseus' work. But the special interest of
the 'half-god' is his connection with the soldier in 'Disabled', a
link suggested by the note '(Thy hands shall be gloved with?)'
among rough workings for the Limehouse poem.

A group of quotations may demonstrate the origins of 'Disabled'
more clearly:[22]

(a) Now approach the days when the evening light draws out
    seductively: tempting all such as have movable hearts and
    movable bodies to stray forth and behold clouds, games,

lamps, stars, riversides, swallows, and the daughters of men. (To Colin Owen, aged fifteen and working on a farm, April 1916)

(b) Of the Last Draught that went out, men I had helped to train, some are already fallen. Your tender age is a thing to be valued and gloried in, more than many wounds. .

Not only because it puts you among the Elders and the gods, high witnesses of the general slaughter, being one of those for whom every soldier fights, if he knew it; your Youth is to be prized not because your blood will not be drained, but because it *is* blood; and Time dare not yet mix into it his abominable physic . . . .

Let your hands be gloved with the dust of earth, and your neck scarved with the brown scarf of sunshine. (To Colin Owen, August 1916)

(c)   Ah! He was handsome when he used to stand
         Each evening on the curb, or by the quays.
         His old soft cap slung half-way down his ear;
         – Proud of his neck, scarfed with a sun-burn band,
         And of his curl, and all his reckless gear,
         Down to [the] gloves of sun-brown on his hand.
              (Cancelled stanza for 'Disabled', autumn 1917
              or later)

(d)   Ah! he was looked at when he used to stand
         In parks each evening [outside cinemas] himself to
              please
         [Who mated with him . . . . 'Oh the *dear!*'
         Wealthy old ladies said quite loud, and scanned
         Unpleasantly the rose behind his ear . . .
         And eyed all up and down his reckless gear]
              (Another attempt at the same stanza)

(e)   Voices of boys were by the riverside
            Sleep mothered them; and left the twilight sad.
              (From 'But I was looking', a fragment
              written at Craiglockhart)

(f)   He sat in a wheeled chair, waiting for dark,
         And shivered in his ghastly suit of grey,
         Legless, sewn short at elbow. Through the park
         Voices of boys rang saddening like a hymn,

Voices of play and pleasure after day,
Till gathering sleep had mothered them from him.

About this time Town used to swing so gay
When glow-lamps budded in the light blue trees,
And girls glanced lovelier as the air grew dim, –
In the old times, before he threw away his knees.
Now he will never feel again how slim
Girls' waists are, or how warm their subtle hands.
All of them touch him like some queer disease.

There was an artist silly for his face,
For it was younger than his youth, last year.
Now, he is old; his back will never brace;
He's lost his colour very far from here,
Poured it down shell-holes till the veins ran dry,
And half his lifetime lapsed in the hot race
And leap of purple spurted from his thigh.
(The first three stanzas of 'Disabled', October 1917)

These interrelated passages imply that Owen had been working
on a poem in 1916 about a young man waiting to pick up a girl,
a subject based on his East End memory and associated with his
awareness that Colin was entering manhood. The 'riversides' in
the first extract would have been the paths along the Severn in
Shrewsbury, perhaps in the Quarry, where games, lamps and
swallows are to be seen in summer, but the setting of the cancelled
stanza seems more urban, 'quays' suggesting the Limehouse
docks. The second letter to Colin introduces the image of the far-
seeing gods, who are detached from human suffering like the
'everliving' in the Yeats epigraph to 'The Show' and the 'half-
god', who had gazed beyond human mortality. Envious of the
Limehouse boy's self-assurance, freedom and detachment, and
attracted by his good looks, Owen brooded on the memory until
it buried itself in his imagination and was eventually (after he
had met Sassoon) released into 'Disabled'. The handsome boy in
'Disabled' is under nineteen, much the same age as the recruits
in 1916 whom Owen had helped to train, and his young blood
has been 'drained' like theirs. Like the 'half-god', he had beautiful
knees ('Someone had said he'd look a god in kilts') but they have
been shot away. He waits again at dusk in the park, this time

sitting impotent in grey hospital uniform instead of standing in 'all his reckless gear', but the women no longer eye him 'up and down', preferring to avoid looking at him. Vermilion and purple have been poured away, leaving only grey. Such is one of Owen's measures for the destructiveness of war. There may be something of the poet himself in the soldier in 'Disabled'. Memories of Paris and London evenings may have gone into the making of the poem, and in October 1917 he described himself as 'an obviously unmarried young man in a reckless soft-cap', using phrases from the cancelled stanza.[23] The sunburnt youth with a handsome neck can be compared with the young poet at Bagnères who was praised for his beauty by Tailhade in the language of the Decadence and who dreamed of enlisting for the sheer romance of it.

The 'half-god' has vermilion lips, dyed with the poet's blood in dreams, just as the lips of the 'painted idol' in 'Long ages past' bear 'the stain of crimson blood' of lovers. These details give some indication of an element in Owen's dreams before 1917, including the 'bloodiness and stains of shadowy crimes' inflicted on his nights by Despondency in 1911–12. It appears from two other poems that the vision took an actual shape in 1917 when Owen saw a young man dying while bleeding at the mouth. One of these poems is 'Has your soul sipped', which seems to be one of the verse exercises he wrote at Craiglockhart before he met Sassoon (it is also possibly his first composition in pararhyme). The poet claims to have been 'witness / Of a strange sweetness', the adjectives 'strange' and 'sweet' introducing a list of such Decadent properties as nocturnes, nightingales, dying loves and martyrdom, but sweeter than all these things

> To me was that Smile,
>   Faint as a wan, worn myth,
> Faint and exceeding small,
>   On a boy's murdered mouth.
>
> Though from his throat
>   The life-tide leaps
> There was no threat
>   On his lips.
>
> [Is it his mother
>   He feels as he slips

Or girls' hands smoother
And suaver than sleep's?]

But with the bitter blood
And the death-smell
All his life's sweetness bled
Into a smile.

There can be little doubt that this grotesque piece was written in the summer of 1917, not in 1916 as was once supposed,[24] but one's response to it should be tempered by the probability that Owen was reading Swinburne at the time. Its unpleasantness may have been a consciously Decadent attempt to be shocking, the repetition of 'sweet' (nine times in various forms) being comparable to the way in which Swinburne harps on that word in describing how the leprous Yolande was 'sweeter than all sweet' to her lover ('The Leper'). On the other hand, 'The lifetide leaps' (originally 'The crimson leaps') and the smoothness of girls' hands anticipate the 'leap of purple' from the soldier's thigh and the 'subtle hands' of girls in 'Disabled'; if Owen was capable of thus turning some of the affected, hackneyed language of 'Has your soul sipped' into such intensely serious imagery only a few weeks later, it probably had some importance for him from the start. The memory of the boy's dying face seems to have been a real one, appearing again in the little poem 'I saw his round mouth's crimson deepen as it fell', where the bleeding mouth is seen as a 'magnificent' sunset. There are more generalised images of bleeding mouths in later poems, notably 'Greater Love' and 'The Kind Ghosts'.

The Swinburnian metaphor of torn mouths as red roses in 'The Kind Ghosts' (1918) brings together Owen's nightmares and his late-Romantic inheritance in an image which is designed to express something of the mysterious 'truth untold' of war. It horrifies the reader, as Owen intended, but it could not have come from a poet whose understanding of the war had been confined to reasoned reflection on external experience. Owen's war poems are not simply protests or statements of pity. They constantly return to certain obsessive images and to guilt, desire, darkness and blood. He might have gone mad as many of his fellow soldiers did, but instead he got his imagination under control and wrote with an increasingly serene self-discipline. His recovery was partly due to his own strength of character but he was greatly helped by his Craiglockhart doctor, A. J. Brock.

DR BROCK

It had always been assumed that the treatment given to Owen at Craiglockhart was much the same as that given to Sassoon, some commentators even following Robert Graves's inaccurate statement that both patients were under the same doctor, W. H. R. Rivers.[25] Rivers was a famous man, made more famous later by Sassoon's portrait of him in *Sherston's Progress*, but he had little or no contact with Owen, who was treated by Arthur Brock (Plate 8) on a system differing considerably from that used by Rivers. According to Sassoon's letters and memoirs, Rivers worked through 'therapeutic conversations', leaving his patients free for much of the day to play golf or otherwise amuse themselves. Brock, on the other hand, regarded spare-time activities as an essential element in therapy. A serious, talkative man, full of ideas, he brought to his wartime job an extensive range of interests in art, classical scholarship, literature and the new science of sociology. Having trained and practised locally before the war, he had many friends in the city. His enthusiasm for sociology, like his commitment to interdisciplinary enquiry, owed much to the celebrated Edinburgh polymath Patrick Geddes, whose teaching strongly influenced his work at Craiglockhart.[26]

Geddes maintained that the ills of modern living were a result of people's having lost touch with their environment; work and life had become separated, towns had become shapeless, communities had fragmented. His formula 'Place–Work–Folk' expressed his belief that the crucial link between people and place is what they *do*, their work in its widest sense. One way to reforge that link was to encourage 'Folk' to undertake 'Regional Surveys' of their 'Place', studying every natural and civic aspect of their surroundings. Seeing the parallel between Geddes's formula and the biologist's 'organism-function-environment', Brock interpreted shellshock as an extreme form of the social failings which Geddes had analysed: the organism had become violently detached from its environment and could no longer relate to it by means of its usual functions. Treatment had to concentrate on 'function' and 'work' if health was to be restored.

Brock had a ready pupil in Owen, who had been interested in biology for years and found Geddesian thinking immediately congenial.[27] The doctor gave him the task of composing an essay on the Outlook Tower, an old house near Edinburgh Castle which Geddes had established as a centre for sociological studies.[28]

Owen's surviving notes for the essay show that he visited the Tower, attending carefully to its symbolic organisation; like all visitors, he would have gone first to the roof, with its view of the city, and then descended through rooms containing 'Regional Survey' exhibitions, first of Edinburgh, then of Scotland and finally of the world as a whole (Plate 9). 'I perceived that this Tower was a symbol,' he wrote, 'an Allegory, not a historic structure but a poetic form . . . . The Tower is suggestive of the great Method of Philosophical Thinking, which is Correlation or Co-ordination.' The Tower embodied Geddes's aim of enabling people to realise their full individuality by growing beyond specialisms, parties and nations towards an understanding of the interdependence of man and nature as a whole. The Tower's chief enemy, Owen noted, was 'the Spirit of exclusiveness'. The outline for his essay contains such typically Geddesian sequences as 'Individual – Family – Township – the Nation – the Internation' and Tennyson's line, 'The Parliament of Man, the Federation of the World'. Later in the year, he was to talk to a school class about 'the international idea' and to make notes for a play set in a federated Europe of the future.[29] It seems clear that the Tower stimulated his political and social thinking, its 'poetic form' offering a purposeful, imaginative set of ideas which revealed, among other things, the unnaturalness of conflict between nations. At the other end of the scale, the 'Individual' made one small step towards regaining a right relationship with his environment by the simple act of looking thoughtfully at the Tower.

Brock's theories are set out in his post-war book and in many articles. Writing to Geddes in 1920, he said that a section of the book was to be on 'Treatment of the War Mind': 'Away from Other-worldliness and back to the Here and Now – i.e. Regionalism'; 'Treatment = Civics beginning by putting each man on his own survey'.[30] This section was unfortunately never published, but the Craiglockhart magazine, the *Hydra*, and Owen's letters show that the doctor's patients were indeed required to study their social and natural environment as a central therapeutic activity. Like Geddes, Brock placed a high value on 'Work', believing that the main symptom of the dissociation of 'Folk' from 'Place' was 'ergophobia', a fear of effort, and that the appropriate treatment was, in his own special word, 'Ergotherapy', a work cure.[31] He expected his patients to work both physically and morally, requiring them to survey not only the region but also themselves, facing up to their past experience and overcoming it. The practical aspects of Ergotherapy came from Geddes but much of its underlying philosophy derived from Bergson, a writer whom Brock much admired, and the Greeks. Bergson insists on the importance of the integrated personality, in whom intuition and imagination make life a process of continuous, creative change. The individual is responsible for his own growth, understanding his past and open to his future, living as spirit and not as machine.[32] Brock saw his task as helping shellshock victims to reconnect themselves with their past, including its terrors, and with their future, as well as with the external world.[33] It followed that he needed to understand their backgrounds, so that in a sense he himself had to make a 'Regional Survey' of each patient, a practice which he found advocated by the greatest doctors of the ancient world, particularly Galen, who believed that an organism could only be understood in terms of its environment.

Brock found that it was common for shellshock sufferers to regress to childhood and long for maternal affection. Owen wrote to an aunt soon after his arrival at Craiglockhart, 'I am not able to settle down here without seeing Mother. I feel a sort of reserve and suspense about everything I do.' He did not 'do' very much, except write a little verse and rashly attend a church service ('It gave me the indigoes, not half'). Mrs Owen hurried up to Edinburgh and was no doubt interviewed by the doctor, who liked to meet patients' families (they were part of the 'environment' which his diagnosis had to take into account). Owen said that his first sight of her was accompanied by the kind of 'exultation' he had felt after getting through the barrage at Savy Wood. He noticed her grey hair, 'the ashes of all your Sacrifices'. This emotional reunion, arousing language associated with his two nervous crises (shellshock and the 'ashes' of his Dunsden sacrifice), seems to have been the starting-point of his cure, for after it Brock was able to start an intensive course of Ergotherapy.

Owen was soon 'full of activities' and enjoying 'a Greek feeling of energy and elemental life' (a phrase which clearly shows the influence of the disciple of Galen and Bergson).[34] Regional Survey began with an afternoon of visits to a factory, a munition works and a brass-foundry, the next morning being devoted, as Geddes would have advised, to some practical metalwork. However, the main elements in the cure were always selected by Brock to suit the special interests of the patient, which meant literature and the earth sciences in Owen's case. On the day after the factory visits, Owen became a founder member of a new Field Club, with Brock as President, and soon he was also busy editing the *Hydra*. He remained editor until the end of September, seeing six numbers through the press and contributing a good deal of unsigned material, his hand being often evident in reviews and stories. At the same time that he took on the *Hydra*, he finished his essay on the Outlook Tower and began work on a poem which Brock had set him on the subject of Antaeus.

The story of Antaeus was one of Brock's favourite myths, often referred to in his writings. An anonymous article in the *Hydra* for November 1917 encourages patients to join in hospital activities, warning them that it might be 'literally suicidal' not to; they needed

> vital contact with our surroundings (physical, organic, and social), and we shall each of us live over again the experience of the giant Antaeus, who gained fresh springs of life at every fresh contact with his Mother Earth.
>
> The Field Club in a sense aims at coordinating all the other scientific groups. Its immediate object is a regional survey, *i.e.*, a survey of the Craiglockhart region, from all the different aspects (geological, botanical, economic, etc.), which will, at the same time, show the absolute interdependence between these aspects. The field of external nature is one . . . .[35]

The January 1918 number explains the myth more fully:

> Antaeus was a young Libyan giant, whose parents were Gaia and Poseidon, Earth and Sea. In a wrestling combat he could not be overthrown as long as his feet were on his Mother Earth. When he was raised off the earth his strength rapidly failed, only to be renewed again at the first contact with the soil. Finally Hercules, seeing this, lifted him bodily up in the air, and holding him there, crushed him to death in his arms.
>
> Now surely every officer who comes to Craiglockhart recognises that, in a way, he is himself an Antaeus who has been taken from his Mother Earth and well-nigh crushed to death by the war giant or military machine.
>
> . . . Antaeus typifies the occupation cure at Craiglockhart. His story is the justification of our activities.

This article continues that the patient must 'act in relation to his environment' and must 'beware of Art for Art's sake', a warning consistent with Outlook Tower teaching. Geddes believed that art should serve the community, so the paintings and other works which he commissioned for the Tower were designed as contributions to its educational function. Artists or poets who concentrated on their own specialisms were scorned by Brock, who would have strongly disliked several of the poems Owen had recently been drafting, including 'The Fates'. Owen's declaration in his 1918 Preface, 'Above all I am not concerned with Poetry', is a statement of Geddesian principle. He had not fully absorbed these ideas when he wrote on Antaeus, but his stock comparisons between seasons, landscape and the human body began to acquire some underpinning from the myth. He took the chance of including plenty of 'Perseus'-like descriptions of male beauty but they have 'a Greek feeling of energy and elemental life' that is new in his verse. The same energy emerges in a bolder use of alliteration and assonance than he had ever tried before.

> the thews and cordage of his thighs
> Straitened and strained beyond the utmost stretch
> From quivering heel to haunch like sweating hawsers . . .

The pairing of 'thews' and 'thighs' here is a reminder that pararhyme was another of the skills which Owen worked on at Craiglockhart. To end the wrestling-match, Hercules tugs Antaeus upward ('Rooted him up') as he had pulled up oaks in Argos, an image of the fighter as a tree uprooted by 'the war giant or military machine' that points to the Geddesian significance of the comparison between trees and soldiers in 'Spring Offensive'. But 'The Wrestlers' is not a very satisfactory illustration of Brock's theories, because Owen is more interested in Hercules than Antaeus, carefully adding the details that Hercules was 'the son of Perseus' and that he gained his wisdom from his beautiful boy companion, Hylas.

'The Wrestlers' and the Outlook Tower essay are the only pieces known to have been written at Brock's request, but he probably encouraged other writing and must have been responsible for Owen's becoming *Hydra* editor. Other Ergotherapeutic activities included teaching in a school (all Brock's patients were expected to do something in the local community), as well as joining in the hospital's debating and dramatic groups. Owen lectured to the Field Club on 'Do Plants Think?' on 30 July; since the ideas in this talk were partly based on information he had gleaned in 1911 from Gunston's *Cassell's Popular Science*, they were hardly new or original but they were very much in line with Brock's.[36] Everyone in the hospital knew the doctor's concern with organism and environment (the January 1918 *Hydra* reports facetiously that 'We hear . . . That a certain stoical M.O. has discovered an organism entirely without environment'), so Owen's lively discussion of plants' responses to external stimuli was well received by the Club. The lecturer felt 'exultation' once more when he was applauded; perhaps he wrote the anonymous *Hydra* report, which said that 'the lecture carried us to the farthest point of modern research'. The Field Club also went on expeditions, including one on 10 August when 'Two wanderers from Shropshire saw no small resemblance between the Pentlands and the Longmynd range'. Owen marked the opening of this sentence for his mother's attention; his memories of the Shropshire landscape were as active as they had been in 1914, when he had seen a hill at Bagnères as 'exactly like' the Long Mynd or one of its neighbours. A further phrase in this *Hydra* article, 'steep grassy hills', again points towards the setting of 'Spring Offensive'.

Doctor and patient must have talked at length about their scientific, social and literary interests. Brock obviously soon discovered that Owen wrote poetry, but whether he saw any of it, apart from 'The Wrestlers', remains a matter for conjecture. It is difficult to imagine Owen showing him the Limehouse fragment or 'Has your soul sipped', for example, although those two curiously personal poems were written while the work cure was in progress. However, two topics which might well have come up for discussion were the techniques of verse and the image of the terrifying face, since the first required hard work which could be regarded as part of Ergotherapy and the second may have recurred as often in Owen's reports of his shellshock dreams as it does in his writing.

Owen seems to have taken a special interest in the technicalities of verse composition during his first months at the hospital, trying his hand at a ballad, sonnets, blank-verse narrative, and a variety of stanza forms and sound-effects. He wrote a small lyric called 'Song of Songs', publishing it anonymously in the *Hydra* (1 September) because Sassoon admired it:

> Sing me at morn but only with your laugh:
> Even as Spring that laugheth into leaf;
> Even as Love that laugheth after Life.

He sent a proof of 'Song of Songs' to Gunston with the comment, 'My first printed Poem!', but he could have added that it was the first published poem in English to use pararhyme as a regular scheme. A closely related piece, 'From my Diary, July 1914', may have been written under the stimulus of Sassoon's praise. These two, with 'Has your soul sipped', seem to be his first complete works in pararhyme, so it may be that his use of the device was one of the fruits of Ergotherapy, although the idea had occurred to him before and probably derived from France. Pararhyme was thus not invented for war poems, as is sometimes claimed, but for sensuous, erotic 'songs' in the Decadent style.[37] 'From my Diary' looks back to the delights of Bagnères, where Tailhade had encouraged him to begin his enthusiastic study of French literature and had joined Mme Léger in awakening him to his own attractiveness and freedom. Despite its being based on memories of that happy summer, the poem is 'seriously and shamelessly worked out' (to borrow a phrase from a 1915 letter),[38] using Owen's well-tried frame of a single day but relating morning, noon and evening to the energy, passion and completion of an imagined sexual relationship. Displaying his skills for his own and possibly his doctor's enjoyment, the craftsman packs in as much rhyme, pararhyme, alliteration and assonance as the lines can hold:

> Birds
> Cheerily chirping in the early day.
> Bards
> Singing of summer, scything thro' the hay.

The careful organisation of these Craiglockhart verse experiments may well reflect Brock's advice.

It was certainly through Brock that Owen made most of his new friendships in Edinburgh. Miss Wyer, for example, was a leading member of the Outlook Tower Association; she showed him round the 'Open Spaces', small plots of land established in the slums by Association members. Owen also met John Duncan and Henry Lintott, two artists who had designed murals and book illustrations for Geddes's many enterprises, and became friendly with two more families who lived nearby, the Grays and the Steinthals. Only in the Légers' house in Bordeaux had he seen a household where art and culture were so much in evidence. Mrs Gray adored him, taking him slum-visiting (no doubt she too was an Association member) and lending him books. At about the time that he completed 'Disabled', in which the young soldier is said to have had 'an artist silly for his face', Mrs Steinthal painted his portrait. What testimony it bore to the beauty and horror which he carried with him cannot be known, for Mrs Owen destroyed it after the war. Although his Edinburgh friends did their best to make his days rewarding, they knew that his nights were hard to bear.

'There is this advantage in being "one of the ones" at the Hospital, that nurses cease from troubling the weary who don't want rest.' There is plenty of evidence in the Craiglockhart letters that Owen deliberately stayed up late in order to shorten his sleeping hours, but he was reticent on the subject of his dreams. He reported 'having had some very bellicose dreams of late' in mid August, but by that stage the worst was over. 'The Barrage'd Nights are quite the exception', he wrote only a week later, adding after another week that, 'I still have disastrous dreams, but they are taking on a more civilian character, motor accidents and so on.' There was 'one horrid night' late in September and no doubt others, but they were not experiences that could be written about easily.[39] The word 'Barrage'd' suggests that the barrage at Savy Wood was a recurrent nightmare, while two references in poems show that other frequent subjects were two horribly blinded faces:

> In all my dreams, before my helpless sight,
> He plunges at me, guttering, choking, drowning.
>
> If in some smothering dreams you too could pace
> Behind the wagon that we flung him in,
> And watch the white eyes writhing in his face . . .

> ('Dulce et Decorum Est')

> Eyeballs, huge-bulged like squids',
Watch my dreams still . . .
> ('The Sentry')

Brock said in his post-war book that shellshock patients often had nightmares of being pursued or rendered helpless by terrifying, devilish apparitions. Claustrophobia was also common, patients fearing to walk 'in long, dark passages' even by day (there were many such passages at Craiglockhart).[40] In 'Strange Meeting', the poet finds himself going down 'some profound dull tunnel' where he meets a dead enemy who holds him with a stare from 'fixed eyes'; this is precisely the kind of 'smothering' dream that was common in shellshock cases and Owen himself had probably experienced it.

It has already been suggested that these horrors were not unlike his pre-war visions. The 'phantasms' of early 1913, the dreams of violence brought by Despondency's stare in 1911–12, the waking tortures described in 'Written on a June Night' – these were the weaknesses which the doctors would have expected to reappear in an exaggerated form in shellshock. The overlap between pre-war and wartime nightmares is evident even in 1918, when Owen's remark that 'my nights were terrible to be borne' refers to his adolescent frustrations, not to 1917.[41] He may also have suffered from claustrophobia before the war; his mother seems to have done so, as his comment on a 1916 incident reveals:

> When I was going up the subway at Liverpool St. . . . . I noticed the passages unduly encumbered, and found the outlet just closed, and Liverpool St. in complete darkness. We were corked down in those subways for close on 3 hours. This should appeal to *your* susceptibilities especially. There was just room to move from one Exit to another seeking an escape. After all the Zeppelins never got over the City, though we heard the guns.

This description may be compared with that of the 'fifty hours' in the dug-out, where 'One entrance had been blown in & blocked' and the guns thundered overhead,[42] and with the 'escape' into the dark 'tunnel' of 'Strange Meeting' where '*encumbered* sleepers' groan; it is in such settings that the dead or disabled figures in Owen's visionary poems are often encountered.

Dr Brock had a Geddesian explanation for dreams of this kind. In folklore, a subject in which he was widely read, the countryman who does his work well is rewarded by benevolent spirits such as Robin Goodfellow, while one who fails in his work and is out of step with his environment is plagued by malicious goblins. In a 1924 article, Brock said that the modern world had lost touch with nature on a massive scale: 'If civilisation is to be saved from perishing, it must rapidly, like Antaeus, regain its footing upon Mother Earth.' He described various legendary spirits which represent man's relationship with his environment, including the

Kobold, a sea spirit which is usually benevolent but which torments idle sailors and is fatal if seen:

> When, in fact, the seaman's morale falls so low that he begins to 'see things', he is indeed in a parlous state . . . he has failed to assimilate his environment and suffers in effect from a kind of nautical 'shell-shock'; hence these nightmares that Morpheus the dream-god (literally 'form-maker') sends him; they are essentially the same as those which haunted the pillows of the soldiers morally disabled by the strain of war; in these latter cases the evil Spirit of the Battlefield constantly took shape as some terrible Kobold or ogre of Frightfulness.[43]

The goblins of folklore and the apparitions in war dreams were thus 'true' in the sense that they represented profound human experience. This interpretation of 'imaginary' beings could easily be extended to art, and in pp. 171–2 of *Health and Conduct* (1923) Brock uses Owen's poems as evidence to prove his point:

> The psychology of all sorts of poetic or artistic creation is, of course, closely allied to the production of dreams or legends. Every work of imagination is a projection into sensory form of the artist's deepest personal experiences. Dante's *Vision of Hell* is an imagery of his own moral struggles; so also with Bunyan's *Pilgrim's Progress*, Mrs Shelley's *Frankenstein*, the gruesome paintings of Wiertz, etc. In the powerful war-poems of Wilfred Owen we read the heroic testimony of one who having in the most literal sense 'faced the phantoms of the mind' had *all but* laid them ere the last call came; they still appear in his poetry but he fears them no longer.

Ergotherapy had '*all but*' succeeded. We do not know what part Brock played, if any, in getting Owen to 'face the phantoms of the mind' through writing poetry; he seemed to regard the poems as only the record of a process which had been achieved by other means. Some of the principal poems about 'phantoms', such as 'Strange Meeting' and 'Mental Cases', were written after Owen left Craiglockhart, but 'Dulce et Decorum Est' and 'The Sentry' were begun while he was still under Brock's supervision and it is possible that the doctor encouraged such writing as a therapeutic exercise. In any case, he gives us a way of reading Owen's war poems which is of great interest; his association of the poems with the *Inferno*, *Pilgrim's Progress* and *Frankenstein* is persuasive.

The mention of Owen in *Health and Conduct* is apparently Brock's only reference to him in print, but Mrs Owen wrote to Blunden after the war, 'You will like to see Dr Brock's letters'; these letters seem to be lost, but they are presumably the source for the quotation which Blunden makes in his Memoir that Brock regarded his patient as 'a very outstanding figure, both in intellect and in character'.[44] Owen's last two and a half months at Craiglockhart were dominated by his friendship with Sassoon but Brock's teaching remained with him. At the heart of his reflections on the nature of war in 1918 lay the conviction that the organism had to live in harmony with its environment and that destruction was bound to ensure from its failure to do so. His own means to wholeness were to face his personal nightmares, recognising them for what they were. Whereas the dying man in 'Dulce et Decorum Est' (one of his 'early' war poems) has a face 'like a devil's' and is blind, the dead man in 'Strange Meeting' is no devil and sees the poet with 'piteous recognition'. Such self-knowledge could not end the war, however; despite Ergotherapy, the recognition in 'Strange Meeting' is the prelude to death among groaning sleepers in a war dream from which there is no awakening.

6 Sassoon

Siegfried Sassoon arrived at Craiglockhart on 23 July 1917, having made a public protest that the war had become one of 'aggression and conquest'. It was easier for the authorities to treat him as a shellshock case than to risk the publicity of a court martial. Some people believed then and later that his being sent to the hospital was yet another example of the unscrupulousness of politicians, but the facts have yet to be fully established. Robert Graves, his friend and fellow officer, said afterwards that Sassoon really had been suffering from shellshock (and hallucinations),[1] but then Graves had played a major part in getting him classified as neurasthenic, believing that his protest had been made at the bidding of pacifists while he was under severe stress. Sassoon himself confided to Lady Ottoline Morrell in April 1917 that he was 'very near the snapping point' and in November that he had 'taken to war nightmares again'. In the following February he admitted that 'I realise now that I couldn't have stood any more French horrors without breaking down.' Worried about his own mental stability, he found Craiglockhart profoundly depressing: 'My fellow-patients are 160 more or less dotty officers. A great many of them are degenerate-looking. A few are genuine cases of shell-shock etc. One committed suicide three weeks ago.' He had to revisit 'the cursed place' briefly in 1918: the 'drifting patients looked more haunted and "mental" than ever. I noticed the same types there, (though they are of course an entirely new crop)'. He does not seem to have taken part in hospital activities or to have found any of the pleasures which Owen enjoyed in Edinburgh; country walks and golf were his only solace.

It was true that Sassoon's protest had been formulated with the help of several pacifists, notably Bertrand Russell, whom he much admired for a time. He told Lady Ottoline in July that he would 'like above all to know that B. R. is satisfied that I've done something toward destroying the Beast of War'. But Russell at a distance was no match for Dr Rivers, who held an hour's

95

consultation with Sassoon every other day. While not suggesting that his patient's nerves were disordered, Rivers maintained that his attitude was abnormal and tried to talk him into modifying his views.[2] A medical officer's job, after all, was to restore his patients' fitness for general service. Rivers would have quickly identified and worked on Sassoon's two most vulnerable points, his affection for his men and his knowledge that they were safest when well led. Quietly but insistently the doctor suggested that the place for an experienced officer was in the battle line. Sassoon's anger against the war did not abate but he began to doubt the usefulness of his protest. Withdrawn and inward-looking at the best of times, he was now in a torment of self-mistrust, his wretchedness made worse by the news that his closest pre-war friend had been killed on 14 August. It is hardly surprising that he was not very interested in Owen when they first met.

Sassoon had published several slender volumes of Aesthete's verse before the war. Like Owen, he was at heart a late Romantic with a fondness for melancholy lyricism, but his early poems are less energetic and interesting than Owen's. Such verse had soon seemed out of place in the trenches. He read Hardy's poems there, saying in March 1917 that Hardy had 'always been more to me than any other writer, in the times I've spent out here. "A thinker of crooked thoughts upon Life in the sere, And on That which consigns men to night after showing the day to them." '[3] His changing attitude to the war, from sacrificial ardour in 1915 to anger in 1916, protest in 1917 and weary acceptance in 1918, can be traced in the unique record which he left in his poems, diaries, memoirs and numerous unpublished letters. In 1916 he began writing his epigrams, forceful and passionately sincere (albeit often clumsy) little poems designed to force civilians into recognising what the trenches were really like.[4] These satires were admired by intellectuals who were trying to turn public opinion against the war. At a time when Germany seemed inclined to seek peace by diplomacy, while the Allies were reluctant to state their war aims as a preliminary to negotiation, the opinion was growing in some circles that Allied politicians were now more interested in 'aggression and conquest' than in liberating Belgium. This change in intention seemed to be supported by profiteering capitalists and a stridently militarist right-wing press. All too many civilians appeared content to acquiesce; Sassoon used satire, realism and straightforward, outspoken language in his efforts to wake them up. He declared in his 1917 protest that he was speaking on behalf of the troops, implying that the officer poet's duty was to put the sufferings of the inarticulate into words, just as writers in earlier periods had spoken up for the poor. His satires were published in the *Cambridge Magazine*, an organ attacked in Parliament in November as pacifist propaganda (which it was not), and he was mentioned admiringly from time to time in its editorials. Other journals also accepted his work, so that by mid 1917 he was beginning to acquire the status he held between 1918 and the publication of Owen's poems in 1920 as the most impressive new poet of the war.

Sassoon's first substantial volume, *The Old Huntsman and Other Poems*, came out in May 1917. It was dedicated to Hardy, who delighted its author by praising the war poems in it and ignoring the lyrics.[5] A contrary opinion came from John Gambril Nicholson, a leading 'Uranian' poet, who praised the lyrics but was doubtful about the war poems. In reply, Sassoon defended the war poems but expressed his own preference for 'The Death-Bed', 'The Last Meeting' and 'A Letter Home': 'they have the *best* part of me in them, the quest for beauty and compassion and friendship'.[6] These three pieces, occupying the final pages of the 1917 edition, are 'lyrical war poems', not satirical epigrams of the kind for which Sassoon is still most generally known. He never regarded his epigrams as his most valuable work, often grumbling in later years at being represented by them in anthologies. 'Am I *never* to be given credit for having written from my heart?' he lamented to Blunden in 1965, referring to the selection made by Ian Parsons for *Men who March Away*.[7] He would have been pleased when Owen agreed with him in September 1917 that 'The Death-Bed' was the best poem in *The Old Huntsman*.[8]

Owen read the book in mid August: 'I . . . am feeling at a very high pitch of emotion. Nothing like his trench life sketches has ever been written or ever will be written.'[9] About a week later he dared to introduce himself. Sassoon later remembered finding him an 'interesting little chap' (he always referred to him as 'little' because of the considerable difference in their heights) but 'rather ordinary' and 'perceptibly provincial'.[10] Owen, on the other hand, was enthralled, his capacity for veneration aroused more strongly than ever before; he persisted in his visits until by mid September he had won Sassoon's confidence. The relationship was always one-sided, more so than is now usually supposed. In contrast to the many fervent passages about 'the Greatest friend

I have' in Owen's 1917–18 letters, Sassoon's letters of the same period contain very few references to 'little Owen'.[11] For Owen it was the friendship of a lifetime, brought about by sheer coincidence like his discovery of Monro's poems in 1911 or his relationship with Tailhade in 1914–15 but far more important to him than either of those encounters. For Sassoon it was a pleasant companionship that brought relief in a period of intense unhappiness.

The first lesson to be learned from Sassoon's precept and example was that truth to experience was essential to poetry, a maxim which Owen had always half known but never seen so clearly before. He realised with sudden excitement that his knowledge of the trenches was not just material for letters. Sending a copy of *The Old Huntsman* home, he said that 'except in one or two of my letters, (ahem!) you will find nothing so perfectly truthfully descriptive of war'.[12] As usual he was quick to imitate, writing 'something in Sassoon's style' immediately after his second visit. This was the first draft of 'The Dead-Beat', which he sent next day to his cousin marked '*True* – in the incidental', adding, 'Those are the very words!' against the doctor's brutal comment in the closing lines.[13] The accurate representation of events evidently seemed a principal characteristic of 'Sassoon's style'; others were colloquial language, deliberately unpoetic imagery, dramatic abruptness and topical references.

> He dropped, more sullenly than wearily,
>   Became a lump of stench, a clot of meat,
>   And none of us could kick him to his feet.
> He blinked at my revolver, blearily.
>
> He didn't seem to know a war was on,
>   Or see or smell the bloody trench at all . . .
>   Perhaps he saw the crowd at Caxton Hall,
> And that is why the fellow's pluck's all gone –
>
> Not that the Kaiser frowns imperially.
>   He sees his wife, how cosily she chats;
>   Not his blue pal there, feeding fifty rats.
> Hotels he sees, improved materially;
>
> Where ministers smile ministerially.
>   Sees Punch still grinning at the Belcher bloke;

> Bairnsfather, enlarging on his little joke,
> While Belloc prophesies of last year, serially.
>
> We sent him down at last, he seemed so bad,
>   Although a strongish chap and quite unhurt.
>   Next day I heard the Doc's fat laugh: 'That dirt
> You sent me down last night's just died. So glad!'

Shown this first attempt at a 'trench life sketch', Sassoon pointed out that 'the facetious bit was out of keeping with the first & last stanzas'. Reluctant to waste the offending section and needing to fill space in the next *Hydra*, Owen hastily revised it; his anonymous editorial (1 September) comments that, when he and his readers had returned from France,

> some of us were not a little wounded by apparent indifference of the public and the press, not indeed to our precious selves, but to the unimagined durances of the fit fellow in the line.
>   We were a little *too* piqued by the piquancy of smart women, and as for the dainty newspaper jokes concerning the men in the mud, we could not see them at all . . .
>   Our reflections, like our reflexes, may have been exaggerated when on first looking round England, we soliloquised thus: –
>
> Who cares the Kaiser frowns imperially?
> The exempted shriek at Charlie Chaplin's smirk.
> The *Mirror* shows how Tommy smiles at work.
> And if girls sigh, they sigh ethereally,
> And wish the Push would get on less funereally.
> Old Bill enlarges on his little jokes.
> *Punch* is still grinning at the Derby blokes.
> And Belloc prophesies of last year, serially.

The style stumbles over itself as Owen tries too eagerly to copy the new way of writing (and to affect a soldierly colloquialism) without abandoning everything from his previous work. As he admitted to Gunston, the line about ministers with its awkward rhyme word was 'years old!!', originating from a 1915 'Perseus' manuscript, and his annoyance at *Daily Mirror* photographs went back at least as far as February. 'The Dead-Beat' was cobbled up from old material as well as new, but it marks a new phase in his poetry, standing at the beginning of his *annus mirabilis*.

He remained dissatisfied with the first draft and its offshoot, revising the poem many times. The final draft is as follows:

> He dropped, – more sullenly than wearily,
> Lay stupid like a cod, heavy like meat,
> And none of us could kick him to his feet;
> – Just blinked at my revolver, blearily;
> – Didn't appear to know a war was on,
> Or see the blasted trench at which he stared.
> 'I'll do 'em in,' he whined. 'If this hand's spared,
> I'll murder them, I will.'

*   *   *

>   A low voice said,
> 'It's Blighty, p'raps, he sees; his pluck's all gone,
> Dreaming of all the valiant, that *aren't* dead:
> Bold uncles, smiling ministerially;
> Maybe his brave young wife, getting her fun
> In some new home, improved materially.
> It's not these stiffs have crazed him; nor the Hun.'

*   *   *

> We sent him down at last, out of the way.
> Unwounded; – stout lad, too, before that strafe.
> Malingering? Stretcher-bearers winked, 'Not half!'

*   *   *

> Next day I heard the Doc's well-whiskied laugh:
> 'That scum you sent last night soon died. Hooray!'

The five quatrains of the first draft, which had been made excessively conspicuous by their heavy rhymes, have been reworked into a more flexible verse paragraph, divided by asterisks where dramatic pauses are needed. Three passages of direct speech have been added, but the doctor's 'very words' of the original have been modified into a single, more forceful line; truth to experience did not necessitate word-for-word reporting. The punctuation throughout has been enlivened (Owen grew fond of the dash). The obscure reference to Caxton Hall gives way to an ambiguous threat from the soldier himself; there is still a momentary puzzle (who is threatened?) but it is worth solving. All the political and topical references are scrapped, because the world of London clubs, ministers, bishops and entertainers, which Sassoon often satirised, was known to Owen only through newspapers (as the *Hydra* verse demonstrates). The 'valiant' civilians in the final draft might be anybody's family, while the 'low voice' which refers to them is that of an unidentified, representative soldier. There is an implied tension, which was to be developed much further in later poems, between Owen-as-officer, using his revolver to enforce discipline, and Owen-as-poet, diagnosing the man's collapse with a sympathy beyond the reach of the war-hardened medical men. The poem has become more thoughtful and dramatic; several other Sassoonish poems went through a comparable process of revision, often spread over many months.

Owen responded to his new friend's first advice, 'Sweat your guts out writing poetry!', with characteristic enthusiasm, making use of everything he could learn from Sassoon's work. One of his Craiglockhart manuscripts shows him making notes for three or four Sassoonish onslaughts against civilian attitudes. He jotted down 'Accidental Death' and 'Killed by accident', presumably titles for what was to become 'S.I.W.', and roughed out a first attempt at 'The Sentry' with an ending in the style of Harold Monro (see above, p.15) as well as of Sassoon. Then he scribbled two fragments, perhaps intended as parts of a single poem, criticising civilians for being more concerned with such things as the sugar shortage than with the scale and significance of the casualty lists.[14] The presence of all this material on one sheet of paper shows how rapidly ideas for poems took shape once he had started to 'sweat his guts out'. It did not take him long to rival and in some respects outdo his new master. Most, possibly all, of his poems 'in Sassoon's style' (except 'Smile, Smile, Smile') seem to have been at least begun at Craiglockhart. Many of them can be matched with poems in *The Old Huntsman*: 'The Dead-Beat' with 'Blighters', for example; 'The Letter'[15] with 'In the Pink'; 'The Chances' with ' "They" '; 'S. I. W.' with 'The Hero'; 'Inspection' with 'Stand-to: Good Friday Morning'. 'The Chances' with its grimly dramatic ending, is as spare and powerful as anything by Sassoon. 'The Dead-Beat', 'S. I. W.', 'Inspection', 'Disabled' and 'Conscious' were all first drafted in quatrains, a form which Sassoon used often, but were then given looser shapes.

'S. I. W.' was further divided up by means of ironic, literary headings, the style of each section being adjusted appropriately so that 'The Action' is terse and broken up by abrupt punctuation, 'The Poem' is elaborately worded, and 'The Epilogue' has a dismissive yet arresting brevity:

> With him they buried the muzzle his teeth had kissed,
> And truthfully wrote the mother, 'Tim died smiling.'

'Truthfully', because the face wore both agony and relief, a macabre joke which prompts the reader to reconsider possible associations between 'Mother', 'kissed', 'smiling', 'muzzle' and the last, loving relationship between Tim and his rifle. One may pause, too, at the unexpected word 'teeth' and notice how Tim has acted out a phrase in the poem's epigraph from Yeats ('that man there has set his teeth to die'). Few of Sassoon's poems offer this kind of interest and concreteness.

Most of Owen's work 'in Sassoon's style' was repeatedly revised, often well into 1918. The multiplicity of versions, and in some cases the absence of first drafts, make it difficult to establish dates of initial composition. 'Conscious', for example, exists in two different versions, either (or neither) of which may represent Owen's final intention. All three drafts of the poem are on types of paper which he used after Craiglockhart, yet it seems more likely than most to be Craiglockhart work in origin because it evidently derives from 'The Death-Bed', the piece which both he and Sassoon considered to be the best in the *Old Huntsman* collection. On the other hand, 'Conscious' does not belong to Owen's first flush of enthusiasm, for there is criticism implicit in his doing in sixteen lines much of what Sassoon does in forty-two. Both poems describe a soldier on the verge of consciousness in hospital. Sassoon uses dreamy imagery of the kind he often introduced into his letters and lyrics:

> He drowsed and was aware of silence heaped
> Round him, unshaken as the steadfast walls;
> Aqueous like floating rays of amber light . . . .

By contrast, 'Conscious' opens with activity ('His fingers wake, and flutter', 'His eyes come open with a pull of will'), and in place of mellifluous generalities there are sharp, isolated details. The man is described in terms of his fingers and eyes, which seem to have wills of their own. His surroundings are perceived as separate, sharply focused objects: yellow flowers, the blind-cord 'drawling' across the window sill, a smooth floor, a rug. Then 'sudden evening blurs and fogs the air'; the things which the patient was beginning to recognise and question blur again as his senses become confused ('Cold, he's cold; yet hot', 'there's no light to see the voices by'). Sassoon's soldier drinks, 'unresisting', but Owen's is aware that 'There seems no time to want a drink of water'. 'Conscious' is full of struggle and effort, whereas the boy in 'The Death-Bed' drifts passively into reverie, almost in the way that Sassoon himself seems to have done in his lyrical moods. Sassoon's dying patient swoons through 'crimson gloom' to darkness', night in the ward and his drink of water bringing him dreams of a river, coloured clouds, and rain on roses, 'passionless music', for some nineteen lines. Owen reduces most of this into three:

> Nurse looks so far away. And here and there
> Music and roses burst through crimson slaughter.
> He can't remember where he saw blue sky . . . .

The second line seems to be an attempt to condense Sassoon's rather obvious descriptions into Symbolist imagery. Owen may even have come across the line, 'L'éclat mystérieux des roses et du sang', in *Poèmes élégiaques*, since he had the book with him at Craiglockhart.[16] Tailhade's craftsmanship still had its value, although Symbolism and Georgian realism would have to be blended more subtly. But truth to experience was the rule above all others which Owen needed to learn and 'Conscious' shows him making good use of it, remembering details such as the yellow flowers from his own stay in the CCS and striving to re-create that sick, visionary sensation of being on the border of life and death that he had felt in dreams, and after his 1912 bicycle accident, and perhaps on the railway embankment after Savy Wood.

Sassoon showed him not only how war poems could be written but also how they could be based on a consistent, reasoned opposition to the war. Owen might have been less easily persuaded by a civilian pacifist such as Russell, although Sassoon seems to have lent him Russell's books and introduced him to liberal periodicals such as the *Cambridge Magazine* and the *Nation*. There can have been few officers in 1917 able to expound the war as clearly as Sassoon did; coming from him the case seemed overwhelming. Owen summed it up in 'The Next War', which he published in the *Hydra* on 29 September in order, he said, to 'strike a note': the war was now being waged for 'flags' (or 'money-bags' and 'empire-dreams', as he wrote in a draft).[17] The poem implies that soldiers understand war more clearly than anyone else, having a special knowledge and comradeship. Owen had acquired some of this knowledge for himself before he met Sassoon, which was why he was so moved when he first read *The Old Huntsman*. His letters from the trenches had expressed anger at the attitudes of civilians, especially churchmen. To the former lay assistant, Sassoon's mockery of priests and bishops would have had a familiar ring. Owen admired 'The Redeemer', a statement of the popular soldier–Christ image which he said he had been 'wishing to write every week for the last three years',[18] but Sassoon would have told him that the poem had been written in 1915 and no longer represented its author's view of the war. Shown the weakness of the image, Owen restated it later as a condemnation of organised religion in 'At a Calvary near the Ancre' and 'Le Christianisme'.

Owen and Sassoon discussed ideas more than experiences, avoiding mention of horrors or their own sufferings, with the reticence characteristic of veterans. The element of swagger in 'The Next War' reflects Owen's pride in being a hardened soldier and a comrade of Sassoon (the poem's epigraph consists of the closing lines of *The Old Huntsman*[19]); 'we', says the poem, have known Death as an 'old chum'. To some extent this was an assumed attitude rather than an expression of Owen's deepest inclinations. It may explain why he took a while to write directly of war's brutality; his first attempt at horrific description, 'Dulce et Decorum Est', was not written until October. Quite apart from soldierly conventions, however, conversation about the trenches was bad for Sassoon's nerves and worse for Owen's. When Sassoon read Blunden's memoir of Owen in 1930, he wrote to its author:

> The passages from W's war letters are a revelation to me, and I believe that their effect on people's minds will be tremendous. At Craiglockhart, he and I talked very little about our experiences of the disgusting and terrible, as seen in France. I discouraged him from reviving such memories, knowing they were bad for him. And little Wilfred was such a modest chap that I never fully realised his imaginative grasp of the scene.

Tonight I have felt that he has grown greater than ever, in my mind.[20]

Although Robert Graves was undoubtedly correct in saying that it was meeting Sassoon which started Owen writing war poems,[21] the stimulus came from Sassoon's example and beliefs rather than from discussions of 'the disgusting and terrible'.

Indeed, the two poets probably talked more about literature than anything else. Owen found that they had been following 'parallel trenches all our lives' and had 'more friends in common, authors I mean, than most people can boast of in a lifetime'. By chance, Sassoon was reading a small volume of Keats which Lady Ottoline had sent him. He shared Owen's interest in the late-Victorian poets, including Housman, whose influence is often apparent in his war poems, but Owen was surprised to find that he admired Hardy 'more than anybody living'. No doubt Sassoon persuaded him to start reading Hardy's poems. In return, Owen showed him Tailhade's book and asked Gunston and Mrs Owen to send all the manuscripts in their possession, Mrs Owen even being instructed to break into a locked cupboard and take out three folders of papers without reading a word. Looking over Owen's manuscripts, Sassoon censured 'the over-luscious writing in his immature pieces'.

> Some of my old Sonnets didn't please him at all. But the 'Antaeus' he applauded fervently; and ['Song of Songs'] he pronounced perfect work, absolutely charming, etc. etc. and begged that I would copy it out for him, to show the powers that be.

Continuing to comment patiently on all he was shown, the new critic 'condemned some . . . amended others, and rejoiced over a few'. Some of the amendments can be seen on surviving manuscripts. 'Song of Songs' met with favourable comment when it appeared (unsigned) in the *Hydra*:

> I have been doubtful whether to [?confirm] the 'Song of Songs' as mine. But now I find it well received by the public and praised by Sassoon with no patronizing manner but as a musical achievement not possible to him. He is sending copies of the *Hydra* to Personages!

Sassoon had clearly been struck by Owen's use of pararhyme, although his reason for sending copies of the magazine to several friends – Robert Ross, Lady Ottoline, probably Roderick Meiklejohn and Edward Marsh, and perhaps others – was that it also contained his own poem 'Dreamers'. Under 'Song of Songs' in Lady Ottoline's copy he wrote, 'The man who wrote this brings me quantities & I have to say kind things. He will improve, I think!'[22]

Having to 'say kind things' helped to draw Sassoon out of his introspection and he was glad of Owen's answering interest in his own work. He had a notebook with him in which he was assembling the poems for his next volume, *Counter-Attack* (1918), a counter-attack against civilian complacency; he read some of them on 7 September to Owen, who thought them 'superb beyond anything' in *The Old Huntsman*. One, written the night before, seemed 'the most exquisitely painful war poem of any language or time'; this was perhaps the last stanza of 'Prelude: The Troops', which is added in pencil in the notebook and dated 'September 1917'. Owen must eventually have heard or read the rest of the notebook's contents, including two pieces which were omitted from the 1918 volume because they were too brutal. The distinction of final place in the book was originally given to 'The Triumph', dated 'Oct. 1917', a poem which Sassoon later suppressed, perhaps feeling that it displayed more of himself than he wished to reveal. 'The Triumph' is not well written but it shows something of that 'quest for beauty and compassion and friendship' which he considered to be the best part of himself in 1917:

When life was a cobweb of stars for Beauty who came
  In the whisper of leaves or a bird's lone cry in the glen,
On dawn-lit hills and horizons girdled with flame
  I sought for the triumph that troubles the faces of men.

With death in the terrible flickering gloom of the fight
  I was cruel and fierce with despair; I was naked and bound;
I was stricken: and Beauty returned through the shambles
          of night;
  In the faces of men she returned; and their triumph I found.

This lyric seems to have caught Owen's attention. The imagery in the first stanza may be compared with similar but sturdier phrasings in 'From my Diary, July 1914', probably composed at this time: 'Leaves / Murmuring by myriads', 'Birds / Cheerily chirping', 'Braiding / Of floating flames across the mountain-brow'. He had described the quest for beauty as 'almost my Gospel' in July, but now he could see that the quest could be fulfilled in war experience.[23]

Owen was Sassoon's follower in writing about the war, but in verse about beauty the two poets were more nearly equal. In fact, there is one small instance of Sassoon imitating Owen rather than the other way about. At the end of August Owen wrote the last of his sonnets on a subject agreed with Leslie Gunston and Olwen Joergens, reading it to Sassoon a fortnight later:

> S. has written two or three pieces 'around' chance things I have mentioned or related! Thus the enclosed scribble is a copy of what he wrote after I had read three sonnets on 'Beauty' (subject) by E. L. G., O. A. J. and me.[24]

The 'Sonnet to Beauty' (also entitled 'The Hour of Youth') was later revised to become 'My Shy Hand', in which 'Beauty' rather than the poet is the speaker:

> My shy hand shades a hermitage apart, –
>   O large enough for thee, and thy brief hours.
> Life there is sweeter held than in God's heart,
>   Stiller than in the heavens of hollow flowers.
>
> The wine is gladder there than in gold bowls.
>   And Time shall not drain thence, nor trouble spill.
> Sources between my fingers feed all souls,
>   Where thou mayest cool thy lips, and draw thy fill.
>
> Five cushions hath my hand, for reveries;
>   And one deep pillow for thy brow's fatigues;
> Languor of June all winterlong, and ease
>   For ever from the vain untravelled leagues.
>
> Thither your years may gather in from storm,
> And Love, that sleepeth there, will keep thee warm.

The poem which Sassoon wrote after hearing the first draft of this is clearly 'Vision' (first entitled 'Poets'), with its echo of Owen's 'heavens of hollow flowers':

Men with enchanted faces, who are these,
Following the birds and voices of the breeze?
Men who desire no longer to be wise,
And bear eternal forests in their eyes.

They are all singing of beauty; yet their dreams
Are mute amid that silence hung with green;
Silence of drifting clouds with towering beams
Dazzling the gloom, silence on earth serene.

No song beyond that archway of the hours,
But beauty breaking in a heaven of flowers,
And everywhere the whispering of trees . . .
Men with triumphant faces, who are these?[25]

In turn, Owen's 'Six O'clock in Princes Street' seems to have been
written 'around' this (although it has more obvious similarities to
Yeats's 'When you are old'):

In twos and threes, they have not far to roam,
    Crowds that thread eastward, gay of eyes;
Those seek no further than their quiet home,
    Wives, walking westward, slow and wise.

Neither should I go fooling over clouds,
    Following gleams unsafe, untrue,
And tiring after beauty through star-crowds,
    Dared I go side by side with you;

Or be you in the gutter where you stand,
    Pale rain-flawed phantom of the place,
With news of all the nations in your hand,
    And all their sorrows in your face.

These interconnected 'scribbles' show the dilemma which Owen
and Sassoon felt themselves to be in. On the one hand, poets had
to 'follow the gleam', like Tennyson's Merlin, the enchanted
enchanter;[26] the 'triumph' which troubled their faces was that of
the vision of beauty. On the other hand, the miserable face of
the Edinburgh newsboy, symbolic of the winter of the present
world, was a reminder that 'tiring after beauty' through a 'cobweb
of stars' might be no more than 'fooling'. The true poet's desire

should be for wisdom and the spreading of wisdom; the sorrows of the nations needed better interpreters than the newspapers would provide. It might have been all very well for Yeats to hide amid a crowd of stars but the soldier poet in 1917 had to be, as it were, 'in the gutter'. Sassoon and Owen knew that beauty and truth were to be found in the faces of the troops, as Owen had begun to say already in 'Has your soul sipped', but the difficulty was to say it in print without allowing civilians to suppose that the troops were contented (or the poets perverted). To write angry satires against civilians and priests was in a sense an evasion of the poet's duty to record his true 'vision' of 'triumph'. Somehow these two tasks had to be brought together. Much of Owen's poetic effort in the bare year that was left to him after Craiglockhart was to go into fusing his lyrical, Romantic bent with his indignation at the war.

Three of his most fertile and deeply felt Craiglockhart poems show him beginning to combine his perception of war with his earlier poetry. 'Anthem for Doomed Youth', 'Disabled' and 'Dulce et Decorum Est' have their roots in his pre-1917 life and writing. All three demonstrate his Romantic inheritance although he failed to put it to full use in 'Anthem'; all three develop the theme of lost youth which he had been exploring in his lyrics before his shellshock. The last stanza of Sassoon's 'Prelude: The Troops', with its lament for the 'unreturning army that was youth', would have shown him how the subjects of 'The Unreturning' and 'Happiness' could be applied impersonally to war and soldiers, enabling him to build on his regret for the lost joys of boyhood and to work towards regaining and strengthening the maturity which he knew Beaumont Hamel had brought him.

'Anthem for Doomed Youth' was completed by 25 September after advice from Sassoon, who recognised for the first time that Owen's talent was out of the ordinary. The differences between the first draft and the last (there were at least seven drafts) show how Owen began to bring his lyrical writing into step with his opinions about the war. The result was a sonorous but rather confused poem; there was still much to get straight, but he had made a start:

What passing-bells for these who die as cattle?
– Only the monstrous anger of the guns.

Only the stuttering rifles' rapid rattle
Can patter out their hasty orisons.
No mockeries now for them; no prayer nor bells;
    Nor any voice of mourning save the choirs, –
The shrill, demented choirs of wailing shells;
    And bugles calling for them from sad shires.

What candles may be held to speed them all?
    Not in the hands of boys but in their eyes
Shall shine the holy glimmers of good-byes.
    The pallor of girls' brows shall be their pall;
Their flowers the tenderness of patient minds,
And each slow dusk a drawing-down of blinds.

This sonnet has come in for some sharp criticism as a relapse
into Owen's youthful Romanticism and as an unintentional
glorification of death in war.[27] The first point seems to me
misleading. The poem's language is certainly Keatsian ('Then in
a *wailful choir* the small gnats *mourn*'[28]) but the allusions are meant
to be noticed, revealing the battlefield as a demented parody of
the Romantic landscape. The second point, that 'Anthem' has a
sanctifying effect on its subject, is more accurate, except that the
first draft (Plate 11) shows that originally this effect was by no
means unintentional. The draft begins by asking, 'What minute
bells for these who die so fast?' Answer: 'Only the monstrous/
solemn anger of our guns'. The only possible response to the
slaughter (of British troops) is that 'our' guns should hurl angry
'insults' at the enemy. The poet explains his function, which is
to arouse grief and remembrance, by saying that 'I will light' the
candles which will shine in boys' eyes (meaning that his poems
will produce tears in the eyes of soldiers' sons or younger brothers).
The funeral ceremonies will not be church services, since battle
conditions prevent such things, but the majestic 'requiem' of
British artillery in France and the sadness of bereaved families in
England. Whether such rites are adequate or not, the poem does
not say; they are the only possible ones, that is all.

Sassoon would have seen the first draft's shortcomings at once.
Even if Owen did not mean it to be a statement in support of
the British war effort, it could be used in that way. It was
uncomfortably close to popular war poems such as Laurence
Binyon's 'For the Fallen' or Beatrix Brice's 'To the Vanguard'.[29]
So Sassoon cancelled 'solemn' in favour of 'monstrous' and
changed 'our guns' and 'majestic insults' to 'the guns' and 'blind

insolence'. Owen followed these pointers in subsequent drafts, removing the anti-German and sanctifying elements from the octave by making shells 'demented', introducing the 'patter' of rifles (the word derives from the meaningless repetition of paternosters) and describing doomed youth as 'cattle' for whom any rites would be 'mockeries'. These changes do not fully conceal the tone of the first draft, but they might have been enough if the sestet had been different. If Sassoon sensed that the last six lines were unsatisfactory, he would not have known Owen well enough to see what was wrong. The difficult transition from battlefields to home is admirably managed by means of bugles, which were familiar in both places (memorial services in 'sad shires' often ended with a bugle call). But the strongest objection to 'Anthem' is that its sestet betrays Owen's hard-won maturity by slipping back into the nostalgia that he had expressed in 'A New Heaven' before he had seen the trenches. The sestets of both sonnets propose that dead soldiers can find immortality in the memory and affection of their families. The first draft of 'Anthem' even says that the men's wreaths will be 'Women's wide-spread arms', but after Beaumont Hamel Owen had said in 'Happiness' that he had gone *beyond* 'the scope / Of mother-arms' (or of 'the wide arms of trees'). It is not difficult to sense the presence of Colin, Mary and Mrs Owen among the weeping boys, pale girls and patient minds in the final sestet of 'Anthem', but there could be no return even in death. The hardest thing of all for a soldier to accept was that even his own family would not understand or remember; Owen was to come to terms with this after Craiglockhart.

It is unjust to treat 'Anthem' as a 'late' poem on a level with 'Strange Meeting' or 'Insensibility', as some critics have done. It should be seen as Owen's first attempt to bring his own style into line with the views he was learning from Sassoon. Unlike his more obviously Sassoonish poems, 'Anthem' draws extensively on what he had heard and read in Bordeaux as a way of resisting his friend's overwhelming stylistic influence. The elegiac tone, elaborate sound-patterns and elegant metaphors are more Tailhadesque than Sassoonish. Phrases in the first draft – 'solemn', '[priest-words] requiem of their [burials]', 'choristers and holy music', 'voice of mourning', 'many [candles shine]' – seem to derive from his account of a French funeral service in 1914:

The gloom, the incense, the draperies, the shine of many candles, the images and ornaments, were what may be got

anywhere in England; but the solemn voices of the priests was
what I had never heard before. The melancholy of a bass
voice, mourning, now alone, now in company with other voices
or with music, was altogether fine; as fine as the Nightingale –
(bird or poem).

A Craiglockhart fragment which contains material used for
'Anthem' experiments with imagery of 'deep' artillery and
'wailing . . . high' shells, like bass and alto voices. This fragment
also shows how Owen reached the metaphor of steady artillery
fire as funeral bells: the 'measured [smiting]' of the guns' 'iron
mouths' suggested the regular beat of minute or passing bells,
rung once a minute for every year of the dead man's life. The
bells also derive from the phrase 'Pacific lamentations of slow
bells' in another Craiglockhart fragment, from which they can
be traced back through 'A Palinode' (1915) to the 'lamentation
pacifique' of the angelus in *Madame Bovary*. Further connections
with Owen's stay in Bordeaux can be seen in the echo from his
1914 Decadent poem 'Long ages past ' ('on thy brow the pallor
of their death') and in the similarity between the bright-eyed
boys and candle-bearing acolytes such as he had seen at Mérignac
and read about in poems by Tailhade and others. These associ-
ations with the French Decadence hint at sinister meanings
behind the poem. Music, beauty and love have become deadly
mockeries of themselves. The girls may be *femmes fatales*, luring
youth to its doom. The domestic funeral rites may be as much a
parody of true religious observance as the rites on the battlefield.
These implications are not brought out clearly (most modern
readers will probably not recognise them at all) ·but they
are indications of how Owen would reconcile his Romantic
inheritance with his understanding of the war.[30]
    The possibilities of applying literary tradition to a war that
seemed to break with all tradition were taken much further in
Owen's next poem, 'Disabled'. Sassoon was beginning to be
impressed, making an unsuccessful effort to get 'Anthem' into the
Nation in October[31] and showing 'Disabled' to Graves, who came
up on a visit in that month. Graves was even more impressed,
writing to Owen soon afterwards with encouragement and some
typically Georgian advice. 'Disabled' was Owen's first thoroughly
original war poem, bringing his new skills and knowledge into
active partnership with his pre-Sassoon verse. As has been
suggested, the poem grew from several related 1916–17 sources

(see above, pp.79–82), including 'Lines to a Beauty seen in Limehouse'. The wounded man can be recognised as the East End 'Beauty', redrawn, disfigured, and perhaps containing elements of the poet himself. Whether or not Sassoon knew of the poem's origins, he would certainly have sympathised with its implications.

The admiring poet had gazed in vain at the Limehouse youth's handsome face and bare knees (an odd detail, but appropriate to a sculptured 'idol'), knowing that his tribute was ignored and that the 'half-god' would spend the night with someone else, presumably a woman. In 'Disabled', the young soldier and former footballer has had 'an artist silly for his face' and has been idolised by women; someone had told him 'he'd look a god in kilts', no doubt having seen him in football shorts. Now he is dressed in a grey parody of sports clothes, with short trousers and no sleeves because he is limbless. 'Voices of boys' are heard in the park – the next generation is perhaps playing football in its turn – until 'gathering sleep' 'mothers' them away from him. For him, sleep and the old happiness are unreturning. The greyness of his hospital suit and of the twilight are contrasted with the 'purple' of his spilt blood, Owen's favourite colour here carrying Romantic, Tailhadesque implications of youthful sexuality and sacrifice. The Limehouse 'Beauty' was unwise to turn to women. Instead of receiving the poet's blood sacrifice, he has become one himself; he has been drained of his blood and potency because he listened to 'the giddy jilts', the Fatal Women who persuaded him to volunteer. The 'hot *race* / And *leap* of purple' which 'spurted from his thigh' was for them an erotic climax (and for him a final athletic triumph); now they turn from him 'to the strong men that [are] whole'. The poem can be read both as a bitter comment on the role of women in wartime and as a study in late-Romantic themes.

'Disabled' contains several literary allusions. The ironic parallel between the soldier's past and present states is now generally agreed to be taken directly from Housman's 'To an Athlete Dying Young'. Another late-nineteenth-century influence is apparent in the Swinburnian juxtaposition of purple (sexual passion) and grey (impotence and repression). There is a less predictable allusion to the classical legend of Adonis, another beautiful youth who was wounded in the thigh – a sexual maiming – while absenting himself from his mistress in pursuit of sport. In Andrew Lang's translation of Bion's lament for Adonis, which Owen bought in December 1917 and might have glanced at before, 'the

dark blood *leapt* forth', leaving Adonis's chest '*purple* with blood'.[32]
It would be consistent with later poems if these associations were
meant to be observed. Readers of Owen's generation might also
have seen ironic relationships between the poem and recruiting-
posters such as those which showed sweethearts urging young
men to enlist or Mr Punch advising a footballer to become a
player in the 'Greater Game' in France. In making its comment
on war, the poem combines the immediacy of Sassoonish satire
with Romantic and Greek material of the kind Owen had used
in 'Perseus' and other work before 1917. At the end of the poem,
the dusk is the Decadent last evening, but the repeated question,
'Why don't they come?', sounds like an echo of a poster which
showed soldiers in need of reinforcements under the slogan, 'Will
they *never* come?' It was too late for anyone to come; the hour of
youth was unreturning.

The bitterness against women shown in 'Disabled' was
continued into 'Dulce et Decorum Est' in mid October. Again,
Owen drew on both literary tradition and contemporary propa-
ganda. 'Dulce et Decorum Est' was originally drafted as a
'counter-attack' against the recruiting-verses of Miss Jessie Pope,
'a certain Poetess' whose doggerel was frequently published in
the right-wing press. More widely, the attack is against civilian
heroic notions in general. Many patriotic versifiers had quoted
the Latin tag or used it as a title; Owen himself had alluded to
it approvingly in 'The Ballad of Peace and War' some years
before. Now, after Beaumont Hamel, the proposition that death
for the fatherland was sweet and decorous seemed nauseating, so
he answered it with a correspondingly revolting 'trench life
sketch', perhaps thinking of Sassoon's most recent work in which
the horrors of war were being described more vividly than in *The
Old Huntsman*. There is a controlled and powerful anger in 'Dulce
et Decorum Est' which for some readers will be the poem's most
valuable quality. The control is partly achieved by a tight formal
discipline. The first half of the poem is a sonnet in all but its final
rhymes, but at the point at which one expects a final couplet
there is instead the first half of a quatrain, so that the sonnet does
not end but instead makes the reader pause in anticipation:

> Dim, through the misty panes and thick green light,
> As under a green sea, I saw him drowning.

The second half of the quatrain comes after a space as an isolated pair of lines, repeating the image of drowning but placing it now not on the battlefield but in dreams:

> In all my dreams, before my helpless sight,
> He plunges at me, guttering, choking, drowning.

These two lines begin another group of fourteen, but this second half of the poem bears no resemblance to a sonnet and is held together only by its rhymes. The organisation and clarity of the first half is replaced by confused, choking syntax and a vocabulary of sickness and disgust, matching the nightmare which is in progress. Owen is directly facing the central experience of his war dreams, the sight of a horrifying face which, Gorgon-like, renders him a 'helpless', paralysed spectator. Some lines which were eventually cancelled tell the reader to think, as the poet thinks, of how the dying man's head was once 'like a bud, / Fresh as a country rose, and keen, and young', an image which has sometimes been regarded as a Romantic intrusion into the poem. The Romanticism is far from irrelevant, however. The soldier had been another beautiful youth but now his bud-like face is compared to that of a devil sickened by 'sin'. Another draft line mentions 'vile incurable sores on sin-kissed tongues'; 'sin-kissed' became 'young corrupted' and eventually 'innocent', a word which makes less sense than those which preceded it, removing what was presumably a reference to venereal disease.[33] These traces of sexual beauty and 'sin' in the poem are puzzling in isolation and Owen was right to reduce them, but they show how his nightmares worked. Once again, beauty and horror meet in the damned and sated figure who is both Gorgon and victim, destroyer and destroyed. The 'white eyes writhing' ('twinging' in one draft) are a version of the sufferers' eyes in 'Purgatorial passions' which 'twinged and twitched'; the simile of the bud comes from 'The cultivated Rose' ('Contused with sap of life like a bursting bud'); the submarine imagery ('flound'ring . . . green sea . . . drowning') is familiar. The Dunsden 'phantasy' has reshaped itself in a wartime setting so that the public statement of the poem is given its force not simply by Owen's anger against Miss Pope but by the pressing intensity of his private, ever-recurring vision (the personal and traditional meanings of the haunting face and its petrifying stare have been discussed in previous chapters).[34] Owen's true courage is evident in his exposing his imagination to war experience as material for poetry;

there is nothing comparable in Sassoon's work except perhaps 'Repression of War Experience', which deals only with waking horror, and 'Haunted', a poem clearly based on a shellshock nightmare but making no direct reference to war.

Rivers's steady work on his patient met with some success. On 24 October Graves wrote to Edmund Gosse that Sassoon had not modified his views about the war but was now applying to be sent back to France, to show that he was not afraid and to share the suffering of the troops.[35] This decision, reached after an intense mental struggle, put Sassoon in a position which many of his modern readers find puzzlingly hard to excuse. The alternatives which he had faced were either to maintain his protest, which was certain to become increasingly a matter of theory and public debate, or to recognise the intense loyalties which bound a serving officer to his men. Most poets who accepted the demands of comradeship felt that protesting was likely to do more harm than good. Sassoon attempted the compromise of returning to active service while remaining opposed to the war as a poet; in doing so, he pleased neither side. Graves said in his letter to Gosse that Sassoon

> thinks he is best employed by writing poems which will make people find the war so hateful that they'll stop it at once at whatever cost. I don't. I think that I'll do more good by keeping up my brother soldiers' morale as far as I can.

On the other side, Russell, Lady Ottoline and the *Cambridge Magazine* were deeply disappointed by Sassoon's decision. Owen tried to dissuade his friend but felt much the same conflict in himself; in the end he made the same decision as Sassoon, directly influenced by his example.

By the time he left Craiglockhart at the end of October, Owen had probably learned as much as he could from Sassoon. His last poem there, 'Soldier's Dream', was little more than a copy of ' "They" ' and other epigrams in *The Old Huntsman*. It was time to move on. But his debt as both soldier and poet to his friend was immense. Sassoon taught him to think for himself about the war and its politics. He taught him how to use experience in poetry and how to be true to it; indeed, like Harold Monro and Graves, he taught him how to be a Georgian. He introduced him to Hardy, Barbusse and other writers. As a later chapter suggests,

1. 'There was born . . . My poethood' : the woods in spring at Broxton, Cheshire.

2. 'As Perseus fearfully beheld the form / Of Gorgon, mirrored in the stilly well.' Edward Burne-Jones, *The Baleful Head* (detail).

3. A 'most dervishy vertigo' : a self-impression of the lay assistant, Dunsden Vicarage (16 November 1912).

4. Owen, Mme Léger and Nénette (front row, second, third and fourth from the left) at one of Tailhade's lectures at the Casino, Bagnères-de-Bigorre (August 1914).

5. Laurent Tailhade introducing Owen to Flaubert in the villa garden at La Gailleste (September 1914).

6. 'By Hermes, I will fly . . .' : a statuette of Hermes bought by Owen, probably in Bordeaux in 1915, and later given to Leslie Gunston.

7. Second Lieutenant WES Owen, Manchester Regiment (1916) :
one of a set of portraits taken by his uncle, John Gunston, to mark
his commission.

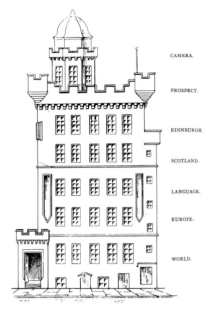

CAMERA.

PROSPECT.

EDINBURGH.

SCOTLAND.

LANGUAGE.

EUROPE.

WORLD.

8. Captain A J Brock, RAMC, probably in his room at Craiglockhart War Hospital, 1916–17.

9. Outlook Tower, Castle Hill, Edinburgh : a diagram taken from Patrick Geddes, *Cities in Evolution*, 1915.

10. 'Shell Shock!' : a cartoon from *The Hydra* (December 1917).

11. The first draft of 'Anthem for Doomed Youth' (September 1917).

ENLIST TO-DAY.

HE'S
HAPPY &
SATISFIED
ARE YOU ?

12. 'When I behold eyes blinded in my stead!' : 'Blinded for You!', a wartime postcard, sold in aid of the National Institute for the Blind.

13. 'Happy the man who...' : a recruiting poster.

Happy With His Vanity Bag Hat.

14. 'Pictures of these broad smiles appear in Sketches / And people say : They're happy now, poor wretches' : a photograph in the *Daily Sketch* (16 September 1918) showing 'Happy wounded Canadians at a casualty station'.

15. Taken at Hastings on the eve of embarkation (30 August 1918) :
'such a badly printed photograph...but looking at a little distance
it is *him*...'.

he is likely to have talked about homosexuality. Above all, he and Owen shared their poetic ideals as their poems show, discussing not only the monstrosity of the war but also the lyrical impulse, the poet's vision and what Sassoon had described to Nicholson as 'the quest for beauty and compassion and friendship'. They were followers of 'the gleam', a difficult role in wartime. In the end, it led them back to France, which may have been why Owen wrote to Sassoon in November 1917, parodying Tennyson:

> I am Owen; and I am dying.
> I am Wilfred; and I follow the Gleam.

Earlier in the same month he told Sassoon,

> you have *fixed* my Life – however short. You did not light me: I was always a mad comet; but you have fixed me. I spun round you a satellite for a month, but I shall swing out soon, a dark star in the orbit where you will blaze.

There are echoes here of 'following gleams' in 'Six O'clock in Princes Street' and of the image of the poet as meteor or errant star (no longer 'lawless') in 'O World of many worlds'. The references to dying and short life imply that Owen had already decided he would have to go back to war, but his youthful Romanticism had always required him to expect an early death. As in 'Storm', the flash of illumination may be fatal but it will make men 'cry aloud and start'. He said in September that some of his poems might 'light the darkness of the world', echoing the first draft of 'Anthem' in which he undertook to 'light' the many candles of grief. He compared his poetry more modestly to a single candle in 1918, saying when Sassoon was invalided home that he would throw his 'little candle' on Sassoon's torch and return to the front.[36]

Sassoon's 'torch' blazed with anger and protest but the anger sprang from his compassion for his men and from his vision of their beauty. In his own and Owen's opinion, his truest vein as a war poet was lyrical and elegiac. If the final stanza of 'Prelude: The Troops' was the piece which Owen described in September as 'the most exquisitely painful war poem of any language or time' (one observes the Romantic words 'exquisite' and 'pain'), it may be taken as an example of Sassoon's writing 'from the heart' as well as from experience ('I write straight from my experiences and heart', Owen said soon after meeting him, describing a letter home[37]). Its echo of Charles Sorley's 'pale battalions' of 'the mouthless dead' places its author with Sorley and Graves. In imagery and diction the stanza is less original than their best wartime work, but it lacks their shield of stoicism. Sassoon's emotion, somehow guaranteed even by the faults in the verse, stands unprotected, movingly exposed:

> O my brave brown companions, when your souls
> Flock silently away, and the eyeless dead
> Shame the wild beast of battle on the ridge,
> Death will stand grieving in that field of war
> Since your unvanquished hardihood is spent.
> And through some mooned Valhalla there will pass
> Battalions and battalions, scarred from hell;
> The unreturning army that was youth;
> The legions who have suffered and are dust.

7 New Influences: Georgians and Others

After Owen was discharged from Craiglockhart on 30 October 1917, he devoted all his spare energies to poetry. Brock had taught him to work, Sassoon had given him purpose and confidence. On 3 December, for example, he finished one poem, drafted three more and determined to get up early next day to 'do a dawn piece'. By the end of the month he was ready 'to revise now, rather than keep piling up "first drafts" ', wishing he could give his 'art' the six hours a day it needed. In February he remembered the Broxton bluebells which had 'fitted me for my job'. That job involved the risk of shellshock nightmares: 'I confess I *bring on* what few war dreams I now have, entirely by *willingly* considering war of an evening. I do so because I have my duty to perform towards War.'[1] In order to define his task he read writers whom Sassoon admired, looking for guidance in both style and ideas from, among others, the Georgians, Barbusse and, almost certainly, Hardy and Russell. Now that there was good reason to bring his 'art' into the immediate service of the age, it was more than time to take account of contemporary writers.

The first moderns to look at were obviously the Georgians, since he already knew three of them personally and had read Brooke. His new posting, on light duties at Scarborough, allowed time for visits to London and the Poetry Bookshop, where he was pleased to find himself remembered. He bought Monro's latest collection, *Strange Meetings* (1917), with its interesting title, and *Georgian Poetry 1916–1917*. This new volume of the anthology, published by the Bookshop in November, included work by Sassoon, Graves, Monro, Robert Nichols, John Masefield, W. W. Gibson, Walter de la Mare and John Drinkwater. Owen eventually possessed at least fifteen volumes by these Georgians and their original leader, Brooke; this was by far the largest representation of modern verse in his shelves, and most of it was

bought and read in November–December 1917. The lessons to
be learned from the Georgians were straightforward. They
all respected Brooke's pre-war language – 'musical, restrained,
refined, and not crabbed or conventionally antique, reading
almost like ordinary speech', as Graves had described it in 1916.[2]
Nineteenth-century diction, vagueness and insincerity were to
be rooted out, and satirised if necessary; realism, technical
accuracy, and fidelity to experience were the modern goals in
composition, and the lifestyle that went with them was expected
to be perhaps unconventional but always plain, sincere and
courageous. One can see the Georgian spirit at work in Owen's
little epigram 'Schoolmistress' (1918), in which a teacher who
has just read the Victorian epic 'Horatius' refuses to acknowledge
the greeting of a modern soldier named 'Orace. The gibe is
against civilian and Victorian double standards, yet by calling
his soldier Horace Owen identifies him as a modern hero.[3]
Similarly, Graves's 'The Legion', which Owen warmly admired
in November, compares Tommies to Romans driving the
barbarians out of Gaul yet makes the Romans sound like ordinary
modern soldiers rather than 'conventionally antique' heroes.

Owen was in the Bookshop in November when copies of
Graves's new book, *Fairies and Fusiliers*, arrived. He wrote 'Asleep'
on the same day, a poem which includes two unintentional echoes
from the book. Graves wrote to him encouragingly, hoping (in
vain as it turned out) to put him in touch with Robert Nichols:
'You must help S. S. and R. N. and R. G. to revolutionise English
Poetry – So outlive this War.' Edward Marsh was told that 'I
have a new poet for you, just discovered, one Wilfred Owen . . .
the real thing; when we've educated him a trifle more. R. N. and
S. S and myself are doing it.' Later, perhaps early in January,
Graves sent Marsh 'the few poems of Owen I can find: not his
best but they show his powers and deficiencies – Too Sassoonish
in places: Sassons is to him a god of the highest rank.' This letter
is marked 'Please return enclosures' without any indication of
what they were. Presumably Graves hoped that Marsh would
accept some of Owen's work for the next *Georgian Poetry*, but
Marsh must have shown his usual caution because Graves wrote
again, 'Owen, I told you, is fearfully uncertain: but he can see
and feel, and the rest will be added unto him in time.' Part of
the 'education' which Graves offered thus seems to have been
advice against being excessively 'Sassoonish'; from January
onward, that quality became less marked in Owen's verse.[4]

Graves also advised him in December to 'write more
optimistically . . . a poet should have a spirit above wars',
apparently in response to 'Wild with all Regrets', which Owen
had written earlier in the month and dedicated to Sassoon. This
may have prompted Owen to take up a poem provisionally
entitled 'The Unsaid' and give it the new title of 'Apologia
lectorem pro Poema Disconsolatia Mea' ('A defence to the reader
of my disconsolate poem'), adding to the manuscript a half-
remembered quotation from Barbusse's *Under Fire*: 'If there be a
bright side to war, it is a crime to exhibit it.'[5] Whereas Graves
wrote for soldiers, as he had told Gosse, Owen still had a civilian
audience in mind; 'Apologia' explains that an 'optimistic' account
of fighting might lead civilians to believe that soldiers were
content in the trenches. That this could happen is evident from
plenty of civilian verse, including, for example, a poem in John
Oxenham's *The Vision Splendid* (1917), a book Owen had read at
Craiglockhart, in which a civilian asks, 'What did you see out
there, my lad?' and a Tommy answers,

> I have seen Christ doing Christly deeds . . .
> I have sped through hells of fiery hail
> With fell red-fury shod;
> I have heard the whisper of a voice;
> I have looked in the face of God.

To which the civilian thanks God for His grace and says the
soldier has a right to his 'deep, high look'. 'I, too, saw God
through mud', Owen admitted in 'Apologia' – but he would have
included Oxenham among the complacent civilians who are
rebuked at the end of the poem. He was not sure that 'the Unsaid'
should be said, but he felt as well qualified as Graves to lay claim
to a 'spirit above wars', remembering the 'exultation' he had felt
in No Man's Land: 'I, too, have . . . sailed my spirit light and
clear / Past the entanglement . . . And witnessed exultation'. To
emphasise the point in his 'apology' to Graves, he borrowed
imagery from 'Two Fusiliers', a poem in *Fairies and Fusiliers* which
describes how Graves and Sassoon had found love at the front
and 'Beauty in Death'. Sassoon had testified in his dreamier way
to similar insights in 'The Triumph', while Nichols, the third of
the Georgian trio, told Mrs Owen after the war that his own
poem 'The Secret' was an 'exact parallel' to 'Apologia'.[6]

'Apologia' denies that beauty and love are as 'old song' had described them; they are now to be found in the experience and comradeship of battle. This seems to be a Georgian rejection of nineteenth-century poetry, but the critic has to be careful here. The poet does not reject Romantic values such as beauty and truth but gives them a new location. The manuscripts show Owen trying out some of the Romantic and Decadent phrasing he had used in erotic verse before meeting Sassoon: 'Sweet ran our sweat' (the pararhyme is from 'Has your soul sipped'); '[glorious lovely] ecstatic [seemed was] the [crimson] purple of our murder'; '[You shall not jest] with them whose wine is fate.'

> Unmeet for you is their mirth
>   By your safe hearths. Close lightning keeps them warm.
>   Only to gods and men grown sick of earth
> Hilarious sound the thunders of this storm.[7]

There are traces of 'Perseus' here, including the rape of Danae and its parallel in 'Storm' ('those hilarious thunders of my fall'). He had recognised in 'The cultivated Rose' that beauty could be found in hell. He did not use this pre-1917 material in drafts of 'Apologia' in order to make some ironic contrast with his earlier verse; its effect is rather to separate the soldiers' knowledge from the civilian's in much the same way that the Romantic poets often saw themselves as possessing a mystery and suffering to which ordinary people had no access. The 'men grown sick of earth' are now soldiers but in literary tradition they had been poets, 'the wise' whose secret knowledge of beauty gave them the power to laugh like gods, their spirits 'floating' far above worldly torment. Owen was to develop the parallel between soldiers and poets in some of his 1918 work.

His new Georgian allegiance led him to reinterpret rather than to reject Romanticism but it did prevent him from approving Leslie Gunston's first and only book. It was bad luck for Gunston that *The Nymph, and Other Poems* came out only a week or two after *Fairies and Fusiliers*. Owen thought the book premature, remarking that it contained to much fictitious kissing. 'I think every poem, and every figure of speech should be a *matter of experience*.' 'Nothing great was said of anything but a definite experience.'[8] He was echoing a new master and an old, not only Sassoon but also Keats, who resolved 'never to write for the sake of writing or making a poem, but from running over with any little knowledge or experience which many years of reflection may perhaps give me'.[9] Owen's 1918 claim that he was 'not concerned with Poetry' was an affirmation of Georgian, Keatsian and Geddesian values, and a dismissal of his own and his cousin's old habit of writing for the sake of writing. Although he never ceased to use his knowledge of Aestheticism, he had no more time for notions of art for art's sake, especially when they resulted in the sort of 'Poetry' that was still appearing in great quantities in the *Poetry Review* and other publications from the house of 'Erskine Macdonald'. There would be no more sonnets on agreed subjects. 'They believe in me, these Georgians', he told his cousin, and referred proudly to 'We Georgians' in January. Gunston was warned not to become a lagoon left by 'the ebbing tide of the Victorian Age' but was doubtful about *Fairies and Fusiliers* and Owen's curious new rhymes. 'Graves's technique is perfect,' Owen replied, and 'I suppose I am doing in poetry what the advanced composers are doing in music.'[10] This determination to be modern and 'advanced' without abandoning accuracy of technique was typical of his Georgian ambitions in the winter of 1917–18. In contradicting 'old song' in 'Apologia', Owen was referring in particular to Gunston's poem 'L'Amour', which had said that 'Love is the binding . . . of lips, the binding of eyes'.[11] 'Apologia' denies this: 'love is not the binding of fair lips / With the soft silk of eyes' as is told in 'old song' but the comradeship of soldiers, 'wound with war's hard wire'. The image from 'L'Amour' is set aside in favour of one taken from Graves's 'Two Fusiliers'. This was not only a literary gesture but also a sign that Owen still thought Gunston ought to be in uniform. But he continued to feel his old affection for his cousin, whose friendship and encouragement had been valuable to his poethood.

Owen's determination not to become a Victorian 'lagoon' himself is apparent in 'Wild with all Regrets' (5 December, later redrafted as 'A Terre'), an unmistakably Georgian poem, its title an ironic reference to Tennyson[12] and its form and style deriving from Masefield by way of Sassoon. The model for this and other Georgian monologues was Masefield's *The Everlasting Mercy* (1911), which had been famous before the war as an example of contemporary realism; Owen may never have read the original but he owned a copy of Sassoon's part-parody, part-imitation of it, *The Daffodil Murderer*.[13] He had marked several pleasing passages in Sassoon's poem, such as:

> I thought, 'When me and Bill are deaders,
> 'There'll still be buttercups in medders . . . .

He used his kind of verse in a number of Sassoonish poems, including 'The Chances':

> 'Ah well,' says Jimmy, and he's seen some scrappin',
> 'There ain't no more than five things as can happen....

But Sassoon had smoothed Masefield's style, going on to tame it still further in the title poem of *The Old Huntsman*, another monologue by a man facing death:

> What a grand thing 'twould be if I could go
> Back to the kennels now and take my hounds
> For summer exercise; be riding out
> With forty couple when the quiet skies
> Are streaked with sunrise, and the silly birds
> Grown hoarse with singing; cobwebs on the furze
> Up on the hill, and all the country strange,
> With no one stirring; and the horses fresh,
> Sniffing the air I'll never breathe again.
>
> 　　　　　. . . . .
>
> You've brought the lamp, then, Martha? I've no mind
> For newspaper tonight, nor bread and cheese.
> Give me the candle, and I'll get to bed.

'Wild with all Regrets' is similar in structure and in some of its subject matter but Sassoon's even tone has been roughened again:

> We said we'd hate to grow dead-old. But now,
> Not to live old seems awful: not to renew
> My boyhood with my boys, and teach 'em hitting,
> Shooting and hunting, – all the arts of hurting.
> – Well, that's what I learnt, – that, and making money.
> Your fifty years in store seem none too many,
> But I've five minutes. God! For just two years
> To help myself to this good air of yours!
> One Spring! Is one too hard to spare? Too long?
> Spring air would find its own way to my lung,
> And grow me legs as quick as lilac-shoots.
>
> 　　　　* 　　　* 　　　*
>
> Yes, there's the orderly. He'll change the sheets
> When I'm lugged out. Oh, couldn't I do that?

'This "Wild with all Regrets" was begun & ended two days ago, at one gasp', Owen told Sassoon. 'If simplicity, if imaginativeness, if sympathy, if resonance of vowels, make poetry I have not succeeded. But if you say "Here is poetry", it will be so for me. What do you think of my Vowel-rime stunt . . . ?'[14] Pararhyme was now not a device for Decadent lyrics but a progressive experiment, a 'stunt' akin to 'what the advanced composers are doing in music'; the harshness and lack of conventional 'beauty' in the poem are deliberate attempts at a modernity which was in fact more extreme than most Georgians would have liked. The once-celebrated ruggedness of *The Everlasting Mercy* seems a tame affair by comparison.

By the end of 1917 Owen felt himself to be a Georgian and a fully fledged poet:

> I go out of this year a Poet, my dear Mother, as which I did not enter it. I am held peer by the Georgians; I am a poet's poet.
> I am started. The tugs have left me; I feel the great swelling of the open sea taking my galleon.[15]

It was a good Masefield-like metaphor and an exciting moment. In the same letter he said he had felt 'sympathy for the oppressed always', which was probably true although it had not often been evident in his verse before Craiglockhart. He had said in a school essay ten years earlier that the Romantics had brought 'a new sympathy with man especially the poor' into literature, and he had found the same quality in Sassoon, Monro and other Georgians. It was not enough to be 'a poet's poet'; like all true poets he was needed as a spokesman. One of the last of the galleon's 'tugs' was Brooke's friend W. W. Gibson, whose *Battle* (1915) Owen read in December. The little poems in *Battle* have rarely had credit as the first things of their kind but Gibson was writing 'trench life sketches' sympathetic to the common soldier long before Sassoon, even though he never actually saw the trenches.[16] Owen may have looked at some of his other books. The introductory poem in *Fires* (1912) symbolises Gibson's sudden change a few years before the war from being a conventional poet of dream and fancy to writing about the sufferings of the poor:

> Snug in my easy chair,
> I stirred the fire to flame.
> Fantastically fair,
> The flickering fancies came, . . .

> Amber woodland streaming;
> Topaz islands dreaming; . . .
> Summers, unreturning; . . .
> Till, dazzled by the drowsy glare,
> I shut my eyes to heat and light;
> And saw, in sudden night,
> Crouched in the dripping dark,
> With steaming shoulders stark,
> The man who hews the coal to feed my fire.

When the newspapers reported a disastrous colliery explosion at Halmerend on 12 January 1918, the poem from *Fires* may have provided the framework for Owen's 'Miners', in which another Georgian sits before his fire and is made aware of the fate of miners rather than of the pleasant dreams which he had been expecting. 'Miners' was the first product of the fully launched poet in 1918, but his consciously Georgian phase was already nearing its end.

Owen's reading in the winter of 1917–18 was not confined to the Georgians. There seem to be traces in his later work of the war poems in Hardy's *Moments of Vision*, which came out at the end of November ('The Pity of It', for example, may be compared with Owen's repeated 1918 phrase, 'the pity of war').[17] Sassoon's admiration for Hardy had probably persuaded Owen to read *The Dynasts*, too, that great epic–drama about war and the pity of war. In tracing the movements of the Napoleonic armies, Hardy describes them from above in stage directions: 'The view is from a vague altitude'. Owen seems to take this up in the first line of 'The Show': 'My soul looked down from a vague height, with Death'. His ensuing description of a battlefield where troops 'writhed' and 'crept' like 'caterpillars' is similar to many of Hardy's descriptions, in which armies move like 'caterpillars' ('a dun-piled caterpillar, / Shuffling its length in painful heaves along'; 'The caterpillar shape still creeps laboriously nearer . . .'). The various Spirits which comment on the action of *The Dynasts* watch from the Overworld 'the surface of the perturbed countries, where the peoples . . . are seen writhing, crawling, heaving, and vibrating' in the beautiful but meaningless patterns which seem in themselves the single 'listless aim' of the controlling 'Immanent

Will'.[18] The Will is solely interested in art for art's sake, like the 'everliving' gods in the quotation from Yeats which Owen chose as an epigraph for 'The Show'. The weary gods breathe dreams on the mirror of the world, the Will weaves its patterns – both are exclusively 'concerned with Poetry'. But in *The Dynasts*, as elsewhere in Hardy, the patterns are observed by the Spirit Ironic and the Spirit of the Pities, and it is the latter which has the truest response. There is no lack of irony in Owen's 1918 poems, but Hardy would have confirmed what experience had already suggested, that 'the pity of war' was 'the one thing war distilled'.

In the first draft of 'The Show' the caterpillars are brown, blue, grey and green, the colours of British, French, German and American uniforms, for the detached view with which the poem begins is based on political awareness as well as on an attempt to see events from the position of 'the Elders and the gods, high witnesses of the general slaughter'. The gods on Olympus used to look down and 'smile in secret, looking over wasted lands'[19] according to literary tradition, and the older generation seemed to be doing much the same in 1917–18, but the poet, too, had to be able to separate himself from the conflict and see it as a whole. Owen met H. G. Wells in November, one of the leading writers about the war and its politics, an advocate of internationalism, efficiency, the defeat of militarism by military means, and the need for personal and communal dedication to a new world order. Owen read at least two of his books in December; if he also knew *The World Set Free* he would have found a description of the last war of the world that used Hardyesque imagery: 'If some curious god had chosen to watch ... he would have noticed ... the long bustling caterpillars of cavalry and infantry, the maggot-like waggons ... crawling ....'[20]

The distance between the poet and his subject in 'The Show' soon closes, however, because this is no Wellsian fantasy but a 'true resumption of experienced things', the high viewpoint having been earned by participation in the very battle which is being described. In this and other ways the poem is much closer to Henri Barbusse's *Le Feu* than to anything by Wells, and its preliminary title, 'Vision', was perhaps a deliberate acknowledgment of Owen's debt to Barbusse's first chapter, 'The Vision', an aerial vision of war-torn Europe watched from above by spirits of dead soldiers ('I can see crawling things down there'). At the end of the book, the battle is seen from the ground through the experience of the squad of French soldiers around whom the story has centred, the author having revealed himself as one of them. Similarly the poet in 'The Show' begins by looking down from a height on crawling armies and ends by falling to earth, where he finds himself at the head of his own platoon. Nothing before *Le Feu* had given such an appallingly vivid description of trench warfare or combined it with such passionate political conviction. The English translation, *Under Fire*, appeared in June 1917 and Sassoon was reading it by mid August; he lent it to Owen, who seems to have read it at Craiglockhart and again in December.[21] Barbusse was fiercely Socialist, presenting his soldiers as victims of profiteers and war-makers, expounding the 'Difference' between those who fought and those who grew rich, and stressing the impossibility of communication from soldier to civilian. The squad is cut off from its exploiters but forms an intense comradeship within itself, thereby becoming a Marxist paradigm of the working class as a whole. The book may well have been the first Socialist polemic Owen had read; its message would have been supported to some extent by Sassoon's reluctant (and in the event temporary) commitment towards the left. However, both Englishmen would have noticed one thing lacking from *Under Fire*. Whether Barbusse was portraying reality or his political convictions, the book gives no evidence of a close relationship between French officers and other ranks. The mutual affection and respect between British subalterns and their men described so often (by officers – not so often by privates) in Great War literature seems to have been generally regarded as peculiar to the British Army and a mainstay of its morale; Owen and Sassoon would have felt that strengthening that bond was one way in which an officer really could ease his men's ordeal. That was another reason why complete detachment was neither possible nor desirable. An officer poet, feeling 'sympathy for the oppressed', had a double duty to lead and to plead, as Owen accepted in 1918. By contrast, the callousness of civilians seemed beyond pardon.

'The Show' and similar poems were designed to shock civilians out of callousness into recognition of actuality, not to arouse pity but to convey the knowledge which could be pity's foundation. Owen was to clarify his thoughts about this process in the spring but in the winter his understanding of 'pity' was only beginning to take shape. The first stage was to shatter civilian complacency, so that priority went to writing poems that would be, like Sassoon's, 'perfectly truthfully descriptive of war'. When he came to revise 'Wild with all Regrets' into 'A Terre' in April, he referred to it as a 'photographic representation'. This may shed light on the legend that he used to carry photographs of mutilated soldiers with which to shock civilians, a story based on the evidence of a single witness, Frank Nicholson, who met him in Edinburgh. Nicholson recalled that Owen put his hand to his pocket to produce the pictures 'but suddenly thought better of it and refrained'; they talked of pararhyme instead. It is difficult to imagine how a subaltern could have obtained such photographs without falling foul not only of the military censor but also of his fellow soldiers.[22] Nicholson may have been under a misapprehension, since he never actually saw what Owen had in his pocket. The evidence which the poet intended to produce may in fact have been one of his new poems in pararhyme, a 'photographic representation' of war's horrors, possibly even an early draft of 'The Show'. It was through the realism of poems such as these that Owen intended to assault the civilian conscience.

If using shock tactics to make civilians see was a short-term aim, the poet's long-term duty was to bring healing and peace to the world, as Shelley had taught Owen years before. It was inconsistent with Shelleyan ideals that poets should participate in war, but the immediate task of protesting had to be done by soldiers because their experience entitled them to tell the truth with unique authority. However, there was a case for Owen and Sassoon to stay out of all further fighting now that they had earned their right to speak, because violence remained inexcusable and a dead poet was of no use to anybody. Graves told Owen to 'outlive this War'. It seemed likely that a shellshock case would not be sent out again anyway ('I *think* I am marked Permanent Home Service', Owen said in November).[23] But Sassoon had decided in October to apply for active service again. Owen tried to dissuade him, though without much hope; writing to him in November, he commented on Graves's 'Letter to S. S. from Mametz Wood', asking, 'If these tetrameters aren't enough to bring you to your senses, Mad Jack, what can *my* drivel effect to keep you from France?'[24] The 'drivel' referred to here seems to be a poem which stated the argument for poets staying out of the fighting in order to work for peace. There is only one surviving poem which meets this description, the untitled piece beginning 'Earth's wheels run oiled with blood'.

'Earth's wheels' has often been regarded as a part-draft of 'Strange Meeting' but it seems to have been originally composed

as a poem in its own right.[25] Owen used the same type of paper
and the same strict pararhymed couplets for it as he did for 'Wild
with all Regrets' early in December, so that 'Earth's wheels'
seems to belong to that period (Sassoon left Craiglockhart on 26
November and reported for duty on 11 December). As in Graves's
'Letter to S. S.', one officer seems to be addressing another: 'We
two', 'Let us forgo our rank and seniority', 'Let us break ranks'.
The military metaphors are maintained, first coming from trench
warfare ('dig') and then taking on biblical characteristics. One
of the five drafts is as follows:

> Earth's wheels run oiled with blood. Forget we that.
> Let us lie down and dig ourselves in thought.
>
> Beauty is yours and you have mastery.
> Wisdom is mine, and I have mystery.[26]
>
> Let us forgo men's minds that are brutes' natures.
> Let us not sup the blood which some say nurtures.
>
> Be we not swift with swiftness of the tigress;
> Let us break ranks and we will trek from progress.
>
> Miss we the march of this retreating world
> Into old citadels that are not walled.
>
> Then, [when] their blood hath clogged their chariot wheels
> We will go up and wash them from deep wells
>
> What though we sink from men as pitchers falling
> Many shall raise us up to be their filling
>
> Even from wells we sunk too deep for war
> Even as One who bled where no wounds were.

This very literary piece, full of allusions appropriate to an
exhortation from one Romantic poet to another, needs some
explanation. The two officers are poets, masters of beauty and
truth. The speaker urges that they should take no more part in
war, which has become, in Bergsonian terms, a machine; the
'war-blood' (as another draft describes it) now oiling the machine
will eventually bring it to a halt. Men have become brutish.

What is supposed to be 'progress' is actually a retreat into outdated, indefensible positions. War is an Old Testament activity, but in the New Testament Christ ('One') is said to bring water from a living well, fulfilling the prophecy that his people would 'draw water out of the wells of salvation' in the day of peace.[27] Christ 'bled where no wounds were' in his 'agony and bloody sweat' before the Crucifixion; the blood which redeems is not blood shed in war, so the popular notion of the soldier-as-redeemer is false. Owen's imagination was still based on the biblical texts and images which he had memorised daily in his younger years, but 'Earth's wheels' also shows the influence of Shelley, the self-declared 'atheist'. Shelley said that *The Revolt of Islam* had grown 'as it were from "the agony and bloody sweat" of intellectual travail', seeing himself as a sort of poet Christ, so it may be that Owen's 'One' is to be understood as a similar figure.[28] The 'wells we sunk too deep for war' are both biblical and Shelleyan:

> Those deepest wells of passion or of thought
> Wrought by wise poets in the waste of years.[29]

In the *Revolt*, Cythna promises Laon to pour

> For the despairing, from the crystal wells
> Of thy deep spirit, reason's mighty lore,
> And power shall then abound, and hope arise once more.[30]

This, then, is the programme which Owen envisaged for himself and Sassoon at the end of 1917. They should be on the side of spirit, not machinery, refusing to take part in violence even if that meant the end of their military careers. They might be able to achieve little until the war machine exhausted itself but in the end their store of beauty and wisdom would be a source of purification and new life for society. Meanwhile they should isolate themselves like Laon and Cythna, using the time for thought and preparation. Owen read Wells's *What is Coming?* in December or January and would have noticed its author's hope that 'we may presently find . . . devoted men and women ready to give their whole lives, with a quasi-religious enthusiasm, to this great task of peace establishment'.[31]

'Earth's wheels' was to be adapted in the spring for inclusion in 'Strange Meeting', where the dead poet describes the pro-

gramme he 'would have' followed if he had lived. The political
prophecy in both poems may owe something to Wells but its
main source seems to be Bertrand Russell, whose work had
strongly influenced Sassoon. Sassoon may well have lent some of
Russell's books to Owen; he certainly wanted to put him in touch
with Russell in November.[32] There is an essay on 'The Danger
to Civilization' in *Justice in War-Time* (1916) which makes a
political forecast very like the one in 'Strange Meeting'. Russell
expects that 'universal exhaustion' will set in if the war continues
('when much blood had clogged their chariot-wheels'), making
true progress impossible ('this retreating world'). Peoples will
have become used to passive obedience or violence, and
governments will have grown accustomed to autocratic power,
so that, when the ruling classes cut back on education after the
war in an attempt to keep the populace ignorant and forcibly
disciplined, either 'apathy or civil war' will result ('men will go
content with what we spoiled, / Or, discontent, boil bloody, and
be spilled'). Russell says past progress has largely been maintained
by young teachers, most of whom are now dead or worn out ('the
undone years, / The hopelessness . . . I would have poured my
spirit without stint'). Russell's other 1916 book, *Principles of Social
Reconstruction*, gives advice to the few who are prepared to 'lie out
and hold the open truth' (to use a phrase from an 'Earth's wheels'
draft). He admits that little can be achieved in the short term.
The aim must be long-term, to prepare for a saner society which
future generations can enjoy. The wise man follows a 'consistent
creative purpose' and is not diverted by external pressures, but
in wartime his reward is bound to be loneliness.

> To one who stands outside the cycle of beliefs and passions
> which make the war seem necessary, an isolation, an almost
> unbearable separation from the general activity, becomes
> unavoidable. . . . The helpless longing to save men from the
> ruin towards which they are hastening makes it necessary to
> oppose the stream, to incur hostility, to be thought unfeeling,
> to lose for the moment the power of winning belief.[33]

Russell held this ground resolutely throughout the war, despite
a prison sentence in 1918 and bouts of near-despair.

But Russell had never led men in battle. Sassoon was persuaded
by Rivers and the call of the troops to abandon his protest as
'futile' and to return to the line, whence he assured his anxious

correspondents that he had made the right decision. Graves, now on home service after a breakdown, wrote a long poem expressing sympathy for what he supposed to be Sassoon's lonely misery, but in reply Sassoon insisted that he was much happier than he had been in 1917. He told Lady Ottoline in May that he was 'driven by an intense desire to do all I can to train the 150 men I am in charge of – because I *know* that it is the only means of mitigating their wretchedness when they get into the Inferno'. Owen understood this position although he was less single-minded himself, advocating 'breaking ranks' in 'Earth's wheels' and allowing friends in 1918 to try to find him a home posting. In February he quoted a Russell-like statement that 'few have the courage, or the consistency, to go their own way, to their own ends', but that might have described Sassoon, who had freely chosen to be true to himself by following a course which served neither pacifism nor militarism. Owen had said at Craiglockhart that 'I hate washy pacifists as temperamentally as I hate whiskied prussianists. Therefore I feel that I must first get some reputation of gallantry before I could successfully and usefully declare my principles.' He was right about his usefulness: a shellshocked officer suspected of cowardice would not have carried any weight with the public without further trench service. He was never really in much doubt. At the end of 1917 he remembered the expression on the faces of the troops ('a blindfold look . . . like a dead rabbit's') and said that 'to describe it, I think I must go back and be with them'. If it was true that 'every poem, and every figure of speech should be a *matter of experience*', the poet had to be with his men at the front.[34]

Owen said in November that poetry for Sassoon had become 'a mere vehicle of propaganda', implying some doubt about using poetry for that purpose, but in fact the propaganda element had already begun to fade from his friend's verse. The dominant force in Sassoon's war poems from that November onwards was not political protest but sympathy with the troops; he told E. M. Forster in the following year that soldiers were 'the only thing in the war that moves me deeply. When I see them in large masses they seem like the whole tradition of suffering humanity'. He wanted to write poems about this in 1918; thinking of *The Dynasts*, Whitman, and the paintings being done by official war artists, he wondered if he might become an official war poet and attempt 'larger canvases, sort of Whitmanesque effects of masses of soldiers' as a detached observer. He said later that this was unconsciously a move towards the kind of work that Owen was doing by then. Owen would not have accepted this, any more than he accepted that poetry should be 'a mere vehicle of propaganda'; if he was less sure of himself as a soldier than Sassoon, he was more certain and determined as a poet.[35]

'The Show' may stand for his achievement in his last winter. It is a large 'canvas', portraying 'masses of soldiers' from the 'vague altitude' of *The Dynasts*, but the poet does not remain an observer. The language is as elaborately patterned as in 'From my Diary' but no longer experimental or decorative, its discordant pararhymes and sound sequences being similar to the sort of work that the 'advanced composers' were producing in music. Technique is not present for the sake of 'Poetry' but as a means of controlling and organising experience, for the poem is not only a Romantic vision[36] but also one of those shellshock dreams that Owen '*willingly*' brought on in the course of following what he believed to be his 'duty . . . towards War'. He was still haunted by the ground at Savy Wood 'all crawling and wormy with wounded bodies',[37] and in the poem this memory combines with an earlier horror, the tormented face, now filling the whole landscape as the maggot-infested face of war:

> Across its beard, that horror of harsh wire,
> There moved thin caterpillars, slowly uncoiled.
> It seemed they pushed themselves to be as plugs
> Of ditches, where they writhed and shrivelled, killed.
> . . .
> I saw their bitten backs curve, loop, and straighten.
> I watched those agonies curl, lift, and flatten.

It is testimony to the help given him by Brock and Sassoon, and to his own dedication as a poet, that Owen was able to write about this twofold nightmare without wavering. 'The Show' is as vivid as anything in *Under Fire* or *Counter-Attack* and more concentrated. As a Georgian, he writes of 'real experience', sending his mind back even to the scene of his shellshock. Paralysed by the sight of the rotting face, the poet falls towards it until he finds himself as another version of it, a severed head, when Death

> picking a manner of worm, which half had hid
> Its bruises in the earth, but crawled no further,

> Showed me its feet, the feet of many men,
> And the fresh-severed head of it, my head.

The image is of a platoon commander lying dead or helpless while his leaderless men find what shelter they can. Sooner or later the memory of that failure on the railway embankment would have to be exorcised by a return to France. Meanwhile, although as an officer he had no real choice, as a poet he still had work to do at home. The newly launched poet, now 'come to the true measure of man'[38] and believed in by leading Georgians, went into 1918 firmly committed to his 'duty . . . towards War'.

8 The Pity of War

In the early months of 1918 Owen decided on the subject of his poetry, stating it in his Preface in the spring as 'War, and the pity of war'. In settling on the subject of 'pity' he was returning to the beliefs of the Romantics, although he was no doubt also influenced by Hardy and the new direction in Sassoon's work. His 1918 poetry has a resonance of feeling, language and ideas which comes from his knowledge of the Romantic poets; whereas his pleasure in being 'held peer by the Georgians' at the end of 1917 soon ceased to represent an ambition to write in an exclusively Georgian way, his allegiance to his first masters had never faltered. His thoughts about the subject and function of his poetry in 1918 are reflected in his plans for publishing a book; the fragmentary Preface and two lists of contents which he drafted in the spring can be seen as a commentary on the poems he was writing at the time.

There was little fighting on the Western Front between mid December and mid March, so that he began to feel more optimistic about his future, even starting to buy furniture for use after the war. His months in Scarborough were busy and sociable. But in February things looked 'stupefyingly catastrophic on the Eastern Front' as Russia collapsed and Germany began to assemble her forces for a final attack in the west. On 12 March Owen was posted to a training-camp at Ripon, one tiny movement in the Army's efforts to gather reinforcements. 'An awful Camp – huts – dirty blankets – in fact WAR once more. Farewell Books, Sonnets, Letters, friends, fires, oysters, antique-shops.' Nine days later the German offensive opened, throwing the British line into desperate retreat. As in 1914, national opinion rallied behind the war effort, leaving only the most dedicated pacifists still demanding peace negotiations. By the end of March Owen was 'trying to get fit', 'Permanent Home Service' having ceased to be either possible or desirable. His writing-career might have ended here, had camp routine been less generous in its allowance of free time, but on

136

the 23rd he found a room in a cottage in Borrage Lane which he was able to rent for use during his long free evenings. Almost all his finest poems (except 'Spring Offensive') and his plans for a book seem to have been composed or revised in this secret 'workshop'. He reported on the 31st:

> Outside my cottage-window children play soldiers so piercingly that I've moved up into the attic, with only a skylight. It is a jolly Retreat. There I have tea and contemplate the inwardness of war, and behave in an owlish manner generally.

Fine spring weather, secrecy and an attic room being the ideal conditions for his poetry to grow, 1918 brought the last and by far the most fruitful of the creative springs of his poethood.[1]

Despite his lightness of tone, that 'owlish' process of contemplating 'the inwardness of war' was a strict, intensely serious discipline, learned, one may guess, from Wordsworth's account of composing from 'emotion recollected in tranquillity'. Owen was 'haunted by the vision of the lands about St Quentin crawling with wounded', the very ground he had advanced over in 1917. 'They are dying again at Beaumont Hamel, which already in 1916 was cobbled with skulls.' Meanwhile the children played soldiers and 'all the Lesser Celandines opened out together' in the lane '(my Lane)'. It was now that Owen earned Murry's later description of him as 'not a poet who seized upon the opportunity of war, but one whose being was saturated by a strange experience, who bowed himself to the horror of war until his soul was penetrated by it, and there was no mean or personal element remaining unsubdued in him'. In order to achieve this imaginative state, Owen trained himself in the impersonal, poetic insensibility which he describes in the poem of that title; he had been working towards this throughout the winter ('Insensibility' may have been in draft before he went to Ripon) but the process was completed at Borrage Lane. Wordsworth had said,

> poetry is the spontaneous overflow of powerful feelings; it takes its origin from emotion recollected in tranquillity; the emotion is contemplated till by a species of reaction the tranquillity gradually disappears, and an emotion, kindred to that which was before the subject of contemplation, is gradually produced and does itself actually exist in the mind.

Owen had been working on similar lines in February when he had willingly brought on war dreams in order to perform his 'duty . . . towards War'. The task was both painful and dangerous for a poet of strong imaginative sensations such as he was, but the first draft of 'Insensibility' shows him working out a solution. Poets cannot shirk their 'duty', but since a mere 'hint', 'word' or 'thought' can smother their souls in blood they must acquire the vision of the common soldier, his senses dulled by the 'scorching cautery of battle'. Owen commented in March that the 'enormity of the present Battle numbs me' and said later in the year after returning to the front that his senses were 'charred'. This dullness of sensation became a necessary preliminary to writing poetry, a means of keeping control over bloodiness and more than shadowy crimes. That 'blindfold look . . . like a dead rabbit's' of the troops was not only a petrifying memory but also a clue to the way in which a poet could still function. However 'great' or otherwise Owen's Borrage Lane poems may be judged to be, his method of working deserves to be recognised as an extraordinary undertaking – a young subaltern training by day for the fighting that would almost certainly kill him, and in the warm spring evenings walking down a country lane to shut himself away in a windowless room and open his 'inward eye' to the intensity of those feelings and experiences that had brought him close to madness a year before.[2]

That his guide in all this was Wordsworth is confirmed by the deliberate literary references in 'Insensibility'. Like Wordsworth's 'Intimations of Immortality' the poem is a 'Pindaric' ode, a form developed in the eighteenth century, and is concerned with the loss of poetic imagination.[3] Several of the key words ('imagination', 'feeling', 'simplicity') belong to late eighteenth-century critical debate, while the opening phrase, 'Happy are men who', is the classical *Beatus ille* construction used, for example, by Pope in 'Happy the man whose wish and care / A few paternal acres bound'.[4] The sanity and order of eighteenth-century literature is used as ironic contrast, showing up the inverted values of war. As the simple Augustan swain was 'happy' in his little world, so the modern soldier is 'happy' when he is back at home 'with not a notion / How somewhere, every dawn, some men attack'. Wordsworth had lamented his own blunted vision but for Owen such a limitation was essential in 1918, when the problem for the 'wise' was an excess of imagination rather than a lack of it.[5] Nevertheless, the aim of poetry was still as Wordsworth had stated it, to reach and ennoble the human heart. Wordsworth ends his ode by claiming that the 'meanest flower that blows' could still give him 'Thoughts that do often lie too deep for tears'. Owen echoed the language but broadened the statement, making it more Shelleyan than Wordsworthian; thoughts about men who 'fade' and 'wither' in war should arouse 'The eternal reciprocity of tears'.

'Insensibility' seems to refer to two great Romantic manifestos, not only Wordsworth's Preface to *Lyrical Ballads* but also Shelley's *Defence of Poetry*. The last stanza contains Owen's first use in a war poem of the word 'pity'. Shelley argues that poetry should arouse man's imagination, making him understand other people and sympathise with them, putting himself 'in the place of another and of many others'. Poetry promotes love, which develops from sympathy and is the key to all moral goodness. Furthermore the power of poetry is such that it 'turns all things to loveliness; it exalts the beauty of that which is most beautiful, and it adds beauty to that which is most deformed; it marries exultation and horror, grief and pleasure, eternity and change; it subdues to union under its light yoke all irreconcilable things'. In the intensity of poetry even the most terrible subjects can be beautiful. One can see how this can be applied to Owen's work; in 'Disabled', for example, the mutilated soldier has lost all his physical beauty, yet the poem 'adds beauty to that which is most deformed' until the reader becomes aware of the man as a fellow human being still fit to be loved. The word 'exultation' occurs in 'Apologia', where it is 'married' with horror. This imaginative process is not to be confused with what Owen dismisses in 'Insensibility' as 'poets' tearful fooling', the sentimental versifying of writers who are more interested in being poetic than in their subject ('Above all I am not concerned with Poetry'). Yet even the true poets could not reach all hearts. The last stanza of his ode condemns civilian 'dullards' (originally 'these old') who, like the 'wise' but for very different reasons, make themselves insensible by choice. This Romantic distinction between the 'wise' and dullards follows that made by Shelley in the Preface to *Alastor* between poets, who suffer from too acute a consciousness of humanity, and men, 'who, deluded by no generous error, . . . loving nothing on this earth, . . . yet keep aloof from sympathies with their kind, rejoicing neither in human joy nor mourning with human grief; these, and such as they, have their apportioned curse'. Owen delivers the curse in one of his most elaborately composed stanzas, using pararhyme and other sound-patterns now with practised ease:

> But cursed are dullards whom no cannon stuns,
> That they should be as stones.
> Wretched are they, and mean
> With paucity that never was simplicity.
> By choice they made themselves immune
> To pity and whatever moans in man
> Before the last sea and the hapless stars;
> Whatever mourns when many leave these shores;
> Whatever shares
> The eternal reciprocity of tears.

In my judgment, this stanza is not quite as successful as some modern critics have made it out to be. Its technical complexity is remarkable – only Owen could have written it – but the imagery lacks substance. The 'last sea' and the 'hapless stars' are no more than clichés, as in Arthur Symons's 'Beyond the last land where the last sea roars' (and Owen's own 'Timeless, beyond the last stars of desire', a line which he had tried out as an ending for 'My Shy Hand').[6] The rest of 'Insensibility' is much more solid, the images coming from hard experience – 'Their spirit drags no pack', 'alleys cobbled with their brothers' (a memory of bones frozen into the streets of Beaumont Hamel[7]) – but in attempting to articulate a fullness of emotion which any twentieth-century poet would have found difficult to handle the last stanza comes too close to Tennysonian cadences and nineteenth-century vagueness. He was to be more successful, and no less original in his technique, in later 1918 poems.

He had probably begun to think about the poetry of 'pity' before the end of 1917, since it is clear that he set himself to read several famous elegies during the winter and following spring. He may have had no very scholarly idea of what an elegy was, remembering only from reference books that it originally meant a song of grief over a dead man and from Tailhade's example that *élégiaque* meant something other than *aristophanesque*, but when he described his war poems at 'These elegies' in his Preface he did not use the word at random. In December he read Lang's translation of the elegies by Bion and Moschus that had been Shelley's model for *Adonais*. In the spring he considered calling his book 'English Elegies' or 'With Lightning and with Music' (a phrase from *Adonais*). Dr Bäckman has pointed out some convincing parallels between the rhetorical structure of 'Asleep' (late 1917) and that of Milton's 'Lycidas', and between the tramp in 'The Send-Off' (Ripon) and the swain in Gray's 'Elegy Written in a Country Churchyard'. 'Futility' (probably Ripon) seems to reflect a famous passage in *In Memoriam*, while Tennyson's description of Hallam as 'strange friend' may be the source of that paradoxical phrase in 'Strange Meeting'.[8] 'Hospital Barge' (December) was written after a 'revel in "the Passing of Arthur"' and is a less serious effort in Tennyson's elegiac mode. Some of Owen's other poems have affinities with the elegies in *A Shropshire Lad* and *The Dynasts*. As early as November 1917 he was aware of a difference between his own verse and Sassoon's, saying that Sassoon wrote 'so acid' while he wrote 'so big'.[9] He described 'Miners' in January as 'sour' but the poem also has a 'bigness' which Sassoon had not attempted, a largeness of expression which is elegiac rather than satirical, universal rather than immediate, even though the poem was inspired by an actual event. His readings in elegy are reflected particularly clearly in the oddly undistinguished 'Elegy in April and September',[10] composed in those months in 1918. On the back of the April draft he made a note about Matthew Arnold, including the titles of two elegies, 'Thyrsis' and 'The Scholar-Gipsy', and '1. lofty, restrained, dignified. / 2. wistful agnostic'. His own 'Elegy', with its search for a lost poet–friend among woods and fields, is an imitation of Arnold's two poems; indeed, the five adjectives which he attached to Arnold could be applied to much of his own 1918 work, which conforms to 'a solemn dignity in the treatment' like the sonnets he had thought of collecting under the title 'With Lightning and with Music' some three years earlier. These traces of Shelley, Tennyson, Arnold and Gray in his late work are a reminder that these were the four poets he had reverently described in a verse letter from Dunsden in 1911. His reading in the winter of 1917-18 was not only in new writers such as the Georgians but also in old ones studied long before.

Critics have argued that elegy is a false response to war because it offers consolation. Although Owen's poems are not wholly devoid of consolation, he said firmly in his Preface that 'These elegies are to this generation in no sense consolatory'. One value of elegy was that it could provoke pity, appealing to hearts which might have been unmoved by satirical attacks. Having read Sassoon's book of press-cuttings, he knew that some contemporary reviewers had dismissed Sassoon's acidity as the product of

immaturity and nervous strain. Edmund Gosse had remarked
disapprovingly in October 1917 that such verse would tend to
weaken the war effort, quite failing to see that that was precisely
what it was intended to do.[11] It was possible to miss the target
entirely with poems in Sassoon's style, devastating though they
seemed to be. In any case, the elegiac convention allowed for
protest; if Milton had attacked priests in 'Lycidas' and Shelley
had savaged critics in *Adonais*, it was legitimate to attack civilians
in war 'elegies'. To accept the elegiac element in Owen's 1918
poems is not to deny that they contain social criticism, but it is
to recognise that their subject is indeed 'pity' and that in defining
it they make extensive use of literary tradition.[12]

At Borrage Lane he returned to 'Wild with all Regrets',
expanding it into 'A Terre'. He had originally imagined the dying
officer in the poem as bookish ('But books were what I liked.
Dad called me moony')[13] but in the finished December 1917
draft the man is given a thoughtless, sporting past. In the 1918
version the bookishness is restored, the officer quoting from *Adonais*
to a friend who seems himself to be the author of a 'poetry book'.
The reference to Shelley suggests that the officer's viewpoint is
Shelleyan throughout in its condemnation of class distinction,
blood sports and war. His somewhat obscure remark that his soul
is 'a little grief' lodging for a short time in his friend's chest may
be compared with the lament in *Adonais* (xxi):

> Alas! that all we loved of him should be,
> But for our grief, as if it had not been,
> And grief itself be mortal!

The hope of becoming one with nature after death, the state
which Shelley claimed for Keats, is a 'poor comfort' in the cruel,
impoverished world of war but it is nevertheless the 'philosophy
of many soldiers'. Although Shelley did not mean it in the sense
in which the 'dullest Tommy' holds it, as a democrat he might
have been pleased to find it so widely valued. There is a scepticism
about poetry in 'A Terre', Owen's as well as Shelley's (a typically
Owenish metaphor is scornfully relegated to the friend's 'poetry
book'), but this is not so much a condemnation of Romanticism
as a Romantic unease like the doubts about the poet's usefulness
which Keats had expressed in *The Fall of Hyperion*. Perhaps poetry
was mere 'tearful fooling'; the poet could only assert his faith by

continuing to write, not for the sake of 'Poetry' but for the sake of humanity.

Some of the poems which Owen wrote at Borrage Lane are less concerned than his earlier war pieces had been with conveying realistic detail to civilians. Instead he takes a subject which a civilian could see or imagine and reveals its significance. Thus, for example, 'The Send-Off' describes a draft of soldiers setting out for France and suggests that they are victims of a 'hushed-up' conspiracy. The situations in these poems are representative rather than specific, sometimes entirely without topical reference so that they become applicable to any war, although they remain in origin 'matters of experience'. 'Arms and the Boy', for instance, may have been suggested by the irony of the children's playing soldiers outside the cottage. Since a boy is not armed by nature, society must provide him with man-made weapons:

> Lend him to stroke these blind, blunt bullet-leads,
> Which long to nuzzle in the hearts of lads,
> Or give him cartridges whose fine zinc teeth
> Are sharp with sharpness of grief and death.
>
> For his teeth seem for laughing round an apple.
> There lurk no claws behind his fingers supple;
> And God will grow no talons at his heels,
> Nor antlers through the thickness of his curls.

This is Owen's 1918 voice, no longer that of Georgian realism though still ironic towards the older generation. War's greatest cruelty is seen to be its destruction of youth and beauty. Its relationship to the young soldier is presented in sexual terms, consumingly urgent on one side ('long to nuzzle', 'famishing for flesh') and innocently exploring on the other ('try', 'stroke'). The imagery is strongly physical, with particular emphasis on parts of the body; the title literary; the language rich but dissonant in the manner of 'advanced composers' of contemporary music. Yet the universality of the statement does not weaken its bitterness, for the boy and the 'blind, blunt' bullets are not mere generalities. In the Easter Sunday letter which mentions children playing soldiers, Owen refers to two boys whom he often remembered:

> I wonder how many a *frau, fräulein, knabe und mädchen* Colin will kill in his time?

Johnny de la Touche leaves school this term, I hear, and goes to prepare for the Indian Army.

He must be a creature of killable age by now.

God so hated the world that He gave several millions of English-begotten sons, that whosoever believeth in them should not perish, but have a comfortable life.

The feeling in 'Arms and the Boy' comes from that kind of reflection, but it is rendered into impersonal terms as a result of deliberate contemplation of the 'inwardness of war'.

Like earlier poems, Borrage Lane work demonstrates how strongly Owen was moved by the waste of young life. One of his first attempts there, 'As bronze may be much beautified', which was begun on Good Friday but never finished, seems to have been first conceived as a lament for a particular youth:

> As women's pearls needs [be refreshed in deep sea,]

> There he found brightness for his tiring eyes
> And the old beauty of his young strength returned –

> Dropped back for ever down the abysmal war.

Perhaps a young soldier, Antaeus-like, was to have been pictured as regaining contact with earth and sea, only to be killed by the war machine and lost underground. In 'Futility' the loss of potential new life is related to all natural renewal, just as Antaeus was the embodiment of all life in nature:

> Move him into the sun –
> Gently its touch awoke him once,
> At home, whispering of fields half-sown.
> Always it woke him, even in France,
> Until this morning and this snow.
> If anything might rouse him now
> The kind old sun will know.

> Think how it wakes the seeds –
> Woke once the clays of a cold star.
> Are limbs, so dear achieved, are sides
> Full-nerved, still warm, too hard to stir?

Was it for this the clay grew tall?
– O what made fatuous sunbeams toil
To break earth's sleep at all?

F. W. Bateson (1979) condemned 'Futility' as an elegant technical exercise in which 'prosodic gadgets' count for more than truth. The 'Hell of trench warfare was already becoming . . . an abstraction' to Owen, according to Bateson, whereas in 'the great war poems' of 1917 grief is an 'authentic' 'personal experience'. It is true that the 1918 poems are less immediately 'realistic' and colloquial than those of 1917, becoming boldly original in technique and firmly grafted into literary tradition, but there is no fault here unless one is determined that all war poems must be of the Georgian kind. Bateson's comments rest on careless reading and a very hazy notion of the dates of Owen's poems. He understands 'Move him into the sun' as a 'curiously inhumane' order to carry a dead or dying man out of a hospital bed into the snow; were that correct, Owen would indeed be shown to have lost touch with true feeling and experience. The setting of the poem seems clear enough: the man has just died from exposure after a night in the open (like 'Exposure', 'Futility' may draw on an actual memory) and his body is to be moved out of the shadow of a parapet or some other object into the light and warmth of the rising sun. Bateson also complains that the second stanza is scientifically nonsense and that it puts the blame for war on the sun rather than on man, but Owen is making use of myth not science (according to ancient legend the sun's rays brought living creatures out of mud). The sun symbolises the source of life; if Owen is blaming it, he is blaming God, which was at least a defensible position to hold in 1918. Much literature has to be dismissed if poets are not to be permitted to question the Creator or to conclude that life is futile. The questions in the poem are not answered, however, so the blame may still be humanity's. Man was made for life and for sowing seed which the sun can ripen; when he turns to killing, nature has to reject him, his potency is lost and he dies. This is consistent with the mythic pattern which Owen had been working on for years. In the 'Perseus' sequence the young lover, 'full-nerved', commits some strange 'Wrong' which results in his being cut off from fertilising sunlight and paralysed (or, as it were, frozen) in darkness. The powerful cadence of the last lines of 'Futility' is passionately felt and far from mere elegance. As Owen felt his young strength returning in the sunlight of the Yorkshire spring while men died again at Beaumont Hamel, his memories of the 'Hell of trench warfare' were very far from becoming an 'abstraction'.

The way in which 'the pity of war' could be evoked, and the relationship between it and anger and disgust, are suggested in the organisation which Owen planned for the book of war poems which was his immediate objective at Ripon. All that remains of this plan is a fragmentary Preface and two rough lists of contents, together with a note of some possible titles ('Disabled and Other Poems' being his preferred choice).[14] The earlier list, written on the same type of paper as the final drafts of 'Insensibility' and 'Strange Meeting' and the first draft of 'Exposure', probably dates from April or early May.[15] It gives an idea of the stage his work had reached after perhaps a month's labour in the cottage. 'Strange Meeting' is included among nineteen or so 'Finished' poems; 'The Send-Off' and 'Mental Cases' await their final titles, as does the first version of 'Exposure'; 'The Sentry' is still 'Only Fifty Yards', the phrase with which the 1917 draft ends. Except for 'Spring Offensive', 'Training', 'The Kind Ghosts' and 'Smile, Smile, Smile', which were written later, almost all his war poems were by now either complete or in draft. It follows that much of his effort in May must have been devoted to polishing existing poems, producing the numerous fair copies overlaid with massive revisions that have been such a minefield for his editors. It was probably in late May or early June that he drew up his second, more detailed list and roughed out a Preface.

The Preface has become so famous that its fragmentary nature is often forgotten. The following version of it attempts to show some of Owen's first thoughts and revisions.[16]

Preface

This book is not about heroes. English Poetry is not yet fit to speak of them.

Nor is it about [battles, and glory of battles or lands, or] deeds or lands nor anything about glory or honour any might, majesty, dominion or power [whatever] except War.

[Its This book] is Above all I am not concerned with Poetry.

[Its The] My subject is War, and the pity of [it] War. The Poetry is in the pity.

[I have no hesitation in making public
                    publishing such]
[My] Yet These elegies are [not for the consolation] to this generation in no sense consolatory to this [a bereaved generation]. They may be to the next. [If I thought the letter of this book would last, I woul might have used proper names;] All a poet can do today is [to] warn [children] That is why the true [War] Poets must be truthful.

   If I thought the letter of this book would last, I [wo] might have used proper names: but if the spirit of it survives – survives Prussia – [I] my ambition and those names will [be content; for they] have achieved [themselves ourselves] fresher fields than Flanders,
              far be, not of war
                         would be
         sing

A following sheet bears the words 'in those days remembers' (perhaps a continuation of the Preface) and the second table of contents. Owen's declaration of poetic intent is in the tradition of the Preface to *Lyrical Ballads* and the *Defence of Poetry*. (It also contains an echo of Keats's poem about art, the 'Ode on a Grecian Urn': 'These elegies are to this generation in no sense consolatory . . . They may be to the next' / 'When old age shall this generation waste, / Thou shalt remain, . . . a friend to man'.) As Wordsworth, Shelley and Keats required, the poet rejects 'Poetry' for its own sake and dedicates himself to the betterment of humanity. There were requirements peculiar to 1918, including the need to refrain from consoling the older generation. It was perhaps because most existing poetic language was consolatory in its effect that Owen considered English poetry to be not 'yet' fit to describe the heroism of soldiers, but the word 'yet' implies that he would have liked to see a kind of poetry fit to speak of heroes and in 'Spring Offensive' he was to move towards a poetry of that kind. The later part of the Preface shows him reaching out to 'children', the future generations who were in the event to be his audience.
   The list of contents which accompanies the Preface is arranged

in a careful sequence, each poem being given a 'Motive' and each group of poems a further label. The first group, which seems in the manuscript to consist of thirteen titles, is 'Protest', beginning with 'Miners' and including 'Dulce et Decorum Est', 'S. I. W.' and 'The Dead-Beat', as well as some newer work such as 'Aliens' (a title for 'Mental Cases' which was suggested by Owen's friend Charles Scott Moncrieff at the end of May[17]). The fourteenth poem, 'The Show', is at the halfway point, its Motive of 'Horrible beastliness of war' sharply contrasting with the next two, 'Cheerfulness' ('The Next War') and 'Cheerfulness & Description & Reflection' ('Apologia'). Two more 'Description' poems follow, then five of 'Grief' and four which all seem to be included under 'Philosophy'. This arrangement was devised to take the reader through a developing, coherent experience. He would begin with 'Miners', a poem based on a civil disaster but leading into the subject of war, then move on to 'Arms and the Boy', a statement of the 'unnaturalness of weapons' and the exploitation of the younger generation. Then comes a series of angry protests at the madness, lies and callousness of war. 'The Show' brings the first half of the book to a climax of horror. Then the mood changes. Having been taught to protest, the reader may now see in 'The Next War' and 'Apologia' that war has a cheerfulness understood only by those who have faced its true nature. 'Exposure' and 'The Sentry' provide more description but check any inclination to make light of the troops' suffering. Then the poems of 'Grief', which include 'Anthem' and 'Futility', establish the mood of elegy, introducing the final 'Philosophy' section ('Strange Meeting', 'Asleep', 'A Terre', 'The Women and the Slain'). The reader was thus to proceed from protest through grief to meditation, a pattern Owen himself had gone through since meeting Sassoon. No stage was invalid but none was complete in itself. Protest was unproductive unless it led to grief, and grief in turn had to bear fruit in new attitudes. Owen seems to have thought of the entire experience as 'pity' – not grief alone but grief arising from re-educated knowledge and feeling, producing a positive, active frame of mind.

'Disabled and Other Poems' was never put together and Owen's notes for it should not be taken as his final thoughts about his poetry. He was never entirely convinced that publishing in wartime would be useful, and his cousin's precipitate rush into print had persuaded him that poetry could not be hurried. He said at the end of May that he could 'now write so much better than a year ago that for every poem I add to my list I subtract one from the beginning of it. You see I take myself solemnly now, and that is why, let me tell you, once and for all, I refrain from indecent haste in publishing.'[18] His departure from Ripon on 5 June perhaps prevented his taking his plans for a book any further but what mattered was to write rather than to publish. His audience was posterity. Poems such as 'Exposure' and 'Strange Meeting' show that he lost hope for the war generation, concluding that civilians could never understand and soldiers could never explain. All that a true war poet could do was to warn children, who might find consolation later in the knowledge that a true voice had managed to speak. His poems might prove that there was something indestructible in the human spirit, but that would be consolation only if future generations acted on his warning and loved their fellow men. On the whole we have not so acted, which may be why we find his 1917 poems of protest more immediately forceful than his later work; prevented by conscience from discovering any kind of consolation in his poems, we are ill at ease when he introduces them as 'elegies'. Nevertheless he meant us to see that protest is an essential stage, but not a final one, in the process of perceiving that 'pity of war' which he described in a draft of 'Strange Meeting' as 'the one thing war distilled'. The task of poetry was the Shelleyan one of arousing imagination, enabling people to share in the experience of others, to sympathise with them and love them, for war was above all a failure of love.

9　To Suffer without Sign

The caution of Owen's commentators about his sexual nature is understandable but no longer necessary or particularly helpful. His interest in young male beauty was one of the sources of his poetry. Having grown up in a world in which homosexuality was unmentionable, if not unthinkable, he may have repressed his preferences for some time, concealing them from himself as well as everyone else (hence, perhaps, the recurrent references to guilt and secrecy in his poems, and the bizarre sexual confusions in works such as 'The time was aeon' and 'Perseus'). His stay in France in 1914–15 seems to have brought him some sexual experience but he is unlikely to have come across any intellectual defence of homosexuality (except as one of the 'strange' sins of the Decadence) until he met Monro or, more probably, Sassoon. Sassoon eventually introduced him into one of the very few literary circles in which 'Uranianism' was accepted and easily discussed. An awareness of these matters illuminates Owen's 1918 poems and his thoughts about religion and war.[1]

After Wilde's disgrace, homosexuals had been obliged to be strictly respectable, so that little advice or leadership was available – except from Edward Carpenter, the celebrated apostle of Socialism and free living, whose essays in defence of Uranian love drew many grateful young men towards him. Sassoon visited him in 1911; Monro spent hours talking to him in 1910–11 when the *Before Dawn* poems were being written; Graves wrote to him in 1914; others who came within his influence included E. M. Forster and D. H. Lawrence.[2] Carpenter preached a gospel of 'beauty and compassion and friendship' (to use the terms in Sassoon's letter to Nicholson), maintaining that Uranian men tended to be musical and artistic, with a highly developed capacity for aesthetic and emotional sensation; they were quick to feel affection for children and pity for the unfortunate, and they could be 'overcome with emotion and sympathy at the least sad occurrence'.[3] Believing (like Geddes) that humanity was out of touch with its environ-

150

ment, Carpenter looked forward to a new order of freedom made possible by the hard work and endurance of the few who were already in a right relationship with nature. Sassoon took a saying of his as a watchword: 'Strength to perform, and pride to suffer without sign.' It is most unlikely that Carpenter was not mentioned at Craiglockhart.[4] There is no certain evidence, but I guess that Sassoon lent Owen some of the prophet's works and that Owen discovered, as Sassoon had done in 1911, that the artistic temperament which he had sought for and found in himself could be seen as essentially homosexual, or, to reverse the equation, that his sexual tendencies were to the benefit of art and humanity. This insight would have been of immense help to his confidence as both man and poet.

When Owen left Craiglockhart, Sassoon gave him an introduction to Robert Ross in London. Sassoon would not have done that lightly. The spirit of Oscar Wilde was still alive in Ross's elegant flat in Mayfair, for Ross had been Wilde's most devoted friend and was still his loyal defender. Other loyal disciples included More Adey, whom Owen met, and Robert Sherard, author of three books about Wilde. Owen read at least one, probably two, of Sherard's books during the winter, as well as *De Profundis* and some or all of Wilde's verse, following his usual habit of reading up an author with whom he found he had personal links. Ross was wholly out of sympathy with middle-class orthodoxy but Wilde's fate had taught him the necessity for extreme discretion. Loathing the war, he had been the first person to encourage Sassoon to write satires but had nevertheless collaborated with Graves in covering up Sassoon's protest in 1917. His nervousness was understandable, because he had suffered repeated persecution from Lord Alfred Douglas in revenge for his publishing *De Profundis*, an abridged version of Wilde's letter to Douglas from prison. Douglas, who had turned violently against his dead lover, maintained that Ross's editing had made a monster sound like a martyr. He had forced Ross to sue him in 1914 by calling him 'the High Priest of all the sodomites in London'; then he triumphantly produced fourteen witnesses. No police prosecution followed, however, as it had done for Wilde, partly because Ross had powerful friends and partly because there had been an advance in liberal opinion since 1895. Witnesses who spoke for Ross included Wells, whose reformist views on sexual matters had been expressed in several novels (Owen read at least two of these in 1917–18), and Arnold Bennett

(Owen read his scandalous *The Pretty Lady* in April 1918). But
Ross's troubles were not over. In January–March 1918 his friend
and secretary, Christopher Millard, Wilde's bibliographer, was
tried and imprisoned for a homosexual offence. At the same time
a Member of Parliament named Pemberton Billing astonished
London with a story that the German Secret Service had listed
in a 'Black Book' no fewer than 47,000 prominent British people
whose private lives were suspect; as an example of national
corruption, he pointed to a current production of Wilde's *Salomé*.
The leading actress sued him for libel and lost, to the loud delight
of press and public, the trial in late May and early June becoming
a grotesque display of hatred for homosexuality and 'the Oscar
Wilde cult'. There was extensive press coverage. Douglas gave
evidence, taking the opportunity to renew his attacks on Ross.
No doubt Pemberton Billing believed that a victory had been
achieved for public morality. Several lives were ruined, including
Ross's, whose health suffered mortal damage (he died in October).
Sassoon and others were distressed for their friend and furious
that attention could so easily shift from the war to a silly scandal.
Owen would have been well aware of all this, although he could
not mention it in letters home; the hysterical public response to
the trial would have strengthened his scorn for civilian opinion
and confirmed his sense of belonging to a secret caste. One side
effect of the affair may have been the loss of headway that seems
to have occurred at the time in plans for 'Disabled and Other
Poems', since Ross had been encouraging Owen as he had Sassoon
and had promised to arrange for publication.[5]

The importance of Owen's friendship with Ross has not been
generally understood. It was not only that 'Owen, the poet' was
introduced to a number of talented literary people, including
Wells and Bennett, but also that in getting to know Ross he came
as near as was possible to knowing Wilde himself. Ross was a
man of culture, charm and excellent conversation, keeping open
house for his many devoted admirers. He lacked Wilde's egotism
and ostentation but stood for Wilde's values in art and life. His
flat must have seemed like a fortress; within its walls of outward
respectability (a fragile protection when court cases were in the
news), Owen was among friends with whom he could talk openly
and yet in secret. Thanks to Sassoon and Ross, the confusions of
earlier years were resolved at last, giving way to a self-knowledge
and self-confidence that are reflected in the strength and sureness
of his 1918 poems. Many, though not all, of Ross's regular visitors

were homosexual. Some believed in the war, some did not, but there was general contempt for 'screaming scarlet Majors' (as Ross called them),[6] 'old men' and unsympathetic civilians. As might be expected among Wilde's followers, there was much lively conversation about art and literature, and an assumption that the outside world was ignorant and wilfully deaf to truth.

In mid May Ross introduced Owen to Osbert Sitwell, a young officer then discovering himself as a poet and Uranian. Sitwell's early verse had been modelled on *Salomé*[7] but in 1917 he had started publishing anti-war poems influenced by Sassoon, whom he knew and admired. Owen had probably seen his work in the *Nation* and may have imitated it. 'The Parable of the Old Man and the Young' is similar to Sitwell's 'The Modern Abraham' (*Nation*, 2 February 1918), while the last stanzas of 'Apologia' and 'Insensibility', and Owen's statement that true poets must be truthful, make the same sort of point as 'Rhapsode' (*Nation*, 27 October 1917):

> Why should we sing to you of little things –
> You who lack all imagination?
> . . .
> We shall sing to you
> Of the men who have been trampled
> To death in the circus of Flanders;
> . . . .
> You hope that we shall tell you that they found their
>   happiness in fighting,
> Or that they died with a song on their lips,
> Or that we shall use the old familiar phrases
> With which your paid servants please you in the Press:
> But we are poets,
> And shall tell the truth.

Sitwell's anger was concentrated against what the *Cambridge Magazine* called 'old men' or, as he himself put it, 'grand old men . . . Who sacrifice each other's sons each day'.[8] His anger was rooted in his detestation for his own father, a feeling which Owen may have understood. Mrs Owen had encouraged her son to keep at a distance from his father; while there is little evidence of hostility in what was certainly an uncomfortable relationship, Owen was always prone to regarding other men as substitute fathers as though his own had proved inadequate. It may be that

an unconscious personal resentment is expressed in the harsh
treatment of fathers, including God the Father, in such poems as
'Parable', 'S. I. W.', 'Soldier's Dream' and 'Apologia'.[9] Owen
had other things in common with Sitwell, including sexual pre-
ferences and a taste for Aestheticism and the Decadence. He did
not try to imitate the clumsy Modernist 'free verse' of 'Rhapsode'
but he does seem to have been impressed by the more talented
work of Sacheverell and Edith Sitwell, whose flamboyantly
'advanced' poetry was in much the same French-inspired style as
T. S. Eliot's 1917 volume, *Prufrock*. Edith's anthology *Wheels*, the
first wholly British collection of Modernist poetry, was deliberately
anti-Georgian (Owen does not call himself a Georgian in later
1918 letters). The fragment 'The roads also', which Owen wrote
after Ripon, is clearly a Modernist street scene in the style of
numerous Sitwell poems. It is almost the only clue on which one
might base an answer to the frequent question as to what he
would have written had he lived. Unlike Sassoon, he would have
admired Eliot and made use of his style, as he had made use of
Monro's, Tailhade's, Sassoon's and others', without remaining a
mere imitator; he might have helped to bridge the post-war gap
between Modernism and the native English tradition. But his
interest in *Wheels* and Sacheverell Sitwell's work did not begin
until July and August, too late for it to bear much fruit.[10]

There were other new friends in 1918 besides Sitwell. In January
Owen went to Graves's wedding, where he was introduced as
'Mr Owen, Poet' or 'Owen, the poet', and people had heard of
him because 'Miners' was in that week's *Nation*. He met Edward
Marsh, Graves perhaps hoping that the anthologist would accept
the new-found poet as a Georgian, and Charles Scott Moncrieff.
The evening was spent at Ross's with Roderick Meiklejohn, one
of Sassoon's regular wartime correspondents, and 'two Critics',
one of whom was Scott Moncrieff. And it was then or not long
afterwards that Scott Moncrieff fell in love with Owen and, being
the eccentric but brilliant literary imitator he was, conceived the
odd idea of expressing his 'passion' in a series of sonnets modelled
on Shakespeare's to 'Mr W. H.'. The relationship did not work
out as he wished, for Owen seems to have been flattered by the
sonnets (he kept one of them, dating it 19 May) but reluctant to
respond to their appeal. Scott Moncrieff was a promiscuous,
quirky and difficult man; Sitwell and Sassoon detested him, and
his view of the war as a chivalric enterprise was quite unlike
theirs. He had deplored Sassoon's war poems in a 1917 review.

On the other hand, he warmly admired Owen's poetry for its adventurous use of pararhyme, assonance and other devices, becoming the first critic to mention him in a review (on 10 May). When he began work in the summer on the *Song of Roland*, the first of his major translations, he drafted a dedication to 'Mr W. O.' (who was thus recognised as the translation's 'onlie begetter', as 'Mr W. H.' had been of Shakespeare's sonnets), 'my master in assonance', adding that 'lessons are to be found in the Song of Roland that all of us may profitably learn – To pursue chivalry, to avoid and punish treachery, to rely upon our own resources, and to fight uncomplaining when support is withheld from us.' Similar heroic values are implicit in some of Owen's war poems; he had enough in common with Scott Moncrieff to find his admiration and encouragement welcome if somewhat excessive.[11]

Owen wrote several lyrics in 1918 which may have been more intelligible to Ross and his friends than they are now. Scott Moncrieff was given a manuscript of 'I am the ghost of Shadwell Stair', a little poem apparently based on Wilde's 'Impression du Matin'; he sent a copy of it after the war to Marsh with the following note:

> The above is a copy of the manuscript. More Adey insisted on reading 'fade' and 'laid' in the last verse, for grammatical reasons. During the influenza epidemic in 1918 I tried to turn it into French prose, rhymed. I give the first verse, on account of the last word, which Owen welcomed rather as tho' it put the key in the lock of the whole . . . .
>
> 'Je suis le petit revenant du Bassin; le long de quai, par l'abreuvoir, et dans l'immonde abbatoir j'y piétine, ombre fantassin.'[12]

This disproves the suggestion made in the *Complete Poems* and elsewhere that the ghost is a female prostitute. The 'petit . . . fantassin' (little infantryman) is 'little' Owen himself, who must have returned since his enlistment to that dock area which he had walked through in 1915 and where, then or later, he had seen the Limehouse boy. The poem is not a mere copy of Wilde, as it would have been if Scott Moncrieff had written it, but 'a *matter of experience*' as the 'key' reveals. Nevertheless, despite a characteristic emphasis on 'physical sensation' and familiar traces of the Little Mermaid and her statue (trembling, purple light, water, shadows, unsatisified waiting), the poem remains enig-

matic. Other post-Craiglockhart pieces which seem to be similarly
in code include 'Reunion' and a group of three curious ballads,
'Page Eglantine', 'The Rime of the Youthful Mariner' and 'Who
is the god of Canongate'.[13] As in earlier lyrics there is a recurrent
suggestion of secret knowledge that cannot be fully communicated,
a theme which reappears in the war poems ('the truth untold',
'Wisdom is mine and I have mystery', 'secret men who know their
secret safe', 'The Unsaid', 'Why speak not they of comrades . . . ?').
'Who is the god of Canongate' seems to be about the secret world
of 'rent boys', well known to Wilde, Ross and Scott Moncrieff,
its subject being a 'little god' who walks the pavements barefoot
(a street boy or Eros) and is visited in his room by barefoot men
(pilgrims to the shrine who need to be secret). Mentions in the
manuscript of Covent Garden, 'Bow St. cases' (Wilde was charged
at Bow Street) and Canongate associate the 'god' of Canongate
with other strange figures seen in London and Edinburgh streets —
the 'phantom' in Princes Street, the 'ghost' of Shadwell Stair, the
'half-god' in Limehouse, and the handsome youth in the lost or
projected poem which provided material for 'Disabled'.[14] The
god of love, who had been hopelessly out of reach in 'To Eros',
'Perseus' and the Limehouse poem, is no longer an inaccessible
deity.

The tradition left by Wilde to his followers was largely borrowed
from French Decadent literature, so Owen was on familiar
ground. Art was an autonomous, mysterious world closed to all
but the privileged few, a world where bourgeois morality had no
authority and where 'strange' sins might be permissible in the
interests of beauty. But it was also a world permeated with
religious values and imagery. When Owen read *De Profundis* and
'The Ballad of Reading Gaol' in the winter of 1917–18, he found
that the older Wilde had much to say about Christ. Since another
of the questions commonly asked about Owen is whether he was
still a Christian in 1917–18, this may be an appropriate point at
which to attempt an answer.

I have said in earlier chapters that Owen was predisposed by
his own nature and his knowledge of Decadent authors towards
imagery of martyrdom and passive suffering. He compared dying
soldiers to Christs as early as December 1914 and in the successive
versions of 'The Ballad of Peace and War'. In May 1917, after
he had been in the trenches, he modified this to correspond with

a general attitude among soldiers that they were not dying for
civilians but for their comrades; Christ was in No Man's Land,
Owen now said, and there 'men often hear His voice: Greater
love hath no man than this, that a man lay down his life – for a
friend'. He recognised, however, that soldiers were killers as well
as victims, so that they had to ignore Christ's essential command,
'Passivity at any price! . . . Be bullied, be outraged, be killed; but
do not kill.' So he felt he was 'a conscientious objector with a
very seared conscience'. These phrases are often quoted. What
tends to be ignored are his later comments. He read John
Oxenham's verse in June, remarking that Oxenham 'evidently
holds the Moslem doctrine – preached by Horatio Bottomley,
but not by the Nazarene – of salvation *by death in war*'. (Bottomley
was a jingo journalist who supported the war with extreme claims
for its religious and moral value.) In August he discussed this
further in an 'important' letter, saying that while he wore his star
as a Second Lieutenant he could not obey Christ's command or
share in the hypocrisy of churchmen who were urging on the war
effort; 'thinking of the eyes I have seen made sightless, and the
bleeding lads' cheeks I have wiped, I say: Vengeance is mine, I,
Owen, will repay'. 'I fear I've written like a converted Horatio
Bottomley', he went on, but he was now convinced that the
notion that 'men are laying down their lives for a friend' was 'a
distorted view to hold in a general way'. So he resolved to suppress
'The Ballad of Peace and War'. This August letter is a remarkable
one, its defiant contradiction of a biblical text ('Vengeance is
mine; I will repay, saith the Lord') being similar to the post-
Dunsden declarations in 'O World of many worlds' and 'The
time was aeon'. The manuscript shows signs of strong feeling;
Owen's handwriting slopes across the page and there are marks
round the phrase 'lads' cheeks' that are either blots or tears.
Those blinded eyes, and the bleeding cheeks once imagined in
the 'Ballad of Peace and War' but now vividly remembered from
experience, belong to the same wounded 'lads' who are described
in 'Has your soul sipped', 'Greater Love', 'The Sentry' and other
poems. Owen's allegiance to poetry, 'physical sensation' and 'the
Flesh' made it impossible in 1917–18, as in 1912–13, to accept
Christian doctrine or to respect clerics who refused to recognise
that impossibility; he was a poet and soldier, and could be false
to neither role. There were 'no more Christians at the present
moment than there were at the end of the first century' – and he
could not be one of them.[15]

He found this comment about primitive Christianity echoed in
De Profundis and quoted Wilde's version of it in a February
1918 letter (but carefully avoided mention of Wilde by name).[16]
Rejecting Pauline doctrine and the established churches did not
prevent respect for Christ as a person. *De Profundis* describes
Christ as the supreme example of pity and individualism, the
perfect artist who apprehended beauty through sorrow and acted
as the 'external mouthpiece' of 'the entire world of the inarticulate,
the voiceless world of pain'. Christ had spoken for those 'who are
dumb under oppression' and had 'made of himself the image of
the Man of Sorrows'. In this interpretation of Jesus the man,
Wilde was defining the role he saw for himself as artist; Owen
would have seen how it parallelled the role of Sassoon and himself
as soldier poets. Some of his comments on his poetic task after
Craiglockhart are similar to Wilde's: he had felt 'sympathy for
the oppressed always', he was 'the poet of sorrows' and he wanted
to act as 'pleader' for 'men, that have no skill / To speak of their
distress, no, nor the will'. No doubt he saw that Wilde's letter
from prison was grossly self-regarding, but there were things to
learn from it.[17]

It may have been reading Wilde that persuaded Owen to
complete 'Greater Love' in 1918, a poem that had perhaps been
in draft for some time. He was always uneasy about it but its
subject had fascinated him throughout the war. The various
drafts reveal the poem's Decadent qualities. In a form and style
taken from Swinburne and Wilde, it compares dying soldiers on
the one hand with Christ and on the other to 'anyone beautiful'
or 'any beautiful Woman'. It began as a kind of Decadent love
lyric, like 'Has your soul sipped', without religious allusions. The
'beautiful woman' has appropriately late-Romantic features (pale
hand, drooped eyelids, red lips), as have the soldiers, whose
bleeding kisses and trembling cramps of death are more 'beautiful'
(later 'exquisite') than her beauty. There are echoes here of the
'Perseus' fragments; the Cultivated Rose had a mouth like blood
and a 'Dangerously exquisite' trembling beauty, and the speaker
in P1 suffers an agonising cramp like 'the first / Terrific minute
of the hour of death'. The old treachery of Eros is answered in
'Greater Love' when the poet himself rejects 'Love' and uses
erotic language to describe violent death. As in the face of
Medusa, the greatest beauty lies in the greatest horror; as the
first draft puts it, 'Your drooped lids lose their lure / When I
recall the blind gaze of men dead'. Several critics have explained

the Romantic language of the poem as an ironic dismissal of 'old song', but in my opinion Owen means what he says: young men dying in battle are more beautiful than any civilian lover. There is no irony in the comparison. He had said much the same in 'Has your soul sipped', as had other soldier poets elsewhere.[18]

Amendments to the poem brought it even closer to the stock poetic notions of 1917–18 by adding the comparison with Christ. Owen chose the title from what was perhaps the war's most frequently quoted biblical text.[19] He changed the original tenth line ('Where love seems not to care'), substituting 'God' for 'love' and thereby allowing later readers to detect an allusion to Christ's 'My God, my God, why hast thou forsaken me?' The original last line was 'O Love, love them, kiss them, and touch me not', where 'Love' is presumably the beautiful woman, but it was rewritten as 'Weep, woman, weep; you may weep but touch them not' and then 'Weep, you may weep, for you may touch them not'. Rosemary Freeman (1963) compared this final version to the risen Christ's words to Mary Magdalene, 'Woman, why weepest thou? . . . Touch me not' (but this may be an over-ingenious reading; the men cannot be touched because they are dead and in France, not necessarily because they are risen). Owen also replaced 'Rifles' with 'Your cross' in the last stanza, reinforcing the theme of sacrifice by alluding to his own very real memory of 'eyes blinded in my stead'. The later drafts of the poem thus imply that soldiers are Christs carrying crosses, being crucified for the redemption of others and, perhaps, rising again. But Owen knew perfectly well that too much of this had been said by sanctimonious people at home, including Bottomley. There was, for example, a popular postcard (Plate 12) showing an injured soldier and the caption 'Blinded for You!', one of many pictures which gave a sacrificial, Christian significance to death in battle. Numerous sentimental poems and newspaper articles had used the 'greater love' text for the purposes of consolation and propaganda. It is not surprising that 'Greater Love' appears only under 'Doubtful' in Owen's second list of contents at Ripon, or that he was never satisfied with the wording of the poem (the third stanza, for example, remains pointlessly repetitious, despite numerous attempts at its last line).

Nevertheless 'Greater Love' is remarkable for the intensity with which it makes its double contrast, recording that element in 'the truth untold' which was hardest to get across to civilians. As an officer away from the front, the poet thinks with guilt and pity of 'eyes blinded in my stead'; as one in sympathy with Wilde and Sassoon, he expresses his conviction that the suffering men are beautiful like lovers and he rejects 'any beautiful woman'. The theme of martyrdom was at the heart of Wilde's aesthetic creed, with Christ the suffering man as its central symbol. If there was a God, though, he was as deaf to human suffering as Hardy's Immanent Will. Owen described this deity in a flippant Wildean ballad, 'A Tear Song' (1918), in which God ignores human prayers but takes a choirboy's tear as a pearl for his jewel box. This God the Father is a pitiless maker and collector of the beauty born of suffering, an 'old man' immune by choice to 'whatever moans in man'. One similarity between Christ and soldiers was that they were sons sacrificed by fathers (or by fatherly officers), a point readily seen by Osbert Sitwell; the famous passage in Owen's letter to Sitwell about teaching Christ to lift his cross by numbers, which has often been quoted as proof of Owen's religious faith in 1918, is a typical example of Wildean imagery, written to impress its recipient.[20] Sitwell, who was at best an agnostic, used Christian themes in his poems to satirise civilians and churchmen. If Owen can be claimed as a Christian in 1918, it is only in some very loose sense of the word that would not have been acceptable to, say, the Vicar of Dunsden. There is no evidence that he acknowledged the divinity of Christ, for example, except occasionally in metaphor. The religious imagery in his 1918 work is not a sign of faith; its function is to reveal the beauty and bitterness of man's life on earth.

Owen's use of the Decadent tradition is especially clear in 'The Kind Ghosts', the only manuscript of which is dated '30/7/18 Scarboro':

> She sleeps on soft, last breaths; but no ghost looms
> Out of the stillness of her palace wall,
> Her wall of boys on boys and dooms on dooms.
>
> She dreams of golden gardens and sweet glooms,
> Not marvelling why her roses never fall
> Nor what red mouths were torn to make their blooms.
>
> The shades keep down which well might roam her hall.
> Quiet their blood lies in her crimson rooms
> And she is not afraid of their footfall.

> They move not from her tapestries, their pall,
> Nor pace her terraces, their hecatombs,
> Lest aught she be disturbed or grieved at all.

Presumably the sleeping figure is Britannia, representing the Nation at Home, especially women, as unaware as ever of doomed youth. The hecatombs, vast public sacrifices, have been of men slaughtered as cattle. It has been suggested that Owen meant 'catacombs' but perhaps he thought 'hecatombs' meant *places* of sacrifice; he probably had in mind pagan sacrifices such as those in *Salammbô*, where parents sacrifice their children to Moloch.[21] The sleeping figure is a languid Fatal Woman much like Salammbô herself, unaware of the death she brings to her lovers. As in Venus's palace in 'Laus Veneris' (Owen brought a copy of *Poems and Ballads* in August), her chambers 'drip with flower-like red'. Her roses are the bleeding mouths often described by Swinburne and the Decadents (Wilde wrote of beautiful men 'whose wounds are like red roses'[22]). The sado-masochism, erotic reverie and elaborate sound-effects of Decadent poetry find what is perhaps their final expression in 'The Kind Ghosts' in an extraordinary but strangely appropriate context. The nation's love for her young men is here the unseeing but consuming love of a *femme fatale*. The 'ghosts' which 'well might' haunt her palace do not do so, because the truth will remain untold. Soothed by the conventional music of the poem, the reader lingers in the garden of England where the roses bloom for ever – and then sees what they are.

By the time Owen came to write 'The Kind Ghosts' he knew he would soon have to return to France. There had seemed to be a chance that Scott Moncrieff would be able to get him a home posting, a plan that was talked of as late as mid June, but on 4 June he was graded fit and sent to his battalion at Scarborough for full duties. The pressures of camp life and the loss of his Borrage Lane retreat made serious reading and writing almost impossible.[23] Then in late July came the decisive news that Sassoon was home with a severe head wound. Owen's letters undergo a striking change from this moment; usually long and conversational, they now became brief but charged with repressed emotion. Sassoon wrote gloomily to him from hospital,

> Overtures are already beginning to make me exchange pride and clean soul for safety and the rest of it.
> But I am too feeble to be able to think it out at all. I only

feel angry with everyone except those who are being tortured at the war.[24]

In the same spirit, now that Sassoon was out of action, Owen decided that it was his duty to 'throw my little candle on his torch, and go out again'. It was his duty because he saw himself as a spokesman, a role he had claimed repeatedly in his poetry from 'On my Songs' and 'The Poet in Pain' to 'Insensibility' and 'The Calls'. Many of the writers he admired had been spokesmen,[25] including not only Dickens and Shelley, both of whom he read again when he went back to France, but also Tailhade, Wilde and other Aesthetes who had made *épater le bourgeois* an obligation on the artist. Wilde had spoken out for the oppressed and inarticulate in 'The Ballad of Reading Gaol' and in his forceful newspaper articles about prison conditions. The satirical war epigrams of Sassoon and Sitwell were directly in the Wilde tradition in their onslaught on bourgeois complacency. But now Sassoon had fallen silent, as he admitted in 'Testament', a little poem which he sent to Owen in the summer: 'O my heart, / Be still; you have cried your cry; you have played your part'. In response, Owen took his place, saying he was glad to be returning to the front because he would be 'better able to cry my outcry, playing my part'.[26]

Presumably Owen applied to be drafted. The ensuing order was issued on 9 August but he was taken off the draft two days later because a medical inspection revealed a cardiac irregularity.[27] The old scares about his heart were apparently true, but a weakness which might have kept him out of uniform three years earlier was discounted now that the Army was desperate for men. Scott Moncrieff pressed the case for a home posting, but later recorded that the authorities refused it on the grounds that special privileges should not be available for anyone who had been sent home with loss of nerve. Owen may have known nothing of this ill-judged attempt at rescue until afterwards. Within a day or two he was on embarkation leave, finding time to see Sassoon and Sitwell in London. On the day before he sailed, he accompanied his mother on a brief visit to his youngest brother at Hastings. The three Owens were photographed together and Mrs Owen later had copies made from this last, crude portrait of him (Plate 15): 'The eyes are touched up badly but looking at a little distance it is *him* he had that look of high *purpose* in his dear gentle eyes. Oh! how he hated war and all its horrors – but he felt he *must* go out

again to share it with his boys . . . .'[28] Now that he was free he
could assure her she was 'absolute' in his affections, writing
devoted letters that were meant only for her. He travelled on
alone to Victoria, where he was met by Scott Moncrieff.

Scott Moncrieff's account of their final evening together seems
to conceal a painful memory:

> I was sickened by the failure to keep him in England, and
> savage with my own unhealed wounds . . . . If I was harsh with
> him, may I be forgiven, as we tramped wearily round the
> overflowing hotels. In the end a bed was found . . . . After a
> few intense hours of books and talk in my lodging, I escorted
> him to his. As we reached it, he discovered that he had left his
> stick behind, but insisted that it was too late now to return.

Scott Moncrieff's attempt to keep his friend off the draft had
succeeded only in uncovering the 1917 accusation of cowardice,
perhaps to Owen's distress and anger. The contrast between Scott
Moncrieff and Sassoon was now obvious: the former ill-tempered
with his friends (he was notoriously quarrelsome), sexually
demanding, preaching knightly virtue yet urging a fit friend to
stay at home; the latter angry with the war and all its cant,
decent in all his behaviour, proud 'to suffer without sign', a
selflessly courageous soldier devoted to his men. It seems that
Owen refused to spend the night at Scott Moncrieff's lodging.
Perhaps it was the bitterness of that parting and jealousy of
Sassoon that drove Scott Moncrieff to write clumsily about Owen
afterwards, making the cowardice story public instead of spreading
the poet's fame as he had once hoped to do. By revealing the
War Office's ruling and omitting any mention of Sassoon, he
gave the impression that Owen would have accepted a job at
home even at the last moment, but Owen's August letters shows
that this was not the case.

Owen embarked next day, pausing for a bathe at Folkestone,
where there emerged from the sea a 'Harrow boy', beautiful,
sympathetic, hating the war, a vision of all that was worth fighting
for, all that the war was destroying. 'And now I go among cattle
to be a cattle driver . . . ', 'a Shepherd of sheep that do not know
my voice'.[29] Men in France had developed a strong sense of
separateness from people at home; the sense of being isolated and
under attack which all Ross's friends must have felt that summer
could easily transform itself into a shared companionship with

the Nation Overseas. A similar transformation had developed since August 1917 as Owen had learned to draw on his erotic verse for his war poems, the beautiful tortured youths in 'The cultivated Rose' and other pieces turning into soldiers, blood-red mouths into Britannia's roses, and the guilt of a love that was 'Against the anger of the sun' ('Reunion') into the guilt of war which the sun had to destroy ('Spring Offensive').

When he went back to France he took his recently purchased copy of Swinburne with him. In October his colleagues teased him for talking too much with some local girls; the 'dramatic irony was too killing', he told Gunston, 'considering certain other things, not possible to tell in a letter./ Until last night though I have been reading Swinburne, I had begun to forget what a kiss was.'[30] A much more serious incident a few weeks before had provided Swinburnian imagery which would have become a poem if there had been time. He had been sent out with a servant, 'little Jones', a talkative, sympathetic and devoted companion. At the beginning of October the battalion went into action, Jones receiving a head wound in the first hour. Three letters give a notion of the poem that was never written.[31] To 'My dear Scott Moncrieff':

> I'm frightfully busy . . . and many glorious Cries of the blood still lying on my clothes will have to be stifled.
> . . . I find I never wrote a letter with so much difficulty as this. Perhaps I am tired after writing to so many relations of casualties. Or perhaps from other causes.

To 'Very dear Siegfried':

> the boy by my side, shot through the head, lay on top of me, soaking my shoulder, for half an hour.
> Catalogue? Photograph? Can you photograph the crimson-hot iron as it cools from the smelting? That is what Jones's blood looked like, and felt like. My senses are charred.
> I shall feel again as soon as I dare . . . .

To 'My darling Mother':

> Of whose blood lies yet crimson on my shoulder where his head was – and where so lately yours was – I must not now write.

The three relationships are distinct. 'Cries' for Scott Moncrieff, because at this formal level Owen was the pleader crying his cry on behalf of 'many' soldiers. It was difficult to know what to say to Scott Moncrieff after their last meeting. Metaphor for Sassoon, and an implied rebuke in answer to some suggestion that catalogues of horrors were material for poetry. More intimately still, Mrs Owen could be told of the parallel between Jones and herself, though she would not have fully understood it. The extreme of 'physical sensation' could only be dealt with under the protection of 'insensibility', the poet's senses 'ironed' in a 'scorching cautery of battle'. The method, the material and the developing imagery are clear; the poet remains a phantom.

10 'Strange Meeting'

The 'Perseus' manuscripts, with their associated poems and fragments, show that Owen's imagination had often been voluntarily or involuntarily occupied with images of bodily entry into hell, a theme which begins to emerge as early as 1911–12 in his 'Supposed Confessions'. The means of entry was a paralysing descent, sometimes into smothering water ('Down-dragged like corpse in sucking, slimy fen'), sometimes into a dark cave. Once in the underworld – an obsessive but not very scholarly compound of the classical Hades, Dante's Inferno, Tannhäuser's Venusburg, and the Hell familiar to an ex-Evangelical – the living visitor from the upper world met a staring face or faces, either in darkness or under a sun 'for ever smouldering blood'. At least three of Owen's trench experiences gave substance to these horrors: his fifty hours in the flooded dug-out where the sentry was blinded, his fall into the ruined cellar, and his sheltering in the 'hole just big enough to lie in' on the railway embankment. He was trapped and helpless in all three places. Ensuing shellshock manifested itself in terrifying dreams, probably often of approaching or pursuing faces, dark tunnels and falling from heights, although the subject matter eventually became less warlike, sometimes reverting to his pre-war 'phantasies'. Soon after his return to barracks after Ripon, war dreams began again, perhaps caused, he thought, by 'the hideous faces of the Advancing Revolver Targets' (presumably mobile dummies which moved towards the marksman as he fired).[1] He had brought on such dreams in the winter by carrying out his 'duty' as a poet and now they were revived by his military duties; the constant threat of nightmare, pressing upon his determination both to give words to the pity of war and to prove himself as a soldier, was accepted for duty's sake.

The smothering hole could be generalised as a shell crater, the individual experience translated into the experience of an anonymous squad:

Cramped in that funnelled hole, they watched the dawn
Open a jagged rim around; a yawn
Of death's jaws, which had all but swallowed them
Stuck in the bottom of his throat of phlegm.

They were in one of the many mouths of Hell
Not seen of seers in visions; only felt
As teeth of traps; when bones and the dead are smelt
Under the mud where long ago they fell . . . .

Several critics have pointed out that the jaw image comes from *Under Fire* ('the story of a squad') and 'The Charge of the Light Brigade', noting that Owen was reading Barbusse and Tennyson in December 1917. As I have suggested elsewhere, 'Cramped in that funnelled hole' can be recognised as work for the 'dawn piece' which he planned to write in that month. The dawn piece was later to take shape as 'Exposure', early drafts of which are in a setting of 'soft mud'.[2] The word 'Cramped' can be associated not only with the soldiers' frozen helplessness in 'Exposure' and Owen's possible collapse in his embankment shell hole but also with P1, where the speaker is 'wrenched with inexplicable weakness' as he enters hell, and with the paralysis described in the 'Supposed Confessions'. In Romanticism poetic vision is often accompanied by sudden bodily weakness, as in one of the poems most dear to Owen in his early days, 'The Ancient Mariner':

Forthwith this frame of mine was wrenched
With a woeful agony,
Which forced me to begin my tale . . . .

As in *The Fall of Hyperion*, the helplessness, the 'cramp', leads to torment but also to re-creating experience in poetry, although Owen, being 'not concerned with Poetry', stresses that the story he is telling is not a vision but a concrete experience which has actually been suffered with all its 'physical sensation' ('not a dream, / But true resumption of experienced things', as he had insisted in that visionary poem, 'The time was aeon').

The funnelled hell mouth, part of the hideous face of war described in 'The Show', has 'all but' swallowed the soldiers. In 'Exposure' Owen changed the metaphor from a mouth to a house. He had first thought of writing his 'dawn piece' during a night in November 1917 when he had tramped the streets of York,

searching vainly for a hotel bed: 'the . . . hotels would not open
to my knocking'. In 'Exposure' the soldiers return home in
imagination but find that 'on us the doors are closed'. The
popular song said, 'Keep the home fires burning . . . . Though
your lads are far away they dream of home', but when these lads
dream of home they find that the fires have been left to die out
by families who have locked up and gone to bed oblivious. Owen
had once liked to imagine that soldiers could 'die back to those
hearths we died for' and even in the trenches had felt protected
from the 'keen spiritual Cold' by the love that reached him from
home.[3] Now, with the maturity that had come with the frost at
Beaumont Hamel, the troops see that they have already joined
the Unreturning. The first full draft of the poem (almost certainly
Ripon work) ends with an outline for an extra stanza:

> Blasts of the shells, blasts of the wind, these are our house.
> Whether we feel no   or yet are   creatures
> Our [hope is waiting] in deepness of dark craters
> We wait till [at our feet] [suddenly] the torn ground gulfs for us
>   And our door opens[4]

After the repeated refrain of 'nothing happens' the poem was to
have ended with an expected event, the opening of the hell door
at the bottom of a crater. This ninth stanza was not completed
but Owen attempted to introduce further house imagery into the
eighth, comparing frozen bodies to bricks and plaster, rubble
awaiting the 'picks and shovels' of the burying-party. Scrapping
most of this, he was left with the burying-party and the corpses,
'their wide eyes ice' (later revised to 'All their eyes are ice'),
thereby returning to the pervasive image of his dreams, the
freezing or petrifying stare. Six years earlier he had described the
Little Mermaid trying to 'thaw' the 'cold face' of her drowned
statue when 'still the *wide eyes* stared, and nothing saw'. Descent,
stare and paralysis were all part of the same complex of imagina-
tive experience.

His table of contents gives 'Description' as the poem's 'Motive'.
As description 'Exposure' is magnificent, its richly elaborate
technique, Romantic in sound and phrasing, working by a kind
of negative principle to evoke the unnatural nothingness of the
scene, the deprivation which the soldiers suffer in mind and body.
The opening echo of Keats ('Our brains ache' / 'My heart aches')
has often been noticed; there are several other literary parallels,

including one between the men's returning to their home fires as 'ghosts' in vain and Tennyson's lotos-eaters, who say that they might as well not return home for 'surely now our household hearths are cold' and 'we should come like ghosts to trouble joy'. These deliberate allusions set up an ironic relationship between the dazed weariness of the soldiers and the languor of the 'Nightingale' ode or 'The Lotos-Eaters'. Keats and the lotos-eaters had relaxed in beautiful landscapes which nevertheless held implicit lessons of morality and mortality. Now the threat is explicit; nature, the moral guardian of man and all life, is compelled to make war on the war-makers, seeming another German army as her clouds advance from the east like grey-uniformed storm troops.

In 'Mental Cases', written at Borrage Lane, the poet has passed the 'door' and sees some of hell's inmates. The title, which took some time to select, is one of several examples of Owen's skill in choosing impersonal military and medical terms – 'Disabled', 'S. I. W.', 'Conscious', 'Exposure', 'Spring Offensive' – for ironic effect. The method is modern irony and understatement but the feeling behind it is learned from earlier writers, especially Dickens, as is evident from the style of a 1912 comment on the word 'Cases', referring to a sick pauper child at Dunsden: 'This, I suppose, is only a typical *case*; one of many *Cases*! O hard word! How it savours of rigid, frigid professionalism! How it suggests smooth and polished, formal, labelled, mechanical callousness!'[5] The subjects of 'Mental Cases' are shellshocked soldiers, as in Sassoon's 'Survivors' and like some of the patients both poets saw at Craiglockhart. Yet Owen's figures have a further dimension, unlike Sassoon's. Words such as 'twilight', 'purgatorial',[6] 'Ever', 'Always' and the opening of what was to have been a fourth stanza, 'Time will not make', all prevent the hell of the poem from being read as a mere simile. The poet is being shown round eternal hell by a guide whom he is questioning: 'Who are these?' The question and its answer are a hellish parallel to the biblical 'What are these which are arrayed in white robes? . . . These are they which came out of great tribulation', and to Dante's questioning of his guide and brother poet, Vergil, in the *Inferno* ('Instructor! who / Are these, by the black air so scourg'd?').[7] Owen's instructor addresses him as 'brother', perhaps as both poet and officer, like Sassoon at Craiglockhart explaining how officers and the educated classes had dealt war and madness to the unfortunate; but readers tend to assume that 'brother' refers to them rather than the poet, so that 'Mental Cases' works as both a traditional poetic vision and a modern public reproach.

Much of the first stanza comes almost word for word from 'Purgatorial passions' (1916) and is thus descended from the various portraits of damned lovers which seem to have been associated with 'Perseus'. The twilit, shuddering figures in 'Mental Cases' are successors to the trembling victims of lust in the 1916 fragment as well as to the lovesick Danae, the Cultivated Rose with his shaking fingers and sweating scalp, the Flesh in 'The time was aeon', and the Mermaid's statue. Only the foxglove simile in 'Purgatorial passions' is missing, but that is replaced by the Decadent image of the bleeding sun in a comparison between dawn and a reopened wound which the young Rupert Brooke would have envied. Decadent authors had often used exquisitely subtle language to describe loathsome subject matter; Tailhade would have appreciated the meticulous care that lies behind the jagged vocabulary and elaborate assonance and alliteration of 'Mental Cases'. But these literary devices are used as means of defining experience, not as ornaments. The third stanza describes tormented eyes (which in draft work 'shrink and smother', 'smother' being one of Owen's nightmare words as in 'Dulce et Decorum Est') and the 'hilarious, hideous' falseness of fixed, corpse-like smiles, symptoms also recorded in Dr Brown's accounts of shellshock patients. These faces of war, like the pock-marked face of the trench landscape in 'The Show' or the 'dead rabbit' look of the troops, were among those 'phantoms of the mind' which Brock saw in Owen's poetry. The impassioned power of 'Mental Cases' lies in the authority and forceful language with which the 'pleader' makes his appeal, an authority which is based not only on the poem's relationship to traditions of Dantean vision and Romantic horror and protest but also on the poet's own knowledge of neurasthenic dreams.

Having entered hell and seen its occupants, the poet might be expected to hear one of them speak. Such an episode seems to be described in a strange manuscript probably written no earlier than late 1917. Conceivably work for 'Perseus', this fragment is only a very rough outline that was never revised:

> With those that are become
> Before the Future and later the Past
> For whom the present is an Absence.
>   and there was one

Whose fingers pinched upon my arm
(As some old hag hissing a tale
[For an unwilling and disgusted listener]
Grips an unwilling youth with vicious finger-bones)
That he might stare into me, madmanlike.
And this was the tale
'You are not he but I must find that man.
He was my Master [whom I worshipped]
Him I wounded unto slow death. God!
Where is he that I ask if he knew me
I loved [him] the more near than brotherly
"For each man slays the one he loves ⎫
The coward   ⎬
   The brave   ⎭
But I must find the hand that pushed mine
   [I will tear it] Emperor's or King's[8]

This has several things in common with 'Mental Cases' and
'Strange Meeting'. 'Those' ('Who are these?') are spirits in a
timeless hell, cut off from the past ('the undone years') and the
future (the 'hopelessness'). The 'madmanlike' figure, who is a
Romantic tale-teller as obsessive as the Ancient Mariner ('He
holds him with his skinny hand . . . He holds him with his
glittering eye'), stares at his listener as the dead man stares with
'fixed eyes' in 'Strange Meeting'. Having fatally wounded his
master ('Wisdom was mine, and I had *mastery*'), he seeks to be
recognised by him ('I *knew* you in this dark'). The words
'wounded' and 'hand' reappear in a draft version of a famous
line in 'Strange Meeting': 'But I was wounded by your hand, my
friend'. (Owen had often associated hands and hand contact with
guilt.) The murderer's hand has been 'pushed' by an Emperor's
or King's (meaning, presumably, that he has been a soldier in a
war attributable to the Kaiser or King George – as in 'Strange
Meeting', nationality is unimportant). He has killed someone he
'loved', and he quotes from Wilde's 'The Ballad of Reading Gaol':

     Yet each man kills the thing he loves,
       By each let this be heard,
    Some do it with a bitter look,
      Some with a flattering word.
    The coward does it with a kiss,
      The brave man with a sword!

Wilde's lines confirm the ambiguity of 'so you frowned . . . through me as you jabbed and killed' in 'Strange Meeting',[9] where the poet is told he has killed a friend with both a bayonet (a sword, the brave man's weapon) and a frown ('a bitter look'). A further gloss on the relationship between the two 'strange friends' is provided by the fragment's reference to more than brotherly love. Wilde's stanza helped to make some sense out of those nights in 1911–12 which Despondency had steeped in 'bloodiness and stains of shadowy crimes'; as the Limehouse poem and 'Has your soul sipped' had already implied, Eros might only be satisfied by the blood sacrifice of the poet or his idol or perhaps both.

The setting of 'Strange Meeting' (probably another Borrage Lane poem[10]) is, as Blunden noted, 'only a stage further on than the actuality of the tunnelled dug-outs'.[11] Indeed, Owen at one stage opened the poem with

> It seemed from that dull dug-out, I escaped
> Down some profounder tunnel, older scooped
> Through granites which the nether flames had groined.

'That' dug-out may have been a remembered version of the one described in 'The Sentry', where he had been tempted to let himself drown. The final draft is less specific in its first line and it omits reference to hell fire:

> It seemed that out of battle I escaped
> Down some profound dull tunnel, long since scooped
> Through granites which titanic wars had groined.
>
> Yet also there encumbered sleepers groaned,
> Too fast in thought or death to be bestirred.
> Then, as I probed them, one sprang up, and stared
> With piteous recognition in fixed eyes,
> Lifting distressful hands, as if to bless.
> And by his smile, I knew that sullen hall, –
> By his dead smile I knew we stood in Hell.
>
> With a thousand pains that vision's face was grained;
> Yet no blood reached there from the upper ground,
> And no gun thumped, or down the flues made moan.

'It seemed': again this is a dream poem, drawing on the Romantic tradition of visionary poetry and on Owen's personal knowledge of nightmare. He had memories of being trapped in holes at the Front and in a London tunnel not unlike the one in the poem. He knew his mother's fear of enclosed spaces, and, as Dr Backman has pointed out, the whole family seems to have had a memory of meeting a ghostly stranger under tunnel-like trees.[12] The poem may have been influenced by Barbusse's appalling description of an underground dressing-station; more certainly it can be related to Sassoon's 'The Rear-Guard', which Owen published in the *Hydra* at Craiglockhart. Sassoon describes an experience of a fellow officer in the Hindenburg Tunnel who had asked directions from a recumbent figure, had found that he was looking at the agonised, staring face of a corpse, and had fled in horror. Owen would also have known Graves's poem, 'Escape', an early draft of which is addressed to Sassoon;[13] Graves mythologises his own narrow escape from death as a descent into Hades, where Proserpine sends him back to sunlight up 'the corridor'. As in other poems, Owen outdoes the two Fusiliers, since his protagonist is answered by the corpse and stands his ground; his escape is into the tunnel, not out of it.

The cavern in 'Strange Meeting' derives from classical and Romantic myth as well as from the Western Front. It has been cut in ancient times by 'titanic wars' (or 'plutonic flames' in one draft), presumably in that war of the Titans which Keats had intended to describe in *Hyperion* (the first of all wars, according to myth). Like many legendary caves it contains sleepers. Owen may have been rereading Spenser's account of the Cave of Morpheus, which is 'farre from enemyes' and full of murmuring sound (but 'No other noyse, nor people's troublous cryes, / As still are wont t'annoy the walled towne').[14] The messenger sent to awaken Morpheus has to push him to get a reply. No noise of war reaches Owen's tunnel, although, in a cancelled line, 'slumber droned all down that sullen hall'. The approach of the protagonist who 'probes' the sleepers, and perhaps the 'citadels that are not walled', suggest a link between the Spenser passage and 'Strange Meeting', and the triangle is completed by Keats's description of the Cave of Quietude in *Endymion*, a cave that was certainly based on Spencer's. Endymion falls from bliss into despair and then into the psychological condition represented by the Cave of Quietude, a 'deep' 'hell' where 'Woe-hurricanes beat ever at the gate' but no sound penetrates. Calm sleep is possible in this state of spiritual deadness but no one can enter the refuge who strives for it.[15] Owen's cavern symbolises a similar state, though less calm; it is a Romantic metaphor as well as a classical setting. The innumerable caves in Romantic literature are often images of the mind, especially in Shelley ('the inmost cave / Of man's deep spirit'). When Owen returned to the Front in 1918 he referred to it as 'Caverns & Abysmals' such as Shelley 'never reserved for his worst daemons' (he was reading Shelley again).[16] The word 'strange' in his title is a late-Romantic adjective, however, and *fin de siècle* writers provide many descriptions of cloistral silence (Dowson), subterranean descents (Wells) and infernal, hopeless landscapes (Thomson). Owen had always been interested in such subjects; in drafts of 'The Unreturning', for instance, the poet calls for the dead but no 'sleeper out of Hades woke' (a draft of 'Strange Meeting' revises this to 'all was sleep. And no voice called for men'). Imagery of silence, sleep and descents into darkness reflect the *ennui* and despair of the late-nineteenth-century sensibility; as Brock later suggested, Europe had been neurasthenic long before 1914.[17]

It is 'hopelessness' (originally 'lethargy') which the Other, the dead man, gives as the principal reason for his mourning, associating it with 'the undone years', presumably the years of youth which are wasted ('the soils of souls untilled', as the first draft defines 'the pity of war', echoing 'Futility) and those of maturity which are not now to come. 'The old happiness is unreturning': this had been a constant theme since Beaumont Hamel.

> 'Strange friend,' I said, 'here is no cause to mourn.'
> 'None,' said that other, 'save the undone years,
> The hopelessness. Whatever hope is yours,
> Was my life also; I went hunting wild
> After the wildest beauty in the world,
> Which lies not calm in eyes, or braided hair,
> But mocks the steady running of the hour,
> And if it grieves, grieves richlier than here.
> For by my glee might many men have laughed . . .

The early 'hope' which the Other has lived for and lost has to do with the näively Keatsian ambitions expressed in some of Owen's lyrics. Poems such as 'My Shy Hand' and 'The Fates' had described a timeless beauty, in pursuit of which the poet had hoped to 'miss the march of lifetime', 'the vain untravelled leagues'. Owen had rejected such hopes as signs of immaturity in 1917; he remained true to Keats, but to the Keats of *The Fall of Hyperion*.

> And of my weeping something had been left,
> Which must die now. I mean the truth untold,
> The pity of war, the pity war distilled.
> Now men will go content with what we spoiled,
> Or, discontent, boil bloody, and be spilled.
> They will be swift with swiftness of the tigress.
> None will break ranks, though nations trek from progress.
> Courage was mine, and I had mystery,
> Wisdom was mine, and I had mastery:
> To miss the march of this retreating world
> Into vain citadels that are not walled.
> Then, when much blood had clogged their chariot-wheels,
> I would go up and wash them from sweet wells,
> Even with truths that lie too deep for taint.
> I would have poured my spirit without stint
> But not through wounds; not on the cess of war.
> Foreheads of men have bled where no wounds were.

This draws heavily on 'Earth's wheels', the exhortation which, as I have suggested, Owen wrote for Sassoon in December. In that poem he had set out a programme of breaking ranks from militarism in order to defend truth until post-war society was once again ready for the peaceful message of the poets. The influence of Bertrand Russell on both 'Earth's wheels' and 'Strange Meeting' has already been discussed (see above pp.132–3). The most conspicuous change from the first poem to the second is the tense ('will' to 'would have'). The Other's pessimistic outline of future events still echoes Russell's prophecies, just as Sassoon still sympathised with Russell's position;[18] but like all soldiers Owen and Sassoon were not free, in conscience or in practice, to stay out of the front line. The hopes outlined in 'Earth's wheels' are now abandoned. One thing that is not abandoned, however, is the sense of apartness described in the earlier poem and by Russell (and the Romantic poets). The two characters in 'Strange Meeting' are cut off by being out of sympathy with the war, by being in hell, by being poets, by their status as soldiers and by the love which seems to be the fatal bond between them.

Apart from Russell, the principal influence on this part of the poem is Shelley, to whom Owen deliberately alludes. Just as the aspirations in 'Earth's wheels' had reflected the ideals of Laon and Cythna in *The Revolt of Islam*, so 'Strange Meeting' is influenced by a passage in *The Revolt* (v.i–xiii) in which Laon is recognised by a friend in a camp full of sleeping men, and then successfully stops a battle by stepping defenceless in front of the first raised spear, receiving its point in his 'arm that was uplifted / In swift expostulation'. As a result of his intervention, friends and enemies are reconciled like brothers 'whom now strange meeting did befall / In a strange land'. Owen, who had known *The Revolt* since Dunsden, must have intended the source of his title and the irony in his allusion to be recognised. The Other has tried to parry a bayonet ('Lifting distressful hands') but has been killed, dying as a fighting soldier not as an unarmed pacifist. Owen's 'strange meeting' takes place after death, unlike Shelley's. The poet in uniform could not hope to emulate Laon.

The last lines of the poem bring a change in style, from the ornate, semi-biblical language of the rest of the speech to a slow pacing of monosyllables that is movingly dramatic:

> I am the enemy you killed, my friend.
> I knew you in this dark: for so you frowned
> Yesterday through me as you jabbed and killed.
> I parried; but my hands were loath and cold.
>   Let us sleep now . . .

Despite their simplicity, these lines complete the ambiguity and 'strangeness' of the poem. The syntax allows two meanings: the Other has been killed not only by a bayonet but also by a frown, the murderous concentration on the poet's face which represents the inhumanity of war, the pitilessness which kills. As Wilde had concluded, 'each man kills the thing he loves', some by 'a bitter look' and some by 'a sword', a look being crueller and more cowardly than a sword. The poet's frown is the means by which the Other recognises him, just as he learns from the Other's 'dead smile' that they are in hell. Each remembers his opponent's expression at the moment the bayonet struck; by looking at one another face to face in hell, they discover the truth. The ambiguous placing of 'through me' draws attention to the double significance of many details in the poem. This meeting in the underworld is a replica of yesterday's action. The poet may have entered hell during an infantry attack, like the men in 'Spring Offensive'; he would still be carrying his rifle and perhaps uses it to 'probe' the sleepers, frowning as he peers into the dark. The Other lifts his hands as if to parry the blow, his face contorted as at the moment of death. He speaks paradoxically: 'I am the *enemy* you killed, my *friend*'. The 'tunnel' (Hindenburg Tunnel or hell) contains sleepers, deep in 'thought' if they are alive or 'death' if they are not, who are 'encumbered' (by packs or war memories). The Other seems both to parry and to bless; he smiles, in agony or in welcome, suffers 'pains' which may be physical or spiritual, and can see despite 'this dark'.

The ambiguities of the poem centre on the identity of the Other. It has been common to regard him as Owen's double, an *alter ego* whose poetic creed and career are those of his author. However, until a late stage of revision, Owen thought of him as 'a German conscript', an enemy counterpart rather than a *Doppelgänger* – and not quite a counterpart, either, since Owen himself was a volunteer and had already turned away from some of the ideals which the Other adumbrates. Tailhade had warned young recruits that they would be expected to kill men whose lives had been similar to their own. Nevertheless, Owen would have been aware that encounters between a man and his other self are common in Romantic literature (they occur in Shelley and Dickens, for example). He may well have read an article by W. C. Rivers in the *Cambridge Magazine* (January 1918) which discussed Yeats's recent use of the double, relating it to literary tradition and Freud. Rivers observed that the double is sometimes represented as having the power to cast its original into hell and that in several stories, including *The Picture of Dorian Gray* (which Owen must have known), the original stabs his other self, thereby causing his own death; traditionally, meeting one's double is likely to be fatal. The event in Owen's poem cannot be reduced to a meeting between a man and his double – he had no intention of presenting war as a merely internal, psychological conflict – but neither is it concerned with the immediate divisions suggested by 'German' and 'conscript' or 'British' and 'volunteer'. The poem is larger and stranger than that. The two men are not identified, except that at first one is alive in hell and the Other is dead ('Whatever hope *is* yours, / *Was* my life also'). The meeting does seem to be fatal, however, since at the end the Other invites the poet to join him in sleep. This sleep is itself ambiguous, being death and rest yet also consciousness and torment. If the idea of the double is present at all, it may be in the mysteriously sexual element in this encounter between two men who meet, discover each other and sleep. There is a trace here of the narcissism evident in Owen's descriptions of those other sufferers in twilight, the Cultivated Rose and the casualty in 'Disabled'. The poet sees himself in the Other but the Other is an independent being.[19]

If the many doubles which have been cited with reference to 'Strange Meeting' are not all strictly relevant, there are other literary parallels which seem convincing, including Dante's pitying recognitions of the agonised faces of spirits who have had to 'abandon hope' in hell.[20] The tortured face and 'fixed eyes' of Owen's 'vision' have no lack of antecedents in Gothic fiction and Romantic poetry. In Landor's *Gebir* (III. 135), for instance, the hero descends into a cavernous underworld and is told how the dead meeting the dead have 'with fixt eyes beheld / Fixt eyes'. Tortured, hypnotic eyes are stock Romantic properties; the Ancient Mariner, the last chapter of *Salammbô* and, above all, Keats's vision in the second *Hyperion*, provide examples which Owen knew well. In Keats's 'Lamia' the philosopher's relentless stare reveals the truth and kills delight. In *The Fall of Hyperion* the goddess of memory unveils her dying yet immortal face and unseeing eyes, thereby allowing the poet to share in her knowledge of the titanic wars of long ago and of the fallen Titans lying 'roof'd in by black rocks . . in pain / And darkness, for no hope':

> deathwards progressing
> To no death was that visage; it had past
> The lilly and the snow; and beyond these
> I must not think now, though I saw that face . . . .[21]

The first draft of 'Strange Meeting' mentions the whiteness of the Other's face: 'With a thousand fears his [strange, white] face was grained'. The *Hyperion* passage is also echoed in 'The Sentry', another description of seeing fixed eyes in a dug-out: 'I try not to remember these things now'. Murry said in 1919 that *The Fall of Hyperion* was undoubtedly Owen's source: the 'sombre imagination, the sombre rhythm [of 'Strange Meeting'] is that of the dying Keats . . . this poem by a boy with the certainty of death in his heart, like his great forerunner, is the most magnificent expression of the emotional significance of the war that has yet been achieved by English poetry'.[22] Owen could have wished for no greater compliment.

It may be that 'Strange Meeting' does not fully tell 'the truth untold'. The *Cambridge Magazine* said on 24 February 1917 that 'anybody who has intimate friends at the front must know ... that a great deal remains untold ... often the most important part of psychological experience'. Critics who are interested in such matters may consider, for example, the relationship between this poem, 'Earth's wheels', 'With those that are become' and Owen's feelings for his friend and master, Sassoon. Certainly, 'Strange Meeting' is one of his most intensely personal poems, despite the grand, impersonal language of its central sections, yet it is also one of his most political and wide-ranging statements. Like the manuscripts of his other 1918 hell pieces ('As bronze', 'With those that are become', 'Mental Cases', possibly 'Exposure', and 'Spring Offensive'), the two drafts of 'Strange Meeting' show signs of his intending to continue the poem. 'Let us sleep now . . . .' is scribbled in as an afterthought in an unusually shaky hand. The classical tradition represented death as a tranquil, silent sleep but the late-Romantic use of the image made the state less desirable; in Swinburne's *Atalanta in Calydon*, for instance, the dying Meleager describes himself as 'gone down to the empty weary house / Where no flesh is nor beauty nor swift eyes'. (Murry might have adduced Swinburne as another source of Owen's sombre imagination and rhythm.) The 'sullen hall' of 'Strange Meeting' is not the Cave of Quietude and the pain there is not only that of loss; the sleepers are 'encumbered' and groaning, carrying with them into an eternity of damnation the wounds and dreams of war.

11 'Spring Offensive'

In his letters from France in September and October 1918 Owen used the word 'serene' to describe himself, privately reassuring his mother and Sassoon that his nerves were now in 'perfect order'. 'You would not know me for the poet of sorrows.' He had no intention of reassuring anybody else, since civilians were not to imagine that any soldier overseas was contented, so he marked a particularly cheerful letter 'Not to be hawked about'. It no longer seemed right to draw attention to his own experiences; whereas in 1917 he had asked for parts of his letters to be circulated, now even his letters about fighting were marked 'Strictly private' and 'Not for circulation as a whole'. While he committed himself to serene activity, his anxious mother had taken to her bed. The last paragraph he ever wrote (31 October) sums up their respective roles:

> I hope you are as warm as I am; as serene in your room as I am here; and that you think of me never in bed as resignedly as I think of you always in bed. Of this I am certain you could not be visited by a band of friends half so fine as surround me here.

'The shades keep down which well might roam her hall'; Mrs Owen's passivity was not to be disturbed.[1]

He was clear about the political nature of the war's closing stages, telling Sassoon that he might find himself in front of a firing-squad if he wrote poems in the dug-outs or talked in his sleep[2] but soon finding that his opinions were widely shared. There had been much talk in Britain of 'the Nation at Home' and 'the Nation Overseas', but the latter now seemed the only true nation, still worth loyalty long after honour had gone from the home front. He was glad to be 'back here with *the Nation*', away from civilians who were still supporting the war without having to fight it.[3] He still disapproved of the Gunston brothers,

180

telling Leslie that 'I must say that I feel sorry that you are neither in the flesh with Us nor in the spirit against war.'[4] In mid October an officer returned to the battalion 'from his first visit to London utterly disgusted with England's indifference to the real meaning of the war as we understand it'. Quoting Sassoon, Owen defined 'we' as 'every officer & man left, of the legions who have suffered and are dust'.[5] Delighted to find that the troops were turning against *John Bull* and the *Daily Mail*, which were clamouring for total victory, he felt a strong sense of solidarity with 'Us', soldiers who knew that they and the dead were all that was left of England:

> (This is the thing they know and never speak,
> That England one by one had fled to France,
> Not many elsewhere now, save under France.)[6]

He was convinced that the war was once again being prolonged by prussianism at home and abroad, urged on by a vindictive newspaper campaign and atrocity stories. 'I have found in all these villages *no evidence of German atrocities*', he told Gunston. 'Do you still shake your befoozled head over the *Daily Mail* & the *Times*?' The damage he saw was caused by British guns, which were killing French civilians because the Allies were refusing to let Germany retreat in peace. The German offensive had made further war inevitable in the spring but circumstances were now very different. That he was by no means alone in his views is suggested by an official order that 'Peace Talk must cease in the Fourth Army'.[7] It was a little like Ross's circle on a much wider scale: a group of friends, who were alienated from press and public but held together by comradeship, a shared secret and common adversity. The bond seemed political as well as comradely; the description in Owen's last letter of his men, his 'band of friends', is unusually detailed and similar to some of Barbusse's accounts of the squad in that political book *Under Fire*.

'FRENCH SENATE THRILLED Clemenceau's Great Speech' (*Daily Mail*, 19 September). *The Times* provided a literal translation of the speech, in which the French Premier had announced France's refusal of an Austrian offer of peace talks on the grounds that peace now would be a betrayal of the troops who were still fighting. Owen incorporated parts of the translation into 'Smile, Smile, Smile', which he finished four days after the speech was reported.[8] The wounded soldiers in the poem smile 'curiously' over such newspaper items and keep the secret of the Nation Overseas.

> Pictures of these broad smiles appear in Sketches
> And people say: They're happy now, poor wretches.

This draft version of the ending is a clue to another newspaper source. On 16 September the *Daily Sketch* had published a picture (Plate 14) of three wounded men, each with a ghastly smile, the caption twice describing them as 'happy'.[9] The three smiles in the photograph may have suggested the poem's title; it was men such as these whom the music-hall song urged to 'Smile, smile, smile'. If the poem is read in conjunction with Owen's letter of 22 September to Sassoon, it can be seen to be a deliberately Sassoonish piece, a 'cry' in the style that Sassoon seemed by then to have abandoned. It is Owen's last poem in his friend's manner, but by this stage in his poethood he could not write anything that lacked his own stamp; the 'secret' is akin to the 'truth untold' in 'Strange Meeting', and the 'sunk-eyed wounded' with their limp heads leaning towards each other are described in the same terms as the damned in 'Purgatorial passions', whose eyes were sunk in 'chasms' and whose necks were 'bowed like moping foxgloves all'.

And indeed he was one of the damned himself, though with no visible wounds. Some of his companions had been with him in 1917 and remembered the railway embankment and the flooded dug-out. He revised his poem about the dug-out in September, sending it to Sassoon with the provisional title 'The Blind' (presumably Sassoon chose the final title, 'The Sentry'). That memory of an injured head was soon replaced in intensity by another when little Jones was shot in fierce fighting in October. The railway bank had been the site of Owen's alleged loss of nerve and he had not forgotten that he needed to 'get some reputation of gallantry' before he could speak out publicly against the war. The October battle gave him his chance. He was awarded the Military Cross, having 'behaved most gallantly' according to the citation, and was glad of it 'for the confidence it may give me at home'. He described his twofold task in a famous statement: 'I came out in order to help these boys – directly by leading them as well as an officer can; indirectly, by watching their sufferings that I may speak of them as well as a pleader can. I have done the first.'[10] He told his mother that he had shot one man with his revolver, captured a machine gun, and taken scores of prisoners, but he did not say what he had done with the machine gun. When the MC citation was published in the *Collected Letters*, one sentence in it was misquoted: 'He personally captured an enemy Machine Gun in an isolated position and took a number of prisoners.' The original citation, of which a typescript on War Office paper is preserved in Tom Owen's scrapbook, gives a different wording: 'He personally manipulated a captured enemy M. G. from an isolated position and inflicted considerable losses on the enemy.'[11] The poet who had hoped to wash the blood off war's chariot wheels had, in the words of his last poem, out-fiended the fiends and flames of hell with 'superhuman inhumanities,/ Long-famous glories, immemorial shames'.

He told his mother,

> I can find no word to qualify my experiences except the word SHEER. (Curiously enough I find the papers talk about sheer fighting!) It passed the limits of my Abhorrence. I lost all my earthly faculties, and fought like an angel.[12]

The language of 'Apologia pro Poemate Meo' and 'Insensibility' was being tested out afresh ('some scorching cautery of battle', 'power was on us . . . Not to feel sickness or remorse of murder', 'Seraphic for an hour'). The word 'sheer' was added to his poetic vocabulary for use in 'Spring Offensive'; he had probably seen it in two typical headlines in the *Mail*: 'ADVANCE BY SHEER FIGHTING The Better Men Win' (19 September) and 'SHEER FIGHTING Both Sides Pay the Price Huns Wait for the Bayonet' (3 October).[13] The poem which he would have written about Jones's wound would not have been in Sassoon's style ('crimson-hot iron . . . That is what Jones's blood looked like, and felt like. My senses are charred').

The only verse which Owen is likely to have written after the October fighting is the later part of 'Spring Offensive'. He had said in his Preface in the spring that English poetry was 'not yet fit to speak' of heroes and his own attempts to write about modern soldiers as, for example, Arthurs ('Hospital Barge') or Horatius ('Schoolmistress') had not been very successful, but in 'Spring

Offensive' he began to fashion a kind of poetry that would be fit
to speak of heroes while denying heroic qualities to war itself. His
last poem seems both a prologue to new writing and an epilogue
to all he had written before. It took him some time to write; he
seems to have begun it in the summer, since '[Attac] Spring
Offensive' appears in a list of titles probably drawn up when he
was choosing work to send to *Wheels* in August, but as late as 22
September he sent Sassoon a version of the first seventeen lines
only, asking 'Is this worth going on with? I don't want to write
anything to which a soldier would say No Compris!'[14] Despite
this awareness that the poem was more 'difficult' than some of
his work, he decided that it was indeed worth finishing, although
the ending which he wrote may be different from, and shorter
than, the one he originally had in mind; he added the last stanza
in a hurried, unrevised pencil and would certainly have rewritten
it had time allowed. The earlier part of the only complete draft
is extensively amended, with illegible, cancelled and alternative
wordings which will always puzzle his editors. There are signs
that he began to break up the stanzas into irregular paragraphs,
as he had done in several other poems, but this job was
not carried through. The version which follows is Professor
Stallworthy's text:

> Halted against the shade of a last hill
> They fed, and eased of pack-loads, were at ease;
> And leaning on the nearest chest or knees
> Carelessly slept.
>   But many there stood still
> To face the stark blank sky beyond the ridge,
> Knowing their feet had come to the end of the world.
> Marvelling they stood, and watched the long grass swirled
> By the May breeze, murmurous with wasp and midge;
> And though the summer oozed into their veins
> Like an injected drug for their bodies' pains,
> Sharp on their souls hung the imminent ridge of grass,
> Fearfully flashed the sky's mysterious glass.
>
> Hour after hour they ponder the warm field
> And the far valley behind, where buttercups
> Had blessed with gold their slow boots coming up;
> When even the little brambles would not yield
> But clutched and clung to them like sorrowing arms.
> They breathe like trees unstirred.

Till like a cold gust thrills the little word
At which each body and its soul begird
And tighten them for battle. No alarms
Of bugles, no high flags, no clamorous haste, –
Only a lift and flare of eyes that faced
The sun, like a friend with whom their love is done.
O larger shone that smile against the sun, –
Mightier than his whose bounty these have spurned.

So, soon they topped the hill, and raced together
Over an open stretch of herb and heather
Exposed. And instantly the whole sky burned
With fury against them; earth set sudden cups
In thousands for their blood; and the green slope
Chasmed and deepened sheer to infinite space.

Of them who running on that last high place
Breasted the surf of bullets, or went up
On the hot blast and fury of hell's upsurge,
Or plunged and fell away past this world's verge,
Some say God caught them even before they fell.

But what say such as from existence' brink
Ventured but drave too swift to sink,
The few who rushed in the body to enter hell,
And there out-fiending all its fiends and flames
With superhuman inhumanities,
Long-famous glories, immemorial shames –
And crawling slowly back, have by degrees
Regained cool peaceful air in wonder –
Why speak not they of comrades that went under?

The poem is loosely based on the assault at Savy Wood in April 1917, the action which preceded Owen's shellshock. Some details, such as the lack of bugles, correspond to those in his 1917 letters but there are differences.[15] For example, the weather in that April had been poor, the land around Savy had already been fought over and the advance was at walking speed, but the troops in the poem 'race' over an undamaged landscape in May sunshine. The reader is evidently meant to recognise the significance of Maytime and the double meaning of the title. May is the traditional setting for poetic experience, in medieval dream

poems, for example, or the 'Ode to a Nightingale'.[16] The term
'spring offensive' was a standard one, referring to the 'Push' that
could be expected when winter weather ended, but here the
spring is the object as well as the time of the attack ('Halted
against the shade of a last hill', '*against* the sun'). The opposition
between attackers and season is crucial to the poem.

The setting is familiar. The unidentified soldiers (as he said in
his Preface, Owen avoided using names and nationalities in his
1918 work) have walked eastwards up a valley, the dew making
buttercup petals or pollen adhere to their slow (reluctant?) boots.
Ahead, an abrupt, grassy hill is silhouetted against the flat glare
of the rising sun, whose rays are already warming the landscape
through which the troops have passed. Like 'Futility' and
'Exposure', this is another 'dawn piece'.[17] Some men take the
opportunity of catching up on the sleep they have lost during the
night march; others (the 'wise', perhaps, for many men in the
Nation now shared the wisdom of poets) stand still as trees, taking
the summer into their veins as a tree draws sap from its roots.
The comfort is only bodily, a 'physical sensation', for the souls
that are alert are acutely aware of the menace of the ridge and
of the unsheltered plateau of 'herb and heather' beyond it. This
landscape is recognisably Salopian, the blessing offered by the
buttercups being very similar to that given by the 'croziers' of
young bracken shoots in a metaphor which Owen had made
years before on Caer Caradoc. Harold Owen even claimed that
the buttercup image was coined near Shrewsbury, a claim which
unfortunately merits some scepticism but which was no doubt
based on an actual memory of the family's yellowed boots in the
Monkmoor fields. The ridge in 'Spring Offensive' resembles
Shropshire hills such as Haughmond, the Wrekin and the
Caradoc, the first two of which Owen mentioned in October. He
said he had been as agile in the fighting as his Welsh mountain
forefathers. He must have been letting his mind dwell on his
native border country where he had spent the happiest times of
his adolescence, no doubt also remembering the steep, heather-
topped hill at Broxton.[18]

The soldiers in the poem have ignored the buttercups and the
'sorrowing arms' of the brambles. In personifying nature Owen
often imagined hands and holding: 'the grip and stringency of
winter', 'Pale flakes . . . fingering', 'the wide arms of trees'. In the
last of these examples, from 'Happiness', the tree branches had
originally been 'mother-arms'; they offer an unfilled, unreachable

embrace, matching the possessive love which Owen knew his
mother still felt for him even though he was no longer 'a Mother's
boy'. In 'Exposure' nature's embrace has the sinister caress of
snow, for nature and love could become fatal when their more
kindly aspects were set aside in the inevitable transition from
innocence to adult knowledge. Spring was the moment of growth,
the season for 'putting forth' poetry (as leaves to a tree) and for
walking in the woods with young companions – with Rampton
in 1912, Henriette in 1914, the Mérignac boy amid the surging
foliage of 'his' woods in 1915. After another such ramble in 1916,
Owen reported that 'we ate the Vernal Eucharist of Hawthorn
leaf-buds. / These are the days when men's hearts (some men's)
become tender as the new green.'[19] Spring's power was both
redemptive and sexual, its new beauty innocent and erotic,
parallelling the 'crucial change . . . from boy to man' in the
human body that Owen had watched in Rampton. Many of his
lyrics had used images of season and landscape to describe the
beauty of youth. The speaker in P1 had imagined that there
would be 'rest for ever' in the 'valleys' between his lover's
shoulders. The valley in 'Spring Offensive' may have offered
'ease / For ever from the vain untravelled leagues' but it, like
youth, has had to be left behind. In 1912 Owen had preferred
'the placid plains of *normal ease*' to the higher 'dangerous air where
actual Bliss doth thrill' but in the 1918 poem the soldiers lie at
ease only as a preliminary to climbing into hilltop air full of the
'even rapture of bullets'.[20]

The spring offensive runs counter to Geddesian and Romantic
principles. Brock's allegory of neurasthenia was of Antaeus
defeated by Hercules, 'the war machine', who tore the organism
from its environment or, in Owen's poem on the subject, 'rooted
up' Antaeus like a tree. The troops in 'Spring Offensive' see the
blessing offered by nature, standing 'like trees unstirred' until the
order to attack comes like a chill wind; then they are stirred, the
contact is broken and they move into action, tree-like no more.[21]
War has uprooted them but this time not against their will; they
are not felled by a storm wind but choose to move, aware of the
consequences. Brock's Ergotherapy was at odds with its own
ideals, curing soldiers in order to send them back into action
where, even if their nerves were in perfect order, their 'work' was
to attack their environment once again. But the environment in
the poem is not only the nature which Owen had studied with
Brock in the Pentlands and with Gunston in Oxfordshire and

Shropshire but also the nature which the Romantics had taught him to revere: 'murmurous with wasp and midge', 'the summer oozed', 'drug' – these phrases are deliberate echoes of Keats's odes ('murmurous haunt of flies on summer eves', 'oozings', 'some dull opiate'). There may also be more distant echoes of a passage in *The Revolt of Islam* (VI. ix–x), where Laon and others gain 'the shelter of a grassy hill' and hold off a murderous enemy with 'stern looks beneath the shade / Of gathered eyebrows', standing 'firm as giant pine'.[22] The soldiers in 'Spring Offensive' reach the 'shade' of a grass-grown hill and direct challenging looks at their enemy, the sun. If the men who have pondered the warm field with its buttercups and brambles may be understood to be as wise as poets, since poetic wisdom was now the 'philosophy of many soldiers', and as observant as naturalists ('Do Plants Think?'), they perceive that they have chosen to attack the landscape of poetry and social health or, less figuratively, the ideals which had been preached by the Romantics and the Outlook Tower. They are unlikely, after all, to become 'one with nature, herb, and stone'.

The attack necessitates a spurning of nature, almost as though it were 'against' the hill and the sun. The only suggestion of a human enemy is the word 'bullets' in a line which Owen revised again and again without completing it to his satisfaction; had there been time he might have seen that the word itself was the course of the trouble. He also tried many wordings for the challenge which the men make by looking at the sun, describing the reflection in their eyes as 'light', 'glory', 'radiance', 'mighty kindle', 'lift and sparkle', 'blaze' and 'flare', before hitting on the pun of 'lift and flare'. As a battle flag is lifted to 'flare' in the wind, so the soldiers, lacking flags, raise their eyes and let them flare in the sunlight. The 'kind old sun' is rejected like a lover. For a moment his smile is outshone by the 'mighty' smile of the advancing infantry. There is something here of the 'exultation' which Owen felt at Savy Wood. 'So, soon they topped the hill, and raced together' was originally less vigorous: 'Turning, they topped the hill, and walked together'. They had already turned to face the sun, so 'Turning' had to go. Owen tried 'Splendid', 'Proudly', 'Glorious', 'Lightly', 'Bright-faced', before settling on 'So, soon' and replacing 'walked' with 'raced', giving the line the speed and exhilaration which he wanted to convey.

'Bright-faced' is interesting. Christ's face shone 'as the sun' at the Transfiguration and God's face is said in Revelation to shine 'as the sun shineth in his strength'.[23] In *God the Invisible King* (1917), a book Sassoon and Owen talked about when they first met, H. G. Wells had said that the God of the new age that was beginning should be represented as 'a beautiful youth' already brave and wise', standing 'lightly on his feet in the morning time', his eyes 'as bright as swords', his lips parted with eagerness, his sword and armour 'reflecting the rising sun'; Christ was no meek victim but a militant hero with a countenance 'as the sun'.[24] Owen seems to be using a version of the soldier–Christ image quite unlike that of the crucified martyrs in 'Greater Love', for he was as clear as ever that he could not follow the Christ who preached 'Passivity at any price'. Wells's book expressed a religious optimism about the war which its author later regretted and which Owen would have found absurd, but the epithet 'Bright-faced' does suggest that Owen imagined the soldiers as being like new gods in their brief splendour. There is no orthodox Christianity in 'Spring Offensive' but there is a commitment to activity. The men's racing may be compared with 'Training' (late June 1918), where the poet prefers the 'clean beauty of speed and pride of style' of cross-country running to love and languor. Like the 'cold gust' in the later poem, 'Cold winds . . . Shall thrill my heated bareness'; but 'None else may meet me till I wear my crown'. (The 'crown' may have been that of martyrdom or an athlete's prize or, perhaps, the crown-shaped badge of a major, the reward for military success.) 'Bright-faced' also suggests sexual and poetic achievement, as in the 'Perseus' fragments, 'Storm', 'A Palinode' (where the 'blessed with gold' metaphor first appears) and other poems. In order to win beauty, poets and lovers had to risk 'the anger of the sun' ('Reunion'); the soldier must take a similar risk to prove his love for his comrades ('they raced *together*').

As the blood of the casualty in 'Disabled' had flowed with a 'race / And leap', so the men in 'Spring Offensive' 'race' over the exposed ground and 'leap' to unseen bullets. In both poems the words mark the climax, though in the second it is not passive. Owen wrote 'Leapt to unseen bullets' and 'Breasted the [surf of] even rapture of bullets' in his draft, implying excitement and voluntary pushing forward as in swimming. In response, the flashing sky[25] suddenly burns with fury against the soldiers and they fall into 'Caverns & Abysmals' such as Shelley 'never reserved for his worst daemons', 'abysmal war' opening 'sheer' at their feet like 'the end of the world',[26] the *fin du globe* image becoming literal. The 'cups' are shell craters, some of the 'many mouths of Hell', infernal chalices for the sacrificial blood. Such is 'the anger of the sun' against the band of friends who have spurned his love but been true to their own.

The 'last hill' has become the 'last high place'. With his background of regular Bible study, Owen would have connected 'high places', mentioned over a hundred times in the Old Testament, with sacrifice. Some pagan high places were associated with Moloch, the deity to whom fathers sacrificed their children by fire.[27] In *Salammbô*, the novel Owen read before enlisting, the Carthaginians feed their sons into a red-hot statue of Moloch, the god of sun, fire, blood and war, in the hope of bringing a disastrous war to an end. Moloch also appears in Osbert Sitwell's war poems as the god to whom 'old men' were sacrificing their sons. Owen's reading of the war's last stages was that fathers were making their sons pass through the fire ('hot blast and fury', 'flames') while women slept like Salammbô the *femme fatale*, unaware of the 'hecatombs' around them. The work of leading boys to the sacrifice was left to officers, priests of the modern Moloch.[28] In the light of this, Joseph Cohen's interpretation of 'God caught them even before they fell' as a 'gesture . . . of compelling blood-lust'[29] is a little less absurd than it seems and certainly nearer the mark than the usual sentimental explanation of the line as pious reassurance. Owen seems originally to have planned to end the poem at this point with 'Of them *we* say God caught them as they fell', as he had said of corpses in 1917 that in 'poetry we call them . . . glorious'.[30] The first person was misleading in 1918 but his underlining of '*we*' shows how the final version of the line should be read: '*Some*' people at home may say that God caught them, but what say those who fought in and survived the offensive? '*Some* say': the myth is brushed aside, rather as Milton dismissed the legend of Mulciber's fall ('thus they relate, / Erring').[31] Pagan slaughter leaves no room for Christian consolation.

The soldiers have faced 'the stark blank sky', as Keats faced the 'blank splendour' of Moneta's eyes. Their smile answers the sun's; as in 'Strange Meeting' and 'Smile', Smile, Smile', there is recognition and shared secrecy. Their door opens 'in deepness of dark craters'. They enter hell in body as well as in spirit, following the poets and heroes of legend who entered the underworld as living men. Like the speaker in P1, they are cut off from the sun. Their fall from light to darkness is 'sheer' like the abrupt descents from delight into loss which characterise Keats's poetry. The sheer fall can be related to Owen's comparison of the sensation of going over the top at Savy Wood to 'those dreams of falling over a precipice, when you see the rocks at the bottom surging up to you'.[32] The nightmare is also sheer in the sense of being complete, for this is his final dream vision, sternly controlled and made impersonal. Hell's fire and darkness are outdone by 'bloodiness and stains of shadowy crimes', called by the world 'glorious' and rewarded with Military Crosses. The upper air purges itself of heat and fury, the sun can smile again, and the survivors regain the May landscape in wonder beneath 'an inoffensive sky',[33] carrying with them the knowledge which Owen had gained from Beaumont Hamel and more recently from his use of the machine gun.

'Why speak not *they* of comrades that went under?' Politicians and journalists were all too ready to speak but the anonymous soldiers stay silent, with 'strength to perform, and pride to suffer without sign'. 'Spring Offensive' takes English poetry a little nearer being fit to speak of heroes. In speaking for his men, the pleader does not after all restrict himself to writing about their sufferings or about passivity, although there is nothing in the poem that could be taken to imply a favourable view of war. The medium is narrative fiction in the epic tradition, as several critics have pointed out; Owen would probably not have described this poem as an 'elegy'.

He does not refer to himself in 'Spring Offensive' yet the poem came – as naturally as leaves to a tree – out of his inner life, rounding off his poetic career and at the same time giving promise of further achievement. Its setting corresponds to the landscapes where his imagination had first been touched by beauty, while its language and imagery show how much he had learned from the great nineteenth-century writers whom he had admired since his schooldays. His use of a short lifetime's experience and reading is characteristic; he brings poetic ways of seeing and evaluating to bear upon contemporary events, with the aim of speaking for the common man as the Romantics had done before him. His own courage is reflected in the men's lack of hesitation in the poem, just as his own self-awareness becomes theirs when they stand like trees; he no longer speaks about them from a distance as he had been obliged to do since Savy Wood, but shares in their action, seeing where it leads. Something of the 'Perseus' pattern survives in the stare, the sudden activity, the fall into hell and the unanswered final question. The question itself is a reminder not only of the ominous divisions that have split twentieth-century society but also of the strangeness and secrecy of his genius.

He was set apart all his life. First, he was his mother's favourite, isolated from the rest of the family. Then his poethood began in secret darkness, born out of a tradition which had made the poet both the prophetic voice of the people and a solitary, damned figure, a dreamer cast out from sunlight. Sexually, he belonged to a group which had to be separate and unseen, though it scorned the morality of the crowd. And he was a soldier in the Nation, that band of friends in France who seemed in the end to be like lovers, poets and heroes. At the moment of their greatest achievement they were superhuman and glorious, yet their deeds were shameful inhumanities and their reward was damnation whether they lived or died. He recorded their story, which was also his, in his poems: 'These elegies are to this generation in no sense consolatory. They may be to the next. All a poet can do today is warn. That is why the true Poets must be truthful.' He was true to his destined task of warning and pleading. For himself, after many doubts and troubles, he was content to follow the gleam into darkness.

Appendix A: Biographical Notes

For abbreviations used in the Appendixes and Notes, see pp.207–8.

1 CLYDE BLACK (1872–1948)

Arthur Clyde Henderson Black apparently became a lay assistant at Dunsden in 1912. Twenty years older than WO and perhaps a recent convert (he feared relapsing 'into his old ways'), he was 'solemn' but forceful, making the household retire to bed at ten. Perhaps he led the Revival; he certainly 'cornered' Willie Montague and elicited confessions of faith from him and at least two other parishioners within two days. (*CL*, 172, 166, 168, 170). London College of Divinity, 1915. Ordained, 1917. Parishes in East London and Sussex. Unidentified in *CL* and not mentioned in JS, but a significant figure in the story of WO's religious crisis.

2 THE LÉGERS

Albine (Nénette) Léger married Jean Loisy, poet, but died young. He recorded his grief in *De la mort à l'espérance* (Paris: Beauchesne, 1952) and quoted a chapter from his wife's unfinished novel (*Tout un monde*). The chapter is a thinly disguised account of Albine and her parents starting a Bagnères holiday *c.* 1909. The relationships match many details in *CL*, although Mme Léger is portrayed as entirely virtuous. M Loisy told me some years ago that Mme Loisy had remembered her mother's English tutor with sorrow and affection. She published three complete novels, as well as translations of *Middlemarch* and *The Rainbow*; even when WO knew her she had written 'astonishing' dramas (*CL*, 271). Her father, Charles Léger, was well esteemed in dramatic circles but had lost his parents' money in experimental theatre. Mme Léger restored the family fortunes by going into partnership with her father-in-law. Like her daughter, she died young. The house at La Gailleste still stands, sadly altered, and still belongs to the Cazalas family.

3 LAURENT TAILHADE (1854–1919)

Born at Tarbes, not far from Bagnères. The latter was a place he loved. 'C'est là . . . que, pour la première fois, j'ai communié de la beauté des choses' (Mme Laurent-Tailhade, 155–6). Accounts of his life are inconsistent. Son of a drunken father and pious, devoted mother, he was correctly pious himself at first, then joined Péladan's mystic order, and eventually became an atheist. 'Le Christianisme n'étant pour lui qu'une pollution de la raison humaine' (Kolney, 47). Settled in Paris, where he became a leading figure in the Decadence (although he later dismissed the word as meaningless and described members of the group with sceptical amusement). A principal contributor to *Le Décadent*, especially of satires against bourgeois philistinism. Friendly with many famous authors; he, Verlaine and Moréas are said to have been an inseparable trio. But also an extravagant dandy, welcome in the best *salons* for his brilliant conversation. His anarchist sympathies appear in his famous comment on the Vaillant bomb in 1893 (see Ch.3, above). A year later another bomb deprived him of his left eye. Imprisoned 1901–2 for criticising France's new ally, the Tsar. Fought many duels, some of them with people offended by his satires. His politics moderated in later life. Married at least twice but responsive to male beauty. By 1914 he was fat, greedy, short of breath and weakened by absinthe and opium. Nevertheless by November he was 'shouldering a rifle' (*CL*, 295) in company with Anatole France, aged seventy, who had joined the ranks to demonstrate publicly that he had abandoned his pacifist principles in the face of invasion; presumably Tailhade was making the same point.

OEF has two letters to WO, 1 Apr 1915 (published in *Yggdrasil*, Paris, July–Aug 1939) and 1 May, both urging him to stay in Paris. On 1 April, Tailhade says he has seen M Léger but had feared to seem indiscreet 'en demandant vos nouvelles'; invites WO to translate 'Les fleurs d'Ophélie' because WO had admired it; and says he has not forgotten 'cet aprés-midi, ni le chemin de La Gailleste, ni Baudéan, ni le Casino de Bagnères'. On 1 May, he asks WO for the name of his Paris hotel and hopes they will dine together. This Paris visit, not mentioned in JS, certainly occurred; WO stayed in a hotel for at least one night and met Tailhade, who gave him *Poèmes élégiaques* on 4 May and introduced him to a composer (CL, 352, 336; JS, 321).

Mme Laurent-Tailhade, *Laurent Tailhade intime* (1924). F. Kolney, *Laurent Tailhade: son oeuvre* (1922). Noël Richard, *Le Mouvement Décadent* (1968) 157–70; *À l'aube du symbolisme* (1961) 148–53. Articles by Ezra Pound and Richard Aldington, reprinted in C. N. Pondrom, *The Road from Paris* (1974).

Tailhade's many books include *Poèmes élégiaques* (1907) and *Poèmes aristophanesques* (1904), his collected poems; *Pour la paix/ Lettre aux conscrits* (1909), the former a ?1908 lecture, the latter an essay dated 1903; *Plâtres et marbres* (1913); *La Douleur* (1914); *Quelques fantômes de jadis* (1920); and *Petuts mémoires de la vie* (1922).

4   ARTHUR JOHN BROCK (1879–1947) AND THE OUTLOOK TOWER

Son of a Scottish gentleman farmer. Edinburgh University (MB, ChB, 1901; MD, 1905). Wanted to be an artist (his mother, Florence Walker, had published verse) but his father forbade it. By 1901 he was under the spell of Patrick Geddes, writing to him about books and ideas. Most of his theories were to be based on Geddes's 'synthesising' principles. Active in Outlook Tower affairs for many years, lecturing on Bergson in 1914, leading natural-history expeditions into the Pentlands, organising the Open Spaces Committee, etc. During the war, served on a hospital ship to India, then at Aldershot. Became (as Temporary Captain, Royal Army Medical Corps) one of the three medical officers at Craiglockhart in 1917 (the others being Rivers and a Dr Ruggles, under the command of an apparently much-liked Major Bryce). After the war, ran his house in North Queensferry as a home for mental patients. He and his Swedish wife, one of the first women physiotherapists, are remembered as impractical, incessantly talkative, keen travellers, full of good works in the local community. AJB was a voracious reader with wide interests, and a prolific contributor to newspapers and professional journals. His articles show that the 'Ergotherapeutic' methods he used in 1917 were developed from his pre-war thought and practice.

Health and Conduct, with a foreword by Professor Patrick Geddes

(Williams & Norgate, 1923). This, Brock's major work, was published with a grant from Victor Branford, but so few copies were sold that the surplus was offered at a cheap rate by the Sociological Society (with its Le Play House label pasted over the original imprint). Translations: *Galen on the Natural Faculties* (Loeb, 1916); *Greek Medicine* (Dent, 1929). Articles (a few of many): 'Ergotherapy in Neurasthenia', *Edinburgh Medical Journal*, May 1911, 430–4; 'The "Moral Factor" in Physical Disease', *Practitioner*, 88 (1912) 315–21; 'The War Neurasthenic: A Note on Methods of Reintegrating him with his Environment', *Lancet*, 23 Mar 1918, 436; 'The Re-education of the Adult: The Neurasthenic in War and Peace', *Sociological Review*, 10 (Summer 1918) 25–40, repr. as *Papers for the Present*, no.4 (Sociological Society, ?1918); 'The Occupation Cure in Neurasthenia', *Edinburgh Medical Journal*, May 1923; 'Dreams, Folklore and our Present Spiritual Distress', *Hibbert Journal*, 87 (Apr 1924) 487–500.

Geddes was in India in 1917. The few Outlook Tower Association members available were struggling to keep the Tower open. Miss Wyer was standing in for AJB as secretary of the Open Spaces Committee. AJB and others tried to revive the place after the war but it seems never to have regained its old vigour. The Victorian *camera obscura* is still open to the public but Geddes's elaborate interiors have long since gone. Sources: Philip Boardman, *Patrick Geddes: Maker of the Future* (N. Carolina, 1944); Amelia Defries, *The Interpreter Geddes: The Man and His Gospel* (Routledge, 1927); Tower records and Geddes MSS (National Library of Scotland); Sociological Society papers (University of Keele).

5 ROBERT BALDWIN ROSS (1868–1918)

Art-dealer (ran the Carfax Gallery with More Adey, 1900–8) and critic (*Morning Post*, 1908–12), benefactor of the National Gallery, patron of many young artists and writers. His housekeeper, Mrs Burton, kept rooms above the flat in Half Moon Street, Mayfair, where friends, including WO, were welcome to stay. As Honorary Adviser, Imperial War Museum (from Dec 1917) and British War Memorials Committee (from Mar 1918), he played a significant part in setting up the Museum's art collection although his grand ideas for it were never realised (M. and S. Harries, *The War Artists*, 1983). He must have been deeply hurt when quietly relieved of these posts after the 1918 trial. For affectionate portraits of him, see SS (1945) 30–2 etc., and OS (1950) 98–101. Margery Ross, *Robert Ross: Friend of Friends* (Cape, 1952) contains letters to him from SS, RG, Nichols and many others. Friendship 'was the chief business of his life' (*Times* obituary, 7 Oct 1918; cf. *CL*, 585).

The many letters and biographies of Oscar Wilde shed light on Ross's earlier life. Accounts of the Ross-Douglas feud are often unreliable. For Douglas's side, see his *Autobiography* (1929); W. Sorley Brown, *Life and Genius of T. W. H. Crosland* (1928); R. Croft-Cooke, *Bosie* (1963). Ross's supporters gave him £700 and a public testimonial after the 1914 trials. *Times* trial reports: Apr, July, Nov, Dec 1914 (Douglas); 30 May – 5 June 1918 (P. Billing); 11 Jan, 4 Mar 1918 (Millard).

6 CHARLES KENNETH SCOTT MONCRIEFF (1889–1930)

Scholar at Winchester, where he rashly published a homosexual story (1908). Read Law at Edinburgh (MA, 1914). Reservist before the war. Mobilised, Aug 1914. Captain, 1915. Repeated illness. Severe leg wound, 1917; awarded Military Cross and put on administrative duties at War Office. Lived in Italy after the war but never recovered his health. Outstanding translator and imitator, his talent evident in his solutions to *Saturday Westminster* competitions; reviews and verse in *New Witness* (harsh comments on SS's war poems, 28 June 1917); translations of *Song of Roland* (Chapman & Hall, 1919), *Beowulf*, Proust, etc. Pre-war friendships with Millard, Philip Bainbrigge and others confirmed his sexual tastes. He and Bainbrigge used to exchange scholarly but highly obscene verses and parodies (d'Arch Smith, 1970). His many letters to Vyvyan Holland (Tex) are obsessively indecent.

According to his own account he met WO at RG's wedding, Jan 1918, after a day giving evidence 'ineffectively, at a Police Court'. This may refer to Millard's trial (at Bow Street? – cf. 'Bow St. cases', MS of 'Who is the god of Canongate'), which would have been a topic of conversation at Ross's flat that evening. In his one surviving letter to WO (26 May 1918, OEF, part-quoted in *CL*, 553 n.1, and not destroyed by HO, who may

not have seen its implications), CKSM says he is writing sonnets
out of 'passion' as a means of both 'vivisecting' their relationship
and discovering how Shakespeare felt(cf. OS's later reference to
CKSM's 'ghoulish process' of trying to inhabit Proust's mind –
Pearson (1978) 211). With the letter is a Shakespearian sonnet
written by CKSM on Half Moon St paper and dated 19 May
1918 by WO, who was staying above the flat for a few days then;
the poet records that he had fallen in love with WO and had
tried to 'draw thy heart to me', but had been found 'unworthy'.
Despite this rejection, he praises WO's poetic 'merit' and hopes
to share in his future fame. On 7 June the *New Witness* published
another 'Sonnet' by 'C.K.S.M.':

> Thinking Love's Empire lay along that way
>> Where the new-duggen grave of Friendship gaped,
> We fell therein and, weary, slept till day.
>> But with the dawn you rose, and clean escaped,
> Strode honourably homeward . . . .
>>>>>> . . . you were gone from sight
> To Honour in an honest House of Shame . . .

The faint traces of 'To Eros' here seem to link this 'coded' poem
with WO. One more 'Sonnet' appeared in the same periodical
on 10 January 1919:

>> When in the centuries of time to come
>>> Men shall be happy and rehearse thy fame,
>> Should I be spoken of then, or they grow dumb –
>>> Recall thy glory and forget thy shame?

The poet goes on to say he does not care, since neither fame nor
'any breath of scandal' could shake him if he were 'in Heaven
with thee . . . Where two contented ghosts together lie'. The echo
of 'I am the ghost of Shadwell stair' ('I with another ghost am
lain'), a poem with which CKSM was somehow associated, is
unlikely to be coincidence. It seems probable that both the *New
Witness* sonnets were among those addressed to WO in May 1918.
A revised version of the second one, entitled 'To W.E.S.O.' and
dated 1918, was published as one of the three dedicatory poems
to friends killed in the war (Bainbrigge, WO, Ian Mackenzie)
which preface CKSM's *Roland*, in place of the dedication to 'Mr
W.O.' which he had drafted in 1918. Changes in wording include

a more discreet fourth line, 'Recall these numbers and forget this name?', as well as 'envy' for 'scandal' and 'stay' for 'lie'.

The cryptic references to shame in these sonnets may allude to WO's alleged cowardice or, more probably, to his relationship with CKSM. There have always been rumours about this relationship, some of them emanating from RG, a notoriously unreliable source (cf. Fussell, 1975, 216, on the 'fatuous, erroneous or preposterous' material in *Goodbye to All That*). Hearsay at several removes is at best doubtful evidence, but there seem to be some grounds for supposing that CKSM at least tried to seduce WO. RG repeated to Martin Seymour-Smith a story from Ross that CKSM had not only tried but succeeded, having got WO drunk, and that WO had been deeply distressed. At any rate, something seems to have happened to cause 'scandal' in Ross's circle, and that may help to explain why SS (1945, 82–3) and OS loathed CKSM. RG also said that WO himself told him in 1918 that he had picked up young men in Bordeaux but had never overcome guilt feelings sufficiently to form any lasting relationship; since RG had by then repudiated the fervent Uranianism he had expressed to Carpenter in 1914, his enthusiasm for WO cooled a little after this confession. Mr Seymour-Smith, who has kindly told me about his conversation with RG on these matters, is convinced that for once RG can be trusted. There is no evidence, incidentally, that there was any physical relationship between WO and SS; SS told RG in a letter that he had never been physically attracted to WO.

C. K. Scott Moncrieff: Memories and Letters, ed. J. M. Scott Moncrieff and L. W. Lunn (1931), includes some verse. CKSM's published memories of WO: letter, *New Witness*, 2 Jan 1920, 117; 'The Poets there are. III – Wilfred Owen', *New Witness*, 10 Dec 1920, 574–5; 'Wilfred Owen' (letter), *Nation and Athenaeum*, 26 Mar 1921, 909–10.

7 HAROLD OWEN AS FAMILY HISTORIAN

By all accounts a charming man of complete integrity, HO knew nothing of literature or scholarship and was in some ways highly eccentric. *JFO*, his absorbing memoirs of the Owen family, is written with considerable artistic licence. Similarities between his memories and WO's poems *may* illuminate the poems or may reflect his long years of guarding and puzzling over WO's MSS, which he hoped one day to edit. Even his one specific gloss on a poem is suspect: *JFO*, I, 176–7, describes his remark that he had feet of gold after a family walk through buttercups, and WO's ensuing comment that 'Harold's boots are blessed with gold'. This has been accepted by all commentators (including myself) as giving the origin of the 'blessed with gold' image in 'Spring Offensive'. But in his 'Working Copy' of EB (OEF) HO wrote against the image, 'The family walk home from Uffington on early summer evenings through the water-meadows when we would look with delighted wonder on our shoes and stockings flushed with gold – unconscious recollection?' This note is convincing, with its intuitive understanding of poem and poet, but the published account may be an imaginative version which quotes from the poem rather than from an actual conversation. The way in which HO's remark is ignored by the family and is taken over by WO, who rewords it to sound priggishly 'poetic', is symbolic, like so much of *JFO*, of the psychological burden that HO laboured under as the obscure, cruelly uneducated younger brother.

HO, and SO before him, did their best to control public perception of WO. It was on WO's own instructions that SO burned 'a sack full' of his papers (EB, 3) but HO thought later that she had probably destroyed more (HO to EB, 13 Oct 1947, Tex). Certainly, remarkably few letters to WO survive. As the portrait of WO the archetypal soldier poet in EB's 1931 memoir is SO's, who supplied all the key information for it, so that in *JFO* of the idealist indifferent to immediate human ties is HO's. Always insisting that only 'members of the family' were able to understand the poet, HO turned away researchers (notably DW) in his efforts to prevent all discussion of WO's personal life. He destroyed some of WO's letters and mutilated others. One of his chief motives was dread that someone might raise the 'frightful implication' of homosexuality. He wrote in 'desperate anxiety' to EB (16 Oct 1950, Tex) for help when some enquiry was made, saying he had 'taxed' WO on the subject but WO had denied all personal involvement although admitting 'abstract' interest because homosexuality seemed to attract so many intelligent people. At a late stage of writing *JFO*, HO inserted a 1918 conversation between the brothers (III, 163–6) in which he revises the information he had given EB. Instead of 'taxing' WO, HO innocently asks for enlightenment about goings-on between sailors, whereupon WO says he had intended making a similar request but since they both knew nothing they might as well talk of other things. No doubt this represents the truth as far as HO saw it. A friend of CKSM and Ross would not have asked for illumination from a puritanical younger brother, but WO's words can be read as regret that HO's evident disgust had prevented confidences. By contrast, as WO may have known, one of SS's younger brothers had eased SS's pre-war worries by admitting to being contentedly homosexual.

If WO did not confide in HO he seems to have done so in ELG, giving him the 'key' to many poems. (CL, 508 – the omitted words refer to one of ELG's girlfriends) and even referring mysteriously to '*mon petit ami*' in Scarborough (*CL*, 544). But ELG says these things were too long ago for him to remember.

Appendix B: Owen's Manuscripts and their Chronology

The odd history of WO's MSS has yet to be unravelled, but almost all of them are now at last in libraries and available to researchers. There are three main collections.

1   BL. Two volumes of verse MSS bought by public subscription in 1934. It seems possible that some or all of these folios were never returned to the family after being lent to Edith Sitwell and SS for *Poems* (1920). Add. MS 43720 (bound for SS before 1930?) consists of the drafts treated as more or less definitive for *Poems* (1920). Add. MS 43721 is a larger volume of further drafts and fragments, read by EB for *Poems* (1931); many of these MSS remained unpublished until *CPF*, and researchers were not supposed to quote from them.

2   OEF. A large, apparently random collection of loose MSS retained by the family. There seems to be no record of why these were kept or what state WO's papers were in at his death, but the family's storage methods were haphazard and these MSS may simply have been overlooked before Mary Owen's death in 1956 (cf. *CL*, 1). Accompanying notes show that HO began to assemble them at about that time in the hope of preparing an edition. It seems that only Patric Dickinson and CDL saw this material before Jon Stallworthy was appointed official biographer and editor. The verse MSS have now been arranged in *CPF* order and numbered by Professor Stallworthy. Other MSS include *Hydra* editorials, some notes on Keats and Dickens (for talks at Craiglockhart?), and fragments of letters (see Lett). ELG has generously added all the WO MSS and books in his possession. OEF also has WO's library and many other

202

items to do with WO and HO.

3   Tex. MSS (described in detail in Lett) of WO's letters home, unfortunately sold after *CL* was completed. Also a curious assortment of letters, photocopies, MSS, etc., connected with WO and other war poets, gathered in the 1950s by Joseph Cohen for a projected 'Wilfred Owen War Poetry Collection'. Whether this was a serious project or just a means of persuading donors to present material is not clear. The more interesting WO items are mentioned in my chapter notes. Tex also has EB's papers, many letters from SS to friends, and other relevant material.

I have not seen the originals of WO's letters to SS, recently bought by Columbia University, nor the few MSS still in private hands.

My own edition, *WPO*, which was put together in 1968–70 during HO's lifetime, had to be based on BL MSS only. I had no access to the material now in OEF, nor was I permitted – by the publishers – to make the substantial changes to the EB–CDL text that were clearly desirable. I was even forbidden to restore WO's 'moans in man' in 'Insensibility' on the grounds that EB and CDL had preferred his cancelled 'mourns' and they as poets knew best. The *WPO* text was an advance on CDL, but *CPF* goes much further.

In general *CPF* and *CL* are meticulously accurate. A few amendments to *CL* are suggested elsewhere (Lett) and to *CPF* in my quotations and chapter notes. Professor Stallworthy and I exchanged many letters but I have not attempted to check his text against MSS except for the passages I have quoted. His generosity and kindness over the years seem poorly rewarded if I criticise any aspect of *CPF*; his edition is a splendid achievement and a great asset to scholarship. But researchers need to bear some caveats in mind. *CPF* cannot show all draft workings, and the conversion of heavily revised manuscript into uniform print has sometimes obscured the sequence of WO's alterations or the relationship between one word and another. Some drafts may still be sundered from the poems they were written for, and a few may be yoked mistakenly together (perhaps I should take responsibility for the debatable separation of 'Purgatorial passions' from 'Mental Cases' and 'Earth's wheels' from 'Strange Meeting'). The arrangement of poems in the order of their final drafts must never be mistaken for the order of composition; WO copied out a lot of early verse in 1917–18 so *CPF* has to put juvenilia among mature work. Finally, researchers should be aware that dates ascribed to MSS are often open to argument, although *CPF* is far more accurate than any previous authority.

One representative problem may illustrate the complexity of the evidence involved in establishing dates for MSS. MS letters show that a particular watermark is invariably limited to one brief period; it follows that any verse MSS with that watermark probably belong to the same period. But this rule is less reliable from mid 1917 because WO bought special paper for his 'job' as a poet and only used odd sheets for letters. Society Bond paper (SB), for example, is used for only four letters (late Jan–28 Feb 1918) but for drafts of eleven poems. *CPF* ascribes the drafts of 'My Shy Hand' (final draft), 'Sunrise' (final) and 'I am the ghost of Shadwell Stair' (first) to January–February, presumably on the basis of the watermarked letters. Puzzlingly, the only drafts of 'Schoolmistress' and 'The Letter', and the final drafts of 'A Tear Song', 'Strange Meeting', 'Dulce' and 'Conscious' are ascribed to January–*March*; the evidence for extending the limit to March in these cases is not clear. (The watermark is also taken as proof that 'The Letter' was 'written' in January–March; that may well be the date of the surviving draft, but the Sassoonish style suggests the poem was first composed at Craiglockhart. There must have been at least one preliminary draft before the SB fair copy; WO certainly fair-copied many of his 1917 poems in 1918.) Moreover, *CPF* implies that the final (SB) draft of 'Insensibility' may be no later than January. (The eleventh of the SB drafts is the first complete version of 'Exposure' but *CPF* does not need to date this because there is an earlier one-line fragment which can itself be dated.) But all these dates seem undermined by one more SB MS, the first of WO's two tables of contents (*CPF*, 538), which lists several poems ascribed by *CPF* to April–May (i.e. late March – early June, the Borrage Lane period). It would be inconsistent with the principles governing *CPF*'s use of watermarks to suggest that this was a stray sheet or that the April–May titles were additions to the list. *CPF* is uncertain in the date it ascribes to the two lists of contents ('March–June', 186, '20 May – 30 July', 537) but it does not suggest that the SB list could be as early as January–February. The strong probability is that both lists of contents were drawn up at Borrage Lane. If WO used one sheet of SB there, *any* otherwise undated SB MS *may* belong to that period. I think one has to conclude that SB was one of the several types of paper which he had available between January and early June 1918. It is a matter of instinct where one places most SB drafts within that period, but I incline to March–June (Borrage Lane) in general. WO composed new poems there and 'realized many defectuosities in older compositions' (*CL*, 543), so one would expect the drafts to include revised 1917 work as well as fresh material. He had been giving time at Scarborough to 'Sonnets' (hence, perhaps, the numerous fair copies of sonnets and lyrics on Pompeian Parchment) but then the war changed. 'Strange Meeting', in particular, seems to me to be a response to the carnage that began on the Western Front on 21 March.

Appendix C: *The Hydra*

OEF has a complete set of nos 1–12 (fortnightly, 28 Apr – 29 Sep 1917) of *The Hydra: Journal of the Craiglockhart War Hospital* and six of the monthly New Series (Nov 1917 – Jan 1918, May–July 1918). WO seems to have become editor for no. 7 (21 July). No. 10 (1 Sep) includes a version of two 'Dead-Beat' stanzas, and 'Song of Songs'; no. 12 (29 Sep) includes 'The Next War'. All three pieces are anonymous, like WO's editorials and prose contributions (which are in the whimsical style then considered appropriate). The November issue reports Mr Owen as being on the Debating Society Committee and as having given an 'interesting' lecture on the classification of soils on 1 October. Many other hospital activities are recorded. WO was succeeded in October by J. B. Salmond, whose experience as a professional writer is evident in the great improvements in design and organisation introduced for the New Series. Salmond said later (letter in Edinburgh University Library, microfilm in Tex) that WO acted as his sub-editor and was responsible for recruiting November contributions from G. K. Chesterton and John Drinkwater. The editorial says Wells and Bennett were also approached (presumably at SS's suggestion). Drinkwater's MS, a poem called 'Reciprocity', is still in OEF; the poem was included in his *Tides* (1917), which is no doubt why WO asked for the book as a Christmas present. The May–July 1918 issues were presumably sent to WO by AJB, who contributed an article in each of them on Edinburgh Regional Survey. AJB marked these articles (with a characteristic cross often found in his own MSS) and a poem which laments that Craiglockhart patients, who apparently had to wear an identifying tab, were stared at in Princes Street ('all people think us mad'), an experience WO may well have suffered in 1917. The January issue announces that Mr Owen's poem on Antaeus will appear in February, but no copies of the missing 1918 issues have yet been traced.

See also DH, 'Some Notes' (1982) and 'A Sociological Cure' (1977).

Notes

The following abbreviations are used in the Notes and Appendixes.

AJB	Arthur John Brock
BL0,1; BL1, 4v; etc.	British Library Additional Manuscript 43720, folio 1; 43721, folio 4 verso; etc.
BNY	Berg Collection (Marsh correspondence), New York Public Library
Casebook	*Poetry of the First World War: A Casebook*, ed. Dominic Hibberd (1981)
CDL	C. Day Lewis *or* his edition of *The Collected Poems of Wilfred Owen* (1963)
CKSM	Charles Kenneth Scott Moncrieff
CL	*Wilfred Owen: Collected Letters*, ed. Harold Owen and John Bell (1967)
CPF	*Wilfred Owen: The Complete Poems and Fragments*, ed. Jon Stallworthy (1983). Numerals refer to *pages*, not poems
DH	Dominic Hibberd
DW	Dennis Welland
EB	Edmund Blunden *or* his edition of *The Poems of Wilfred Owen* (1931)
ELG	E. Leslie Gunston
Geo	Dominic Hibberd, 'Wilfred Owen and the Georgians', *Review of English Studies*, 30 (Feb 1979) 28–40
HO	Harold Owen (brother)
JFO	Harold Owen, *Journey from Obscurity*, 3 vols (1963–5)
JS	Jon Stallworthy, *Wilfred Owen: A Biography* (1974)
Lett	Dominic Hibberd, 'Wilfred Owen's Letters: Some Additions, Amendments and Notes', *Library*, 4 (Sep 1982) 273–87
OEF	English Faculty Library, Oxford (Wilfred Owen Collection). Numerals refer to MSS in this collection
OS	Osbert Sitwell
RG	Robert Graves
SO	Susan Owen (mother)
SS	Siegfried Sassoon
Tex	Harry Ransom Humanities Research Center, University of Texas at Austin
TO	Tom Owen (father)
WO	Wilfred Owen
WPO	*Wilfred Owen: War Poems and Others*, ed. Dominic Hibberd (1973)

Page references to *CPF* are not given when the title or first line of the poem or fragment is obvious.

Books and articles are identified only by surname of author/editor and date of publication (of the edition referred to), except that an abbreviated title is given when confusion might otherwise result: AJB (1924); Bäckman (1979); DH, 'Rival Pieces' (1976); etc. All items thus referred to are listed in full in the Bibliography or Appendixes.

A reference to '*CL* [Lett]' indicates that a quotation from a letter involves an amendment or addition to the *CL* text.

In some cases several consecutive references are contained in one note and identified where necessary by key words.

Readers unfamiliar with *CPF* may find the following list of fragments helpful; it includes those I have discussed as P1–6 under 'Perseus'.

P1: 'What have I done, O God, what have I done', BL1, 155–6v (*CPF*, 467–70).

P2: 'The cultivated Rose', BL1, 153 (*CPF*, 465–6).

P3: 'Shook and were bowed before embracing winds', OEF 216 (*CPF*, 464).

P4: 'The sun, far fallen in the afternoon', OEF 209 (*CPF*, 449).

P5: 'About the winter forest loomed', OEF 208 (*CPF*, 448).

P6: 'Speech for King', BL1, 154 (*CPF*, 470).

The fragment about Broxton: 'Instead of dew, descended on the moors', OEF 203 (*CPF*, 433–4).

The fragment about touching a boy's hand: 'We two had known each other', OEF 204v (*CPF*, 437–8).

The following titles used (and in some cases invented) by earlier editors may still be more familiar than the more accurate versions given in *CPF*:

'All sounds have been as music', *now* 'I know the music' (*CPF*, 485).

'Antaeus', *now* 'The Wrestlers' (*CPF*, 520).

'Bold Horatius', *now* 'Schoolmistress' (*CPF*, 139).

'Bugles sang', *now* 'But I was looking at the permanent stars' (*CPF*, 487).

'Shadwell Stair', *now* 'I am the ghost of Shadwell Stair' (*CPF*, 183).

'Sonnet to a Child', *now* 'Sweet is your antique body, not yet young' (*CPF*, 129).

'To a Comrade in Flanders', *now* 'A New Heaven' (*CPF*, 82).

'To my Friend', *now* 'With an Identity Disc' (*CPF*, 96).

'Voices': *see* 'Bugles sang'.

CHAPTER 1. THE ORIGINS OF A POETHOOD
[1893–1911]

1   WO's surviving books and other possessions may be assumed to be in OEF unless otherwise stated.

2   *CL*, 271.

3   'Instead of dew . . . ' (*CPF*, 433–4). This 1914 fragment says 'ten ye[ars]' have elapsed since Broxton. For another reference to the Bagnères moon, see *CL*, 464.

4   *CPF*, 68 (Welsh blood). *CL*, 581 (forefathers), 256 (uncle, aunt).

5   *CL*, 68, 186 n.1. Cf. 'Perversity', line 14.

6   *CPF* ascribes 'To Poesy' to 1909–10 but without clear evidence, and
     'Written in a Wood, September 1910' to 1910 on the basis of the title.
     The wood seems to be Hampstead, visited by WO in September 1911,
     but '1911' in the title would have required 'ninety-one' in the poem,
     ruining the metre.

7   Quoted by Patric Dickinson in a BBC talk, 17 Aug 1953 (script at Tex).
     HO showed Dickinson some early MSS, now lost, including verse (*CPF*,
     xxv) and another prose sketch (for a sonnet on poetic desire). CDL, 14–
     15, quotes a third sketch.

8   In WO's Keats, I, 10–11 and 14–15.

9   *CL*, 273 n.1.

10   JS, 78, and *CPF*, 409n., need slight amendment. Keats's house was not
     yet open to visitors. The Dilke Collection, including MSS and a lock of
     hair (*CPF*, 447) was presented to the Hampstead library in 1911 and
     displayed there. (Information from Assistant Curator, Keats House.)

11   *CPF*, 447, 409.

12   T. S. Eliot, 'Little Gidding'. Eliot's many sources may include 'Strange
     Meeting', a poem he admired (see his contribution to Walsh, 1964).

13   *CL*, 112.

14   For titles, inscriptions, etc., see JS, 308–23, and DH, 'WO's Library'
     (1977). When WO's books were transferred to OEF, the Librarian, Miss
     M. Weedon, shelved them as HO had listed them in 1920.

15   Keats to Taylor, 24 Apr 1818; cf. *CL*, 325, and 'To Poesy'. *CL*, 150
     (King). Lett, 286–7 (Collingwood).

16   SO's (Anglican) Evangelicalism is shown by her attendance at the
     Evangelical St Julian's rather than her parish church, the Abbey, despite
     a steep walk. WO's name is on war memorials in both churches, in the
     former as a 'member of the congregation', in the latter as a parishioner.
     Among the notes in SO's Bible is 'Feb 22nd 1909 Wilfred spoke at
     Frankwell', perhaps a record of his first public talk or prayer. See also
     Alec Paton in Walsh (1964).

17   *CPF*, 447.

18   *CL*, 118, 150, 106.

19   *JFO*, I, 120. Unlike HO, WO praised SO's self-sacrifice (*CL*, 32, 479).

20   SO to EB, n.d., *c*.1930 (Tex).

21   JS, 27; *CL*, 68. JS tends, I think, to overrate SO's intellectual ability and
     interests.

22   *CL*, 99. I assume WO is answering a comment from SO.

23   JS, 28; *JFO*, I, 103. Here as elsewhere JS seems a little too ready to
     accept HO's record. HO was writing years later about an event which
     occurred in his absence when he was five.

24   See DH, 'Images' (1974).

CHAPTER 2. THE FIRST CRISIS: RELIGION [1911–13]

1   'O World of many worlds'.

2   *CL*, 75.

3   *CL*, 102. *CPF*, 394 (CPF may be mistaken in treating this fragment as part of 'Spring not . . . '; the two fragments differ in form and subject). WO was worried about his heart at Dunsden (cf. *CPF*, 36; *CL*, 131, 271).

4   *CL*, 273 n.1.

5   *CL*, 123.

6   *CPF*, 16, 397. *CPF* follows my suggestion in identifying the first piece as a 'chorus' rather than a hymn. Evangelical choruses are informal verses on scriptural themes, to be chanted at meetings; this one is on God's promises. WO composed another in February (*CL*, 115).

7   For details see DH, 'Rival Pieces' (1976).

8   *CL*, 122, 73 (Sept 1912: letter misdated in *CL*, see Lett, 278). Beckett (1879); WO's copy has a Reading bookshop label.

9   Rossetti (n.d.) 158.

10   *CL*, 93.

11   'I simply daren't be sincere' (*CL*, 155).

12   Black: see Appendix A1.

13   *CL*, 174. Cf. n. 38 below.

14   'O hard condition!' (*CL*, 181).

15   JS, 85–6. I quote from MS (OEF 259v) with slight simplification. The Keats quotations are from 'Eve of St Agnes' and 'Lamia'.

16   'Spring Offensive'.

17   *CL*, 131. WO misquotes from Magnus (1902) 146; his copy has a Reading bookshop label. With 'wolfish', cf. Dickens, *Hard Times*, ii.vi ('Reality will take a wolfish turn, and make an end of you'); 'press upon' echoes Keats (to Dilke, 21 Sep 1818).

18   *CPF*, 387. Symonds (1878) quotes Mrs Shelley's note on *The Revolt*.

19   *CL*, 96, 109–10. For details see Geo, 28–9.

20   *CPF*, 396.

21   Monro (1911) 130. *CPF*, 372.

22   Geo, 30 (quoted, *CPF*, 107).

23   Monro was friendly with Carpenter in 1910–11. See Grant (1967).

24   *CL*, 167. Cf. Lord Henry Wotton's typically Decadent thought, 'One could never pay too high a price for any sensation' – Wilde (1948) 55.

25   *CL*, 171.

26   *CL*, 206 (phantasies), 212 (horrors), 235 (phantasms: here he records that they began in late February 1913).

27   The scene of Perseus showing Andromeda the head's reflection in a well or pool occurs several times in ancient and Pre-Raphaelite art. With WO's description of Medusa, cf. his feeling 'helpless' before the 'thrilling eyes' of a girl in a painting, 1912 (Lett, 278).

28   *CL*, 135, 137 (Borrow); 153 (bicycle). Discussed in DH, 'Images' (1974).

29   *CL*, 339.

30   *CPF*, 12. JS, 71, seems to overstress the conclusion to this poem; WO is not 'in the throes of an almost Christlike suffering' but enjoying the pleasure of *recovering* from indigestion. 'Bliss' may imply sexuality or it may refer to religious ecstasy (with 'dangerous air', cf. 'madness-giving air' in 'Unto what pinnacles').

31   *CPF*, 228 (mother-arms), 378 (rapture).

32   *CL*, 175 ('On my Songs', Jan 1913).

33   *CL*, 186 n.1.

34   *CL*, 161. Tom Coulthard suggests a parallel with Trelawny's snatching the heart out of Shelley's burning corpse, a story WO had read in Symonds (1878).
35   *CL*, 536.
36   *CL*, 137.
37   *CPF*, 403.
38   *CL*, 400 (eyes, school), 123 (tea), 119–20 (piano), 118 (Ramble), 174–5 (furor). *CPF*, 437 ('We two had known each other'; *CPF* follows my suggestion in identifying the subject as Rampton). The Librarian of Reading School tells me V. C. Rampton (born 23 Nov 1899) entered the school in September 1915 and left in July 1917 (for war service?).
39   Draft refers to pines, beeches, one June/August day (*CPF*, 207). I am not quite convinced by *CPF*, 58, that a parish outing is referred to since it was over before dusk and WO was not alone with one child (*CL*, 145).
40   *CL*, 181.
41   *CPF*, 269 (draft). Cf. the sermon WO read to an old parishioner: 'Not more frail are flowers . . . or more fleeting meteors than Human Life' (*CL*, 154).
42   *CPF*, 413. *CL*, 400; Simon Wormleighton recently met an elderly Dunsden resident who remembered how Wigan used to 'preach and preach and preach'.
43   *WPO*, 31 (quoted, *CPF*, 72). Other sources of WO's imagery may include Tennyson, 'The Silent Voices', and Keats, 'The Poet'.
44   DH (1975), 10; Geo, 30 (both quoted, *CPF*, 74). With the image in the poem, cf. E. Vedder's Decadent painting, *Superest Invictus Amor* (P. Jullien, *Dreamers of Decadence*, 1971, pl. 71).

CHAPTER 3. AESTHETE IN FRANCE [1913–15]

1   *JFO*, iii, 52–6. Typically, HO says WO did not start the 'Sir Thomas' rumour. But who else could have done? It paid off. The Légers lived in one of the grandest streets in town. Miss de la Touche had been governess to princesses, her sister was a baroness, her nephews went to an English public school; WO told her he was 'preparing for Oxford', more hopeful than true (*CL*, 299,305).
2   WO had affected purple ink, tie, slippers (*CL*, 111, 127). His early Aestheticism also appeared in 'Wilfred's Church' and burying SO in flowers (*JFO*, i, 77–8, 150–1). (Flower burials occur in Morris, 'The Wind', and d'Annunzio, *The Triumph of Death*.)
3   I use the word loosely to include more specific movements such as Symbolism and Decadence. For more substantial accounts, see Carter (1958), Gaunt (1945), Kermode (1957), Nordau (1895), Praz (1970), Stephan (1974), and many others.
4   Tailhade: see Appendix A3.
5   Baudelaire, 'Le soleil s'est noyé dans son sang qui se fige' ('Harmonie du Soir'); Flaubert, 'Legende de St Julien l'Hospitalier'; d'Annunzio, see Praz (1970) 279; Wilde, 'Panthea'; Hardy, *Tess*, xxi; Dickens, *Our Mutual Friend*, iv.i. Cf. SS, 'Last Meeting'; Rossetti, 'A Last Confession'; Flecker, *Hassan*; etc.

6   Nordau (1895) 2.
7   'Hymn to Proserpine'.
8   Locke (1905) 77. The best and easiest way to get bloodshed, says the character, will be to challenge and 'exterminate Prussian Lieutenants'.
9   Brooke to St John Lucas, Oct 1907 (MS at King's College, Cambridge). Seven years later Brooke really did see fire and men hurt in Antwerp, finding 'release there' ('Peace') as he had lightly hoped in 1907.
10   Quoted in Gaunt (1945) 119.
11   Wilde (1948) 90.
12   But it was also to have had type like *Before Dawn* (BL1, 163v).
13   The 'chasms' round mad eyes in 'Mental Cases' began as 'blue chasms' in 'Purgatorial passions'. Such marks usually signify sexual excess in Decadent imagery.
14   *CL*, 441.
15   *CL*, 431.
16   *CPF*, 465, a 'Perseus' MS. A list of pararhymes headed 'Nocturne' on a draft of 'The Imbecile' (JS, 105) matches pararhymes in 'Has your soul sipped' (1917), a poem WO might well have intended to call 'Nocturne', and may thus be much later than 'The Imbecile' itself (1913). For WO's rhymes and their French–Welsh origins, see Bäckman (1979), DH (1978), Masson (1955), DW (1950), etc. It would be pleasing to prove us all wrong by finding that his pararhymes originated as a solution to a literary competition, as 'The Imbecile' did – DH, 'Problems A' (1980).
17   *CL*, 234 [Lett, 280].
18   *CL*, 243–5. WO quotes the 'One remains' line from *Adonais* in this letter, which reinforces the link between Henriette and the sonnet. He had recently been given a Shelley for his twenty-first birthday.
19   *CL*, 280, 295.
20   Léger family: see Appendix A2.
21   *CL*, 271.
22   Appendix A2.
23   *CL*, 271–2. WO's playing of Chopin was admired at home (*JFO*, ii, 756; cf. ELG, 'Music'). The *Marche* was one of his favourites.
24   The book cover in OEF corresponds with the one in the photograph.
25   *CPF*, 435–6. 'Ballade élégiaque pour le morose après-midi' (*morose* was a favourite Decadent adjective).
26   WO seems to have lent the first volume to SS, the second – now lost – to Monro (*CL*, 361, 493), which implies he was proud of the friendship despite HO's later attempt to play it down (*CL*, 2).
27   Tailhade (1913). For sources for this paragraph, see Appendix A3.
28   *CL*, 282.
29   Kolney (1922) 32.
30   Lett, 286.
31   Cf. Tailhade's titles: 'Lundi de Pâques', 'Vendredi-Saint'.
32   *CPF*, 433–8.
33   *CL*, 286, 291.
34   *CL*, 350, 348. I assume WO read *Bovary* in 1915. A phrase from it is echoed in 'A Palinode' (Oct); see *CPF*, 78, but the point was first made by Bentley (1970).
35   Steiner (1971) 25.
36   *CL*, 347.

37 *Pace* DW (quoted, *CPF*, 70), the poem seems nearer Tailhade and Flaubert than Wilde and Swinburne. Cf. Salammbô's prayer to the moon (*Salammbô*, iii).

38 *CPF*, 444.

39 *CL*, 322 (novelists); 320 [Lett, 281] (soundings); 285 (hospital).

40 See Appendix A6.

41 *CL*, 333 (writings, trees), 325 (boy), 352 (heather), 295–6 and 300 (useful to England), 342 (Vigny quotation).

42 *CPF*, 471, 545, gives some dating-evidence. P1–2 could as well be 1914 as 1915, I think. P3–5 have the same watermark as the 'certain writings' letter (Apr 1915). *CPF* groups under 'Perseus' only P3, P2, P1, P6, in that order. P1 is a large double sheet, of which *CPF* treats the first and second sides as separate pieces, breaking the fragment in mid stanza. The third side is blank. The fourth has four isolated lines about Pluto (*CPF*, 470). Other MSS which may be 'Perseus' work include *CPF*, 528 (winged sandals); 492, interesting for its links with 'Strange Meeting'; 463; and possibly 'Purgatorial passions' (455).

43 *CL*, 439. ELG has no recollection of 'Icarus' but it may have begun as a tribute to Gustav Hamel, a celebrated aviator who had given displays from the racecourse in front of the Owens' house and who crashed into the sea in 1914. There is a poem to his memory in ELG's book. ELG once told me the cousins liked H. J. Draper's painting *The Lament for Icarus* (Tate).

44 My readings differ from *CPF*. In addition to those shown in my reconstructions, I read 'no heat', 'soul' 'drenched the fires', for *CPF*'s 'us heal', 'rough', 'drenched the flowers'. I think WO wrote 'I touch the god', altered it in stages to 'I hav touched the godess', and then left it unrevised. MS shows that the two lines in *CPF* about Persephone's body and soul were afterthoughts.

45 Quoted from BL1, 11, the earlier draft.

46 For Decadent hermaphrodite imagery, see Busst (1967).

47 MS appears to read 'feel' but I assume WO intended 'fell'. With WO's details in 'Perseus', 'Storm' and 'Supposed Confessions', cf. Morris, 'The Doom of King Acrisius' (*Earthly Paradise*), including: Zeus as sunlight, thunder; Perseus a 'fair' child; 'aged crone'; Gorgon's head reflected in a pool. WO was reading about Morris in 1915 and thinking of poetic creation as flight (*CL*, 315–16). With Danae's captivity, cf. Henriette's 'plaints of captivity . . . she is watched and warded everywhere' (*CL*, 244).

48 *CL*, 408. *CL*, 334, mentions Perseus as a sailor, referring to HO's tribulations in the Navy.

49 *CL*, 348, 353.

50 *CL*, 458.

51 *CPF*, 463.

52 Endymion falls from love into hell, where he meets Age. The blank verse of P1 and P6 reads like a crude imitation of speeches in *Atalanta*. Pluto and Persephone: appear in P1 only, perhaps dropped thereafter.

53 WO mentions buying 'Casts ' to ELG in 1915 (*CL*, 355). The statuette, presumably a copy of a Roman votive figure, came to ELG after WO's death. Cf. 'By Hermes, I will fly' (*CL*, 408).

54 Brown (1934) 95.

55   *CPF*, 76. See also Lett, 287.
56   *CL*, 332.
57   *CL*, 341. WO knew the area, his uncle having been a doctor there.

CHAPTER 4. PREPARING FOR WAR
[Oct 1915 – Dec 1916]

1   Chapple (1970) 262 (war scare). A. Paton to Joseph Cohen, 7 Feb 1954 (Tex) (toy soldiers). *Christian*, 22 July 1912, 15.

2   Pound (1964) 55.

3   Beerbohm (1911) 291. Before the sacrifice the *Marche funèbre* was played and grey morning clouds 'massed themselves . . . an irresistible great army' (207). Cf. Ch.3, n. 23, above, and dawn 'massing . . . her . . . army . . . in ranks on . . . ranks of grey' ('Exposure').

4   ' . . . the highest moral act possible, according to the Highest Judge' (1916 – *CL*, 387).

5   Murry (1921), in *Casebook*.

6   *CPF*, 151, 487–8. *CPF* suggests July 1917 for the 'Artillery' sonnet without clear evidence; content seems pre-SS but the poem could have been written in France, possibly in response to Sorrell's challenge in March (*CL*, 441).

7   *CL*, 304. Cf. 160 (Severn), 310 ('the End'; quoting the prophecy).

8   *CPF*, 500–9. WO probably meant this poem when he referred to 'that War Ballad' in 1916 and the 'Ballad' in 1917 (*CL*, 416, 476). A 1915 version was called 'The Ballad of Purchase Moneys' (cf. Acts 20:28).

9   *Christian*, 3 Sep 1914. WO probably saw this number (*CL*, 279).

10   *CL*, 484. For examples of soldier-Christ poems and paintings, see DH and Onions (1986).

11   *CL*, 388.

12   *CL*, 381.

13   *CL*, 393. *CPF*, 114, and JS, 139, identify the addressee as Johnny de la Touche, but I suspect Professor Stallworthy attaches rather too much importance to him. If the poem refers to old memories, there are several more likely addressees: if it refers to 10 May 1916, de la Touche is unlikely to have been able to visit London from his Somerset boarding-school on a termtime weekday.

14   *CPF*, 223. Draft version quoted for its botanical metaphor ('die back') and the detail that war memorials were beginning to appear even in 1916. Another draft substitutes 'brows' (cf. 'Anthem') for 'breasts', more appropriate to 'Acropole'. Another title: 'To a Comrade in Athens' (hence 'Acropole') or 'Flanders'. The comrade may have been Lt Briggs, 'my closest chum', who was warned he would be sent out in September (*CL*, 391, 407). The many current rumours may have included talk of being sent to Athens, where the Navy was involved in a local crisis, but in the event Briggs no doubt went to Flanders.

15   *CPF*, 228.

16   Draft last line. With 'mock', cf. 'mockeries' in 'Anthem'.

17   *CL*, 492.

18   See DH, 'Rival Pieces' (1976) and 'The End' (1983).
19   Kyle: Monro MSS (BL Add. 57739); *The Times*, 17–23 Mar 1922.
     'Macdonald' was a major publisher of 'soldier-poetry'. For WO's Little
     Books, see Lett, 287, and Geo, 32. 'Minor Poems' MS (OEF) includes:

> Points to note about my Sonnets
> 1 They are 'correct' as regards rime, but the system of rime is not
>   necessarily classical.
> 2 [They range from the simplest to the] Such as I send you here
>   conform to the essential   of a sonnet unity of idea – and a
>   solemn dignity in the treatment. At the same [time I] The only
>   corrections I have made have been [on the side] by way of
>   simplification. I can write nothing simpler, & at the same time,
>   poetical than the Sonnet 'The One Remains'.

'Sonatas': *CL*, 454; BL1, 163v. In the numbered sequence of MSS (all
watermarked 'Pompeian Parchment', so second half of 1917 or first half
of 1918), 1–9 are the sonnets numbered 100–8 in *CPF*; 10–14 are missing
(but *CPF* nos 95 and 113–16 have drafts on Pompeian); 15–20 are *CPF*
nos 109–11, 154, 112, 119 ('The End', a tailpiece).

20   Quotations selected from OEF 333 (partly reproduced in *CPF*, 323–6).
     With drums and trumpets in 'The End', cf. 'The thunder of the trumpets
     of the night' ('Laus Veneris', last line).
21   *CL*, 354.
22   Joergens's 'Attar of Roses' is subtitled 'Tannhäuser" and begins 'Great
     Venus, at thy knees I am lying low' (ELG has MS). No doubt the three
     sonneteers knew Wagner's opera and perhaps that attar was his favourite
     scent.
23   'I looked and saw' ('1915'), 'Afar off, afar off' ('Ideal Love'). The latter
     has stresses marked; perhaps WO was looking for a drumbeat to go with
     his 'drummers drumming'.
24   BL1, 31v (mentioned, *CPF*, 496). Several images from BL1, 31–2,
     reappear in 'Purple'.
25   *CPF*, 457. With 'my heart has failed . . . in sleep', cf. *CPF*, 36 (Dunsden
     hypochondria) and 'Mental Cases', lines 8–9.
26   BL1, 127.
27   WO confused Inferno and Purgatorio, using both terms to describe the
     war zone (*CL*, 425, 440). He knew the *Inferno* (*JFO*, II, 71) but may not
     have read further. Purgatorio is not subterranean.
28   *CL*, 383–4. For Monro's influence on WO, see Geo, 28–34. They may
     have met more often than *CL* records; WO may even have been at one
     of Monro's drinking-bouts (*CL*, 501).

CHAPTER 5. THE SECOND CRISIS: SHELLSHOCK [Jan–July 1917]

1   DH, 'Concealed Messages' (1980).
2   *CL*, 427. *Tale of Two Cities*, closing lines.
3   *CL*, 431 ('unnatural' is underlined in MS).
4   *CL*, 424, 449, 427, 425, 429.

5   *CL*, 432.
6   *CL*, 424, 427.
7   *CL*, 95, 211, 285, 322.
8   *CL*, 429.
9   *CL*, 428. Several sharp comments on the Gunstons, usually Gordon, are omitted from *CL*, ranging in date from July 1916 to October 1918. Cf. Ch. 11, n. 4, below.
10   The battalion felt 'bitterly towards those in England who might relieve us, and will not' (*CL*, 453). And see other comments in these letters (e.g. on Somme films, 429, 440).
11   *CL*, 425 (Poems), 434 (Leslie's), 482 (Tennyson). Benson (1912) 79. 'Adolescens' appears on BL1, 3, and Bodleian draft of 'Happiness'.
12   'Happiness' draft and notes: *CPF*, 88, 227–30.
13   *CL*, 444. JS, 171n.
14   *CL*, 448 (rest), 452 (hole). WO ascribed his shellshock to the shellburst and the proximity of Lt Gaukroger's shattered, presumably decaying corpse (cf. JS, 182n.). *CL*, 475 (coming-to). JS, 183, presumably paraphrases from a reliable source in saying the Medical Officer found 'him to be shaky and tremulous and his memory confused' (he was still slightly concussed from the cellar fall). The gaps and confusions in his letters about Savy Wood, which he always called 'Feyet', seem to confirm the Medical Officer's view.
15   Sources for this paragraph: CKSM (1920, 1921); SS to SO, '20 February' (OEF); E. Sitwell (1921); RG (1929), end of ch. xxiv (modified in later editions); EB's draft memoir and correspondence (Tex). See also DW (1978) 159–60.
16   Brown (1934) 88. My information on shellshock comes mainly from Brown, Brock, MacCurdy and Rivers (see Bibliography). Brown worked in France in 1916–17, treated WO in May 1917 (*CL*, 455–6), and was put in charge of Craiglockhart in 1918 (presumably in the upheaval there referred to in *Sherston's Progress*).
17   Brown (1934) 91. Pre-war stress emerged in war dreams which had 'their source in the patient's earlier life'; treatment was by recall and analysis of pre-war and war experience.
18   The notebook (BL1, 157–64) includes drafts of 'With an Identity Disc' and 'Sunrise'; the fragments 'When on the kindling wood', 'It was the noiseless hour', 'Hide ah! my Flower'; notes for 'Sonatas in Silence'; and a Shakespeare sonnet.
19   *CPF*, 460–1. *CL*, 234.
20   Craiglockhart registers, Public Records Office (MH 106.1887).
21   *CL*, 473, 478. A mock ballad? Cf. his hospital parodies of the Bible (458–60), medical chart (465) and litany (557–8 – 8 June 1917, misdated in *CL*).
22   (a) *CL*, 389 (b) 406–7; (c) *CPF*, 353, (d) 351, (e) 487, (f) 175. For other dock imagery, cf. 'A Palinode' and 'I know the music'. Drafts of 'Disabled' show that WO imagined the soldier sitting 'between his crutches in the park' (no longer a 'movable' body).
23   *CL*, 502.
24   The only surviving MS has a July–August 1917 watermark; however, *CPF* does not add that EB seems to have seen another draft of unknown

date (CDL, 113–14). CDL suggested 1916 because MS has a note of Sorley's 1916 book, but perhaps SS or RG recommended Sorley, whom they both admired, in 1917 as an antidote to the lushness of WO's poem.
25   RG made this mistake several times. Cf. Seymour-Smith (1982), 97, 113.
26   AJB: see Appendix A4.
27   WO found Outlook Tower people held 'my own – almost secret – views of such things as sculpture, state-craft, ethics, etc. etc.' (*CL*, 491).
28   *CL*, 476. MS notes in OEF (I amend slightly). WO acquired one Tower publication, Branford (1913), an essay by a leading Geddesian which AJB's book recommends as a study of poetic idealism–hysteria.
29   *CL*, 497, 481 n.3.
30   AJB to Geddes, 17 Mar, 16 Apr 1920 (National Library of Scotland, Geddes MSS 10546).
31   *Hydra*: see Appendix C. AJB (1911) first defines Ergotherapy. 'Effort and work are the instrument of all attainment' (WO, Tower essay).
32   Bergson (1915) argued that Germany had become a machine and would therefore be defeated.
33   *Health and Conduct*, 278.
34   *CL*, 473 (Mother). Lett, 283 (indigoes). *CL*, 479 (Sacrifices), 475 (activities), 479 (energy). The Craiglockhart letters repay careful reading. SO would have heard AJB's theories and WO promised her 'an hour on the Tower' (477), so subsequent letters to her assume a knowledge of Ergotherapy.
35   Article possibly by WO. The January one, signed 'Acturus' (he who is about to act), probably by AJB.
36   MS in OEF. *CL*, 478. WO had studied at a more advanced level than Cassell's, marking passages about plant behaviour in Keeble (1911).
37   See Ch. 3, n. 16, above.
38   *CL*, 255.
39   *CL*, 482 (WO first wrote 'wicked' for 'weary'), 484, 488, 490, 496.
40   *Health and Conduct*, 150.
41   *CL*, 536.
42   *CL*, 377, 427. Bäckman (1979) 103.
43   AJB (1924) 494.
44   SO to EB, n.d., *c*.1930 (Tex). EB, 29.

CHAPTER 6. SASSOON [Aug–Oct 1917]

1   RG (1930) 56. Seymour-Smith (1982) gives RG's side of the protest affair. There are many other published and unpublished sources.
2   SS's letters in Tex unless otherwise stated. These quotations: to Morrell, 26 Apr 1917 (snapping), 13 Nov 1917 (nightmares); to Meiklejohn, 25 Feb 1918 (horrors); to Morrell, 30 July 1917 (dotty), 21 Aug 1918 (cursed), 8 July 1917 (B. R.). Information on Rivers: SS to Meiklejohn, 1 Aug 1917; to Morrell, 30 July 1917.
3   SS to Meiklejohn, 25 Mar 1917, quoting Hardy, 'Night in the Old Home'.
4   For some criticism of SS's war poems, see *Casebook*.

5   SS to Morrell, 21 May 1917.
6   SS to Nicholson, 21 June 1917 (Harvard). For Nicholson, see *Diaries* (1983) 33, and d'Arch Smith (1970). Beauty, compassion and friendship were Uranian values.
7   SS to EB, 4 Aug 1965.
8   *CL*, 486.
9   *CL*, 484.
10 SS (1945) 58.
11 *CL*, 567. SS's first mention of WO in a letter seems to be in answer to RG's enthusiasm in October (*Diaries*, 191). Evidence suggests that RG admired WO's verse before SS did. SS's silence about WO contrasts with his 1918 excitement to many correspondents about Frank Prewett (cf. *CL*, 482).
12 *CL*, 489 [Lett, 283]. Proof, were any needed, that WO wrote no trench poems before meeting SS.
13 For poem, drafts and associated comments, see *CPF*, 144, 298–300; *CL*, 485–6; *Hydra*, 1 Sep 1917; *CL*, 436 (*Mirror* photographs). WO was probably mistaken in marking the Belloc line as old; he should have marked the line from 'Perseus' about the Kaiser (*CPF*, 449).
14 OEF 249 (*CPF*, 255–6, 372). *CPF* treats both fragments about civilians as work for 'Six O'clock', although that poem is different in tone and style.
15 *CPF*, 137, ascribes 'The Letter' to 1918 but 1917 seems more likely. See Appendix B.
16 *CL*, 493. 'Hymne a Dionisius', Tailhade (1907) 105. DW (1960), 127, suggests this echo.
17 *CL*, 497. BL1, 60.
18 *CL*, 489 (Aug 1917).
19 1917 edition. SS reshuffled the sequence in his *Collected Poems*.
20 SS to EB, 12 Nov 1930 ('2.30 a.m.').
21 RG (1929, 3rd impression) 326. DW (1951), 349, disagrees with RG; the argument seems to depend on what date one gives to 'Exposure'.
22 *CL*, 494 (parallel). SS to Morrell, 19 Aug 1917 (Keats). *CL*, 487 (Hardy). *CL*, 492 (the folders may have included work by ELG). SS (1945) 59 (some confusion here: SS quotes from a 1918 poem as an example of 'lusciousness'). *CL*, 486 (Sonnets), 491 (condemned). *CL*, 490 [Lett, 283] (doubtful); 'Song of Songs' was published anonymously. The annotated *Hydra* is among SS's letters to Morrell; another, unmarked copy is in BNY, presumably sent by him to Marsh. He also sent a copy to Ross and promised one to Meiklejohn (SS to Meiklejohn, 9 Sep 1917).
23 See DH, 'Some Notes' (1982) for references for this paragraph. 'The Triumph' is last in the notebook, eighth from the end in SS (1918) and omitted from SS (1961).
24 *CL*, 494.
25 MS in OEF. JS, 212, says WO echoes SS, but WO's letter shows his poem preceded SS's.
26 Tennyson, 'Merlin and the Gleam'. Tennyson explained 'the gleam' as 'the higher poetic imagination' but it may have had some further meaning for WO and SS. Cf. *CL*, 512, and 'follow gleams more golden and more slim' (*CPF*, 184).

27   For example, Silkin (1972) 210–11.
28   An echo pointed out by David Perkins in a perceptive discussion of WO's
      Romanticism (*Casebook*).
29   Binyon, 'At the going down of the sun ... We will remember them'
      (1914). Brice, 'the voice of monstrous guns' (1916). WO liked Binyon's
      poem in 1915 (*CL*, 355).
30   *CL*, 248 (funeral); liturgical details in 'Anthem' drafts are Roman
      Catholic, so in calling them 'mockeries' WO was in line with his
      Evangelical past and not necessarily condemning all formal observance.
      Craiglockhart fragments: 'But I was looking' (*CPF*, 487–8), 'I know the
      music' (*CPF*, 485–6). Bells: cf. *CL*, 205, and 'passing-bell' (*Hyperion*, I. 173).
      Acolytes: favourite Decadent–Uranian subjects; cf. 'Maundy Thursday',
      and *CL*, 311.
31   Final draft marked '*Nation*'. Cf. *CL*, 506–7 (despite the footnote, WO
      could not have been referring to 'Miners' so early); SS (1945) 59–60.
      Two of RG's letters are in *CL*, 595–6; a third is in OEF.
32   Lang (1906) 172 (my italics). WO bought a copy of this edition (OEF),
      inscribing it 'W. E. S. Owen   Scarborough   Dec: 1917' (cf. *CL*, 520 n.
      3).
33   For *CPF*'s 'small ... vile ... kissed' and 'turning ... turning ... writhing',
      I read 'sin ... vice ... kissed' and 'turning ... twinging ... turning ...
      writhing' (*CPF*, 293).
34   Cf. Shelley's image of the face of war, eyes starting 'with cracking stare',
      tongue 'foamy, like a mad dog's hanging' (*Revolt*, lines 2476–83).
35   RG to Gosse, 24 Oct 1917 (Brotherton Collection, Leeds).
36   Gleam: *CL*, 512 (cf. n. 26, above), 505 (comet). 'Storm': cf. WO's early
      phrase 'Consummation is Consumption' (*CPF*, 384). *CL*, 492 (light the
      darkness), 567 (candle).
37   *CL*, 492.

CHAPTER 7. NEW INFLUENCES: GEORGIANS AND
OTHERS [Nov 1917–Jan 1918]

1   *CL*, 513 (3 December), 520 (revise), 525–6 (art), 535 (bluebells), 533–4
     (duty).
2   RG to Marsh, 1 Jan 1916 (BNY).
3   ''Orace Cockles' in draft (cf. Horatius Cocles).
4   For details, and references for this and preceding paragraph, see Geo,
     and DH, 'WO's Library' (1977).
5   'It would be a crime to exhibit the fine side of war, even if there were
     one!' – Barbusse (1929 edn) 342.
6   Nichols to SO, 10 Dec 1920 (OEF).
7   OEF 284. This hurriedly amended version of the last stanza is arguably
     later (but not better) than that given in *CPF*. Cf. imagery of gods,
     laughter and the exclusiveness of art in 'Sweet is your antique body'
     (*CPF*, 129).
8   *CL*, 510. Second sentence from a passage about ELG's book omitted from
     CL, 516. In May WO had sent ELG a roundel, having found it easy to

write without 'either emotion or ideas' (*CL*, 250; for date see Lett, 281); there are five roundels in ELG (1917). So the cousins had been in disagreement about truth to experience before WO met SS.

9 Keats to Haydon, 8 Mar 1819. Cf. 'Nothing ever becomes real until it is experienced' (to George Keats, 19 Mar).

10 *CL*, 520, 526, 531.

11 *WPO*, 122. *CL*, 416. 'L'Amour' first published in *YM*, the YMCA magazine, 10 Nov 1916, reprinted in ELG (1917).

12 'Tears, idle tears'. WO was reading Tennyson again with pleasure despite this gibe (*CPF*, 127). Cf. *CL*, 152.

13 WO got SS to autograph at least two copies (ELG still has one), having read the poem before meeting him (*CL*, 494).

14 *CL*, 514.

15 *CL*, 521. Cf. 'I suffer a temptation . . . to remain a poet's poet!' (*CL*, 520).

16 Two *Battle* poems were in *Nation* in October 1914. See DH and Onions (1986). Possible traces of Gibson in WO's poems include a parallel between 'Makeshifts' (*Livelihood*, 1917) and 'Disabled' and 'A Terre'.

17 WO first wrote in his Preface that his subject was war and 'the pity of it' (the phrase originates from *Othello*). With another Hardy title, 'The Souls of the Slain', cf. phrases in WO's list of contents, 'The Soul of Soldiers' and 'The Women & the Slain'. WO described Hardy as 'potatoey' in 1917, perhaps alluding to the potato conversation in *Under the Greenwood Tree*; he may not have been aware of Hardy as a poet before meeting SS (*CL*, 487).

18 In Hardy's 'To the Moon', the moon sees life as a 'show'. *Dynasts* quotations: iii.iv.1, ii.vi.1, iii.i.9, Fore Scene. Some of these parallels are noted by Cohen (1957).

19 *CL*, 406. Tennyson, 'The Lotos-Eaters', line 159.

20 Wells (1914), 113–14. Cf. 'the last War of the World' (*CL*, 274).

21 SS to Morrell, 19 Aug 1917. *CL*, 520. Glover (1980) shows how Fitzwater Wray's spirited translation influenced WO's diction and imagery in 'Dulce' and other poems.

22 *CL*, 545 ('A Terre'). EB, 134 (Nicholson). Ross used such photographs (OS, 1950, 96); perhaps he got them from a senior civil servant such as Meiklejohn, who could also have given some to SS. But if SS avoided talking of horrors to WO, 'knowing they were bad for him', he is unlikely to have given him nightmarish pictures.

23 *CL*, 509.

24 *CL*, 512.

25 *CPF*, 514–17, gives three of five drafts, treating them as fragments. *Poems* (1920) included one as an 'Alternative Version' of 'Strange Meeting'. I assume they represent a complete, independent poem. I quote a fourth draft (BL0, 5) and fragments from others.

26 Cf. WO to SS: 'my principles and your mastery' (*CL*, 582). Cf. 'Had such a mastery of his mystery' (Tennyson, 'The Last Tournament', line 327).

27 Ezekiel 25:10: 'the noise . . . of the wheels, and of the chariots . . . as men enter into a city wherein is made a breach'. Joel 2:5, 7: destroyers shall come like 'the noise of chariots' and 'they shall not break their ranks'. Wells of water: John 4:14; Isaiah 12:3 (cf. also 58:11, one of WO's 1903 'promise texts').

28 See Mrs Shelley's note on *The Revolt of Islam*. Shelley's Prometheus is referred to as 'One' several times and has 'Drops of bloody agony' on his white brow (*Prometheus Unbound*, I.564). Cf. 'the wise and free / Wept tears, and blood like tears' ('Ode to Liberty', line 269). Bäckman (1979) suggests other interesting parallels, including war's red chariot wheels in *Queen Mab*.

29 'Letter to Maria Gisborne', line 121. With 'wise', cf. 'wise and free' (preceding note) and 'We wise' ('Insensibility').

30 *Revolt of Islam*, line 1042.

31 Wells (1916) 22. *CL*, 527.

32 *CL*, 504. A visit to Lady Ottoline would have established a contact with Russell.

33 Russell, *Principles* (1916) 10. Cf. 'Those who are to begin the regeneration of the world . . . must be able to live by truth and love, with a rational unconquerable hope; they must be honest and wise, fearless, and guided by a consistent purpose' (246).

34 RG's poem, in his unpublished book *The Patchwork Flag* (1918), and associated letters are in BNY. SS to Morrell, 28 May 1918. *CL*, 530 (quotation unidentified – it is perhaps nearer Wells or even Wilde than Russell), 498 (washy), 521 (blindfold).

35 *CL*, 520 (propaganda). SS to Forster, 1 May 1918, quoted in P. N. Furbank, *E. M. Forster* (1978) 47. SS to Marsh, 18 July 1918 (BNY); SS (1945) 70–1.

36 'My soul looked' – still a trace of Joergens ('I looked and saw') as well as Shelley.

37 *CL*, 458, 544.

38 *CL*, 521.

CHAPTER 8. THE PITY OF WAR [Mar–May 1918]

1 *CL*, 535 (catastrophic), 538 (Farewell), 543 (get fit, cottage-window). WO, *CL* and JS spell 'Borage'; WO probably never saw it written down but then as now it was apparently 'Borrage' (from 'burgherage', not 'borage'). 'No one here knows of my retreat' (*CL*, 547): JS, 259, may be mistaken in implying WO actually lived in the cottage, since he would presumably have had to inform his superiors. He was free daily from about 3 p.m. to Lights Out. Borrage Lane compositions probably include 'As bronze', 'Arms and the Boy', 'The Send-Off', 'Strange Meeting', 'Futility', 'Mental Cases', 'Elegy in April' (four stanzas). Many poems begun earlier were extensively revised, including 'Exposure', 'A Terre' and 'Insensibility'.

2 Wordsworth, Preface to *Lyrical Ballads* (1802). *CL*, 544 (public attention was on the German breakthrough at St Quentin), 524 (Hamel), 542 (Wordsworth wrote three poems to the 'small' celandine). Murry (1921). *CL*, 543 (numbs), 581 (charred).

3 *Pace CPF*, 147, 'Insensibility' is hardly a reply to Wordsworth's 'Happy Warrior', which is not a Pindaric ode and contains little that WO would have disagreed with (cf. Ch. 11, n. 23, below).

4 'Happy': a key word in Keats's odes but also in wartime propaganda (cf. 'Smile, Smile, Smile', and Plates 13, 14).

5   The 'wise' in 'Insensibility' are poets (cf. Ch. 7, n. 29, above, and *Adonais*, line 312). WO does not imply any comment on class or education as some critics have supposed.

6   Symons, 'To the Merchants of Bought Dreams', *Poems* (1906) II, 175. BL1, 15.

7   The first draft (*CPF*, 304) refers to frozen bodies underfoot. Cf. *CL*, 542.

8   *English Elegies*, etc.: titles on verso of first list of contents (*CPF*, 538; cf. JS, 265, and *CL*, 561 n. 3, an inaccurate note). Lang: see Ch. 6., n. 32, above. Milton, Gray: Bäckman (1979) 40–3. Tennyson: DH, *WO* (1975) 32–3; *In Memoriam*, cxxix.

9   *CL*, 511 (acid). EB, 125 (sour).

10   MSS, like 'An Imperial Elegy', have musical annotations. At one stage entitled 'Ode for a Poet reported Missing: later, reported killed', this may be the 'Ode' in the 1918 lists of contents (*CPF*, 147 headnote). Subtitle, '(jabbered among the trees)', from SS, 'Repression of War Experience'. In stanzas 1–4 (Apr) the poet seeks a companion missing in spring; in stanzas 5–7 (Sep) he laments him killed in autumn. Presumably the poem was meant for SS, but who is its subject?

11   *CL*, 526. Gosse in *Casebook*, 44–5.

12   Some careless remarks of mine years ago on protest and elegy have been rebuked. DW (1978) 167–8 rescues me from an absurd position with characteristic generosity. Silkin (1980) seems less persuasive.

13   '[And have I shut the last book I shall read?]' OEF 339–42, not in *CPF*.

14   For both lists, see *CPF*, 538–9. They are of war poems only, but WO continued to plan work unconnected with war, assembling sonnets at Scarborough ('Farewell . . . Sonnets' – *CL*, 538). A note of 5 May 1918 (OEF; *CL*, 551 n. 1) lists four 'Projects': verse plays on old Welsh themes, like Tennyson's English and Yeats's Irish dramas (so WO envisaged a role as a Welsh poet); *Collected Poems* (1919); 'Perseus'; 'Idylls in Prose'. But he would have been less old-fashioned than this if he had lived; he had yet to encounter Modernism.

15   For the date of Society Bond MSS, see Appendix B.

16   MS reproduced as frontispiece to *CPF* and in DH (1975).

17   CKSM to WO, 26 May 1918 (OEF).

18   *CL*, 554.

CHAPTER 9. TO SUFFER WITHOUT SIGN [1918]

1   See also Appendix A 5–7.

2   Carpenter Collection, Sheffield Central Library, has letters from SS, including five in 1917, and one from RG (1914). SS sent a copy of his protest to Carpenter, who satirised the official response to it in 'Lieutenant Tattoon, M. C.' (*Three Ballads*, 1917). SS considered taking a factory job near Carpenter in August 1918. See also Tsuzuki (1980), Grant (1967).

3   'The Intermediate Sex' – Carpenter (1911) 130 – an essay which SS said had 'opened up a new life' for him in 1911. Cf. 'We wise who with a thought besmirch / Blood over all our soul' ('Insensibility').

4   WO and SS seem to have shared confidences; see WO's allusions to Sodom, beautiful bodies, 'exposed flanks' (*CL*, 506, 512, 582). Cf. n. 31

below. Homosexuality was on SS's mind at Craiglockhart – R. Gathorne-Hardy, *Ottoline at Garsington* (1974) 230.

5   For Sherard, see JS, 242, 320. Ross wrote to Gosse about covering up SS's protest (19 July 1917, BL Ashley MSS). SS often asks after Ross in 1918 letters. For other sources for this paragraph, see Appendix A5, and *CL*.

6   SS (1945) 29.

7   OS (1949) 115. WO sent him a crudely spelled copy of 'Long ages past', perhaps to show that his own juvenilia had included *Salomé*-like verse.

8   'Armchair', prefatory poem in *Wheels 1917*. For 'old men', see 'Adelyne More', 'The one thing needful', *Cambridge Magazine*, 7 (19 Jan 1918) 315–17.

9   TO's war scrapbook (OEF) shows the simple patriotism for which WO sometimes criticised him. It contains reports of actions fought by WO's regiment; the report of WO's death is accompanied by news of Victoria Crosses won at the time and some consolatory newspaper poems.

10   WO ordered *Wheels 1917* in late July (cf. S. Sitwell's 'Barrel-Organs' in this volume with 'The roads also'). CKSM gave him S. Sitwell (1918) in August (JS, 320). For an assessment of what WO might have achieved, see P. Hobsbaum in *Casebook*.

11   Details in this paragraph from OEF MSS and sources given in Appendix A6.

12   TS in BNY, n.d.

13   The evidence for *CPF*'s 1917 date for the first draft of 'Reunion' is not clear; the second draft is almost certainly early 1918. The three ballads are on Clarence Gardens paper (like Nov–Feb letters). WO may have sent them to a *Bookman* competition, announced in January; the results (May) list him (Clarence Gardens address) and ELG as runners-up in the ballad section ('Song of Songs' won a consolation prize and was printed in the lyric section). In February WO saw much of P. Bainbrigge, skilled author of 'ballads of a . . . private kind' (CKSM, 1920).

14   Cf. WO's poems about the 'god' Eros, and the 'phantoms' seen in his 1913 illness.

15   *CL*, 461 (cf. Tailhade, 'Ne tue pas!'); WO gave his religion as 'Primitive Christian' in June (467). *CL*, 468 (Oxenham), 483–4 (*CL* gives 'lad's cheeks'; MS is ambiguous; plural seems more likely).

16   *CL*, 536 ('as one says'). WO misquotes from Wilde (1905), 116. The style of *De Profundis* is evident in this letter.

17   Wilde (1905) 88–9. *CL*, 521, 573, 580. WO, 'The Calls'.

18   But see Breen (1974) 177, Silkin (1972) 234–5, etc. My comments on and quotations from 'Greater Love' drafts are based on MSS, not *CPF*. Unlike *CPF*, I take BL1, 40 (a version of lines 1–18) and OEF 269v (lines 19–24) to be the earliest surviving draft. These and BL1, 38v and 39v, were scribbled out on the backs of fair-copied sonnets at some point in the period summer 1917 to spring 1918. Two later drafts are probably summer 1918.

19   But 'greater love' also occurs in Keats ('Isabella', xl).

20   WO imitates OS's epigram 'Ill Winds' (*CL*, 561–2). He copied it for his family, adding, 'I need not show unto you this Jesus. For myself, I have seen him with my eyes, and touched his blood with my hands. / I am now engaged in teaching him to lift his cross by numbers, and inspecting

his feet, that they be worthy of the nails. WEO' (MS in OEF). R. Nichols described WO himself as a crucified, gospel-bringing Christ: 'You owe it to his wounds, received for your sake, . . . to try and realise what war is, as he has shown it, and, having learned, to teach others' (cutting dated 1920, OEF). WO might have preferred N. Royde-Smith's comparison of his work to 'the torso of some unimaginably beautiful antique marble, mutilated, unrestorable, as splendid as dreams' (*Time and Tide*, 13 June 1931).

21 With the walls and terraces in 'The Kind Ghosts', cf. the terrace in *Salammbô*, xiii, so heaped with bodies that it seems to be made of them.

22 Wilde (1948) 56.

23 *CL*, 563. *CPF* perhaps ascribes too many drafts to Scarborough (July–Aug); WO had much less time there than at Ripon (Mar–May).

24 SS to WO, c. 7 Aug 1918 (OEF); cf. *CL*, 567.

25 Mrs Gaskell defined the Victorian author's role as spokesman in saying she wrote *Mary Barton* 'to give utterance to the agony which, from time to time, convulses the dumb people' – K. Tillotson, *Novels of the 1840s* (1961), 205.

26 *CL*, 568, 570. WO misquotes 'Testament' (See DH and Onions, 1986).

27 WO was willing to go out again but it is not clear whether he volunteered or awaited orders. Recorded events as follows: 9 August: draft order issued (OEF). 11th: taken off draft by Medical Officer. What happens next is uncertain (*did* the War Office intervene?) but he gets a few days' leave (*CL*, 16, says 12–18 Aug but is probably guessing). 17th (Saturday): returns to Scarborough after a London afternoon with OS (1950, 108–9) and SS (1945, 71–2). 26th: embarkation order (OEF) issued at Scarborough, the Medical Officer having now certified him fit to proceed overseas (how could a cardiac irregularity have disappeared in a fortnight?). 30th: in Hastings with SO and Colin, returns Victoria alone late, met by CKSM. 31st: 7.35 a.m. train, Victoria-Folkestone; embarks later that day. WO's letter about his last evening in London has been mutilated by HO. I have not seen WO's War Office file.

28 SO to Alec Paton, 27 May 1919 (Tex).

29 *CL*, 570–1.

30 *CL*, 589. A fellow officer in October later recalled that WO 'mentioned that he had the highest regard for the Poet A. C. Swinburne and very often I found him studying a volume of his works' (Lt J. Foulkes, unsigned notes used by EB, *c*. 1930, Tex). For the volume, see JS, 321.

31 DW (1978) 158–9. *CL*, 580–1. WO told SS he was glad Jones was 'happily wounded: and so away from me. He had lived in London, a Londoner.' This may be a coded message, and 'Who is the god of Canongate' may be relevant to an interpretation of it; Jones seems in fact to have come from Hereford (*CL*, 582, 560).

CHAPTER 10. 'STRANGE MEETING' [1918]

1 *CL*, 560.

2 DH, 'The Date of . . .' (1976). MS of 'Cramped' has draft lines used in 'Exposure' and 'Mental Cases' (*CPF*, 513).

3 'A New Heaven' (*CPF*, 223). *CL*, 424.

4 Reconstructed from BL1, 28v. For other workings, see *CPF*, 367.

5 *CL*, 126.

6 Cf. Ch.4, n.27, above.

7 Revelation 7:13–14 – Sinfield (1982) also makes this point. Dante, *Vision of Hell*, tr. Cary (1814) v.50–1; 'Mental Cases' is reminiscent of many passages in this translation, which both WO and Keats knew.

8 *CPF*, 492. I reconstruct a little. MS has features in common with those of 'Spells and Incantation' (late 1917) and possibly 'Mental Cases'. It ends '[or clo]', another echo of Keats ('emperor and clown').

9 An ambiguity first pointed out by Gose (1961).

10 I prefer a Ripon (March – very early June) date to *CPF*'s January– March (see Appendix B).

11 EB, 128.

12 Bäckman (1979) 101–2. As elsewhere, HO's memory may have been influenced by WO's poetry but Bäckman's suggestion is striking.

13 MS in BNY.

14 *Faerie Queene*, i.i.41–2. The preceding stanza is quoted in the Hazlitt volume WO read in January. He summarised *Faerie Queene*, i, at school.

15 *Endymion*, iv.512–42.

16 'Ode to Liberty', lines 256–7. *CL*, 571.

17 A recurrent theme in *Health and Conduct*.

18 SS to Forster, 30 June 1918 (King's College, Cambridge), records his respect for and disagreement with Russell's views. SS's political understanding of the war was now that German militarism was preventing peace.

19 The *alter ego* reading was proposed by DW (1960) and subsequently widely accepted (but see Silkin and DH, *Stand*, 1980). Earlier examples of doubles include Shelley, *Prometheus Unbound*, i.192–9; Dickens, *Our Mutual Friend* (Headstone–Riderhood), *Dombey* (Phiz illustration to ch. xl). See Miyoshi (1969). The sexuality in 'Strange Meeting' is noticed by John Bayley (*Casebook*, 156–7).

20 Ser Brunetto is the obvious example, familiar from 'Little Gidding' (cf. Ch. 1, n. 12, above).

21 *Fall of Hyperion*, i.462–3 (an echo suggested by Bäckman); i.260–3.

22 Murry (1919) 1284. Murry deals admirably with borrowing: 'no danger to the real poet. He is the splendid borrower who lends a new significance to that which he takes . . .'.

CHAPTER 11. 'SPRING OFFENSIVE' [Sep–Nov 1918]

1 *CL*, 571 (serenity); 580–1 (nerves); 573 (sorrows); 575 [Lett, 284] (hawked); 580 (Strictly); 583 (circulation); 591 (band of friends; cf. 'band of brothers', *Henry V*, iv.iii.60, and *Revolt of Islam*, line 2407).

2 *CL*, 572.

3 *CL*, 574. The Harrow boy was 'the best piece of Nation left in England' (570). By chance, in February WO had read Vachell (1905), a Harrow story, in which a boy redeems past failings by dying a hero in South Africa. The scene possibly influenced 'Spring Offensive': troops are 'halted

at the foot of the hill, halted in . . . a storm of bullets. Then the word was given to attack . . . fire from invisible foes . . . He ran . . . as if he were racing for a goal', dying at 'the highest point', 'smiling at death' (295). Harrow Hill reminded WO of Broxton, his own place of education (*CL*, 535).

4 *CL*, 589 [Lett, 284]. An ensuing sentence about Gordon Gunston is silently omitted from *CL*, one of three similar comments omitted from late-1918 letters.

5 *CL*, 585.

6 'Smile, Smile, Smile'.

7 *CL*, 589 (atrocities), 583–5 (Peace Talk).

8 WPO, 134.

9 'Happy': cf. 'Insensibility', and Ch. 8, n. 4, above. Anger against newspaper optimism had been an Army grouse for some years; WO is acting as spokesman.

10 *CL*, 498 (reputation), 582 (confidence), 580 (pleader).

11 The *CL* wording (580 n. 2) follows a carbon TS preserved by HO (OEF), who may have thought it genuine. The TS contains at least one error and has no official mark. The type of carbon looks early. Is it a forgery by SO? John Bell cannot explain the discrepancy between it and the apparently official wording given (with slight variations) in TO's scrapbook, Higham (1922), Walsh (1964), and JS, 279 (where the puzzle is not remarked on).

12 *CL*, 580. Cf. 'one seraphic lance corporal' (582).

13 Two reports by William Beach-Thomas (cf. *CL*, 584).

14 *CPF*, 540, 193.

15 *CL*, 458.

16 Years before WO had asked for a poetic vision like those granted to 'old dreamers on May Morn' (*CPF*, 385).

17 *WPO*, 135, gives the time as late afternoon, an inexcusable error.

18 *CL*, 510 (croziers; quoted from ELG, 'From the Caradoc in June'). Appendix A7 (HO's memory of buttercups). *CL*, 588 (Haughmond), 581 (forefathers; HO perhaps remembered this when saying he too thought of them in times of danger – *JFO*, ii, 77).

19 *CL*, 381.

20 *CPF*, 12, 378.

21 Cf. imagery of men as trees in Monro's 'Trees' (*Strange Meetings*, 1917), a poem strongly influenced by Carpenter.

22 Cf. 'Stand ye . . . Like a forest . . . With . . . looks which are / Weapons of unvanquished war' (Shelley, *Mask of Anarchy*, lines 319–22).

23 Matthew 17:2; Revelation 1:16. Cf. *CPF*, 194 n. 2, and Wordsworth, 'Happy Warrior', lines 51–2 (the soldier called to fight is 'happy as a Lover; and attired / With sudden brightness, like a Man inspired').

24 Wells (1917) 77–8, 123. *CL*, 487 (WO had deplored a passage from the book when it was published in May – 461).

25 'Fearfully flashed', 'the whole sky burned': cf. rape of Danae ('the whole sky fell / In . . . flashings' – P3); and 'Fitfully flash' (*Dynasts*, iii.iii.2).

26 Cf. 'the last sea' ('Insensibility'). Men thought the end of the world had come at Roncesvalles.

27   WO was not erudite enough to have been aware of the arguments about what is really meant by the many Old Testament references to 'high places', and to Moloch (Molech) and child sacrifices by fire; but he would have remembered Milton's description of Moloch, and such biblical phrases as 'They have built also the high places of Baal, to burn their sons with fire' (Jeremiah 19:5), 'no man might make his son or his daughter to pass through the fire to Molech' (2 Kings 23:10), 'Then did Solomon build an high place . . . for Molech' (1 Kings 11:7).

28   Moloch's priests wear scarlet (cf. WO's battledress soaked in Jones's blood and his simile for it, 'crimson-hot iron'). Another *Salammbô* chapter WO may always have remembered is the last, which brings together key images of scarlet, blood, fatal love and stare, passivity, sacrifice, etc., in a ghastly climax.

29   Cohen (1965) 259–60.

30   *CL*, 431.

31   *Paradise Lost*, i.746–7, referring to a 'Sheer' fall (James McLaverty suggests this parallel). WO's line is persistently misread. In Arthur Bliss's war oratorio *Morning Heroes* (1930), it is intoned as Christian consolation. But Bliss did see the heroic element in the poem. Rutherford (1978) is one of the few modern critics to write perceptively about heroism in this and other Great War poems.

32   *CL*, 458.

33   *CL*, 432.

Bibliography

A select list of published works consulted (for MSS, see Notes and Appendixes).

Space prevents a complete list of Owen articles. William White, *Wilfred Owen (1893–1918): A Bibliography* (Kent State University Press, 1967) gives a near-complete record to 1965. The following books, in addition to others listed in (3) below, contain discussion of Owen's work: A. Banerjee, *Spirit above Wars* (1975); Bernard Bergonzi, *Heroes' Twilight* (1965); D. J. Enright, essay in *Pelican Guide to English Literature*, v, ed. Boris Ford (1961); Paul Fussell, *The Great War and Modern Memory* (1975); John H. Johnston, *English Poetry of the First World War* (1964); Philip Larkin, *Required Writing* (1983); David Perkins, *A History of Modern Poetry* (1976); C. H. Sisson, *English Poetry 1900–1950* (1971); Hilda D. Spear, *Remembering, We Forget* (1979); C. K. Stead, *The New Poetic* (1964). *Poetry of the First World War: A Casebook*, ed. Dominic Hibberd (1981), reprints studies by Sassoon, Blunden, Murry, Day Lewis, Welland, Bayley, Johnston, Perkins and others.

For 1914–18 poets, see Catherine W. Reilly, *English Poetry of the First World War: A Bibliography* (Prior, 1978) and the biographical–bibliographical notes in *Poetry of the Great War: An Anthology*, ed. Dominic Hibberd and John Onions (1986).

Books marked * are a small selection of those known to have been read and/ or owned by Owen (in the edition shown, where this can be ascertained). (*) indicates probability rather than certainty. Standard works by major authors are usually omitted.

Abbreviations: *ELT*– *English Literature in Transition 1880–1920*; *N&Q*– *Notes and Queries*; *RES*– *Review of English Studies*. Place of publication (books) London unless otherwise stated.

1   POEMS PUBLISHED DURING OWEN'S LIFETIME

'Song of Songs', *Hydra*, 1 Sep 1917, and *Bookman*, May 1918.
'The Next War', *Hydra*, 29 Sep 1917.
'Miners', *Nation*, 26 Jan 1918.
'Futility' and 'Hospital Barge', *Nation*, 15 June 1918.

2   EDITIONS OF OWEN'S WORKS

Poems by Wilfred Owen, ed. Siegfried Sassoon [actually mainly ed. Edith Sitwell] (Chatto & Windus, 1920).

228

The Poems of Wilfred Owen, ed. Edmund Blunden, with a memoir (Chatto & Windus, 1920).
The Collected Poems of Wilfred Owen, ed. C. Day Lewis, with an introduction and notes (Chatto & Windus, 1963).
Wilfred Owen: Collected Letters, ed. Harold Owen and John Bell (Oxford University Press, 1967).
Wilfred Owen: War Poems and Others, ed. Dominic Hibberd, with an introduction and notes (Chatto & Windus, 1973).
Wilfred Owen: The Complete Poems and Fragments, ed. Jon Stallworthy, 2 vols (Chatto & Windus, The Hogarth Press and Oxford University Press, 1983).
Wilfred Owen: Selected Letters, ed. John Bell (Oxford University Press, 1985).
The Poems of Wilfred Owen, ed. Jon Stallworthy (Chatto & Windus, The Hogarth Press and Oxford University Press, 1985).

3 GENERAL

Bäckman, Sven, *Tradition Transformed: Studies in the poetry of Wilfred Owen*, Lund Studies in English 54 (Lund: C. W. K. Gleerup, 1979).
*Barbusse, Henri, *Under Fire: The Story of a Squad*, tr. Fitzwater Wray (Dent, 1917). Originally *Le Feu* (Paris: Flammarion, 1916).
Bateson, F. W., 'The Analysis of Poetic Texts: Owen's "Futility" and Davie's "The Garden Party" ', *Essays in Criticism*, 29 (Apr 1979) 156–64.
Bebbington, W. G., 'Jessie Pope and Wilfred Owen', *Ariel* (Leeds), 3 (1972) 82–93.
*Beckett, Sir Edmund, *On the Origin of the Laws of Nature* (SPCK, 1879).
Beerbohm, Max, *Zuleika Dobson, or an Oxford Love Story* (Heinemann, 1911).
*Bennett, Arnold, *The Pretty Lady* (Cassell, 1918).
*Benson, A. C., *Tennyson* (Methuen, 1912 edn).
Bentley, Christopher, 'Wilfred Owen and Gustave Flaubert', *N&Q*, 17 (Dec 1970) 456–7.
Bergson, Henri, *The Meaning of the War: Life and Matter in Conflict* (T. Fisher Unwin, 1915).
*Branford, Victor, *St Columba: A Study of Social Inheritance and Spiritual Development*, illus. John Duncan (Outlook Tower and Chelsea: Patrick Geddes and Colleagues, 1913).
Breen, Jennifer, 'Wilfred Owen: "Greater Love" and Late Romanticism', *ELT*, 17 (1974) 173–83.
——, 'Wilfred Owen (1893–1918): His Recovery from "Shell-Shock" ', *N&Q*, 23 (July 1976) 301–5.
Brock, A. J.: see Appendix A 4.
*Brooke, Rupert, *1914, and Other Poems*, 13th impression (Sidgwick & Jackson, May 1916).
Brown, William, *Psychology and Psychotherapy*, 3rd edn (Arnold, 1934).
Busst, A. J. L., 'The Image of the Androgyne in the Nineteenth Century', in *Romantic Mythologies*, ed. Ian Fletcher (Routledge, 1967).
Carpenter, Edward, *Love's Coming-of-Age: A Series of Papers on the Relations of the Sexes*, 7th edn (George Allen, 1911).
——, *Three Ballads (an Intermezzo in War Time)*, pamphlet (Oct 1917).

Carter, A. E., *The Idea of Decadence in French Literature 1830–1900* (Toronto: University of Toronto Press, 1958).

Chapple, J. A. V., *Documentary and Imaginative Literature 1880–1920* (Blandford Press, 1970).

Cohen, Joseph, 'Wilfred Owen's Greater Love', *Tulane Studies in English*, 6 (1956) 105–17.

——, 'Owen's "The Show" ', *Explicator*, 16 (Nov 1957) item 8.

——, 'Owen Agonistes', *ELT*, 8 (Dec 1965) 253–68.

*Colvin, Sidney, *Keats* (Macmillan, 1907 impression)

Cooke, William, 'Wilfred Owen's "Miners" and the Minnie Pit Disaster', *English*, 26 (Autumn 1977) 213–17.

*Dante, *The Vision, or, Hell, Purgatory, and Paradise of Dante Alighieri*, tr. H. F. Cary (Warne, n.d.).

d'Arch Smith, Timothy, *Love in Earnest: Some Notes on the Lives and Writings of the English 'Uranian' Poets from 1889 to 1930* (Routledge, 1970).

Das, Sasi Bhusan, *Wilfred Owen's 'Strange Meeting': A Critical Study* (Calcutta: Firma KLM Private, 1977).

——, *Aspects of Wilfred Owen's Poetry* (Calcutta: Roy & Roy, 1979).

(*)Flaubert, Gustave, *Madame Bovary* (first published 1857).

*——, *Salammbô* (first published 1862).

*——, *La Tentation de Saint-Antoine*, Collection Gallia (Paris: Crès; London: Dent, n.d.).

Freeman, Rosemary, 'Parody as a Literary Form: George Herbert and Wilfred Owen', *Essays in Criticism*, 13 (Oct 1963) 307–22.

Gaunt, William, *The Aesthetic Adventure* (Cape, 1945).

Geddes, Patrick: see Appendix A 4.

*Gibson, Wilfred Wilson, *Battle* (Elkin Mathews, 1915).

——, *Collected Poems, 1909–1925* (Macmillan, 1926).

(*)——, *Fires*, 3 vols (Elkin Mathews, 1912; repr. as one vol., 1915).

Glover, Jon, 'Owen and Barbusse and Fitzwater Wray', *Stand*, 21, no. 2 (Spring 1980) 22–32.

——, 'Whose Owen?', *Stand*, 22, no. 3 (1981) 29–31.

Gose, E. B., 'Digging in: An Interpretation of Wilfred Owen's "Strange Meeting" ', *College English*, 22 (Mar 1961) 417–19.

Graham, Desmond, *The Truth of War: Owen, Blunden and Rosenberg* (Manchester: Carcanet, 1984).

Grant, Joy, *Harold Monro and the Poetry Bookshop* (Routledge, 1967).

(*)Graves, Robert, *Over the Brazier* (Poetry Bookshop, 1916).

(*)——, *Goliath and David* (Chiswick Press, ?Dec 1916). [Owen referred to Graves's 'books' in Oct 1917.]

*——, *Fairies and Fusiliers* (Heinemann, 8 Nov 1917).

——, *Goodbye to All That: An Autobiography* (Cape, 1929, extensively revised in later editions).

——, *But It Still Goes On: An Accumulation* (Cape, 1930)

——, *In Broken Images: Selected Letters 1914–1946*, ed. Paul O'Prey (Hutchinson, 1982).

*Gunston, E. Leslie, *The Nymph, and Other Poems* (Stockwell, Nov 1917). [Dedicated to Owen.]

(*)Hardy, Thomas, *The Dynasts: An Epic-Drama of the War with Napoleon* (Macmillan, 1903–8).

*——, *Under the Greenwood Tree* (Macmillan, 1907).

Hassall, Christopher, *Edward Marsh: A Biography* (Longman, 1959).
———, *Rupert Brooke: A Biography* (Faber, 1964).
Hibberd, Dominic, 'Images of Darkness in the Poems of Wilfred Owen', *Durham University Journal*, 56 (Mar 1974) 156–62.
———, *Wilfred Owen*, Writers and their Work 246, (British Council and Longman, 1975), repr. in *British Writers, VI* (New York: Scribner, 1983).
———, ' "Rival pieces on a chosen theme": A Note on Some of Wilfred Owen's Minor Poems', *Four Decades of Poetry 1890–1930*, 1 (Merseyside, Jan 1976) 70–5.
———, 'The Date of Wilfred Owen's "Exposure" ', *N&Q*, 23 (July 1976) 305–8.
———, 'A Sociological Cure for Shellshock: Dr Brock and Wilfred Owen', *Sociological Review*, 25 (May 1977) 377–86.
———, 'Wilfred Owen's Library: Some Additional Items', *N&Q*, 24 (October 1977) 447–8.
———, 'Wilfred Owen's Rhyming', *Studia Neophilologica*, 50 (1978) 207–14.
———, 'Wilfred Owen and the Georgians', *Review of English Studies*, 30 (Feb 1979) 28–40.
———, 'Some Contemporary Allusions in Poems by Owen, Rosenberg and Sassoon', *N&Q*, 26 (Aug 1979) 333–4.
———, 'Silkin on Owen: Some Other War', *Stand*, 21, no. 3 (Spring 1980) 29–32.
———, ' "Problems A": The Solution to Wilfred Owen's "The Imbecile" ', *N&Q*, 27 (June 1980) 232–3.
———, 'Concealed Messages in Wilfred Owen's Trench Letters', *N&Q*, 27 (Dec 1980) 531.
———, (ed.), *Poetry of the First World War: A Casebook* (Macmillan, 1981).
———, 'Some Notes on Sassoon's *Counter-Attack and Other Poems*', *N&Q*, 29 (Aug 1982) 341–2.
———, 'Wilfred Owen's Letters: Some Additions, Amendments and Notes', *Library*, 4 (Sep 1982) 273–87.
———, ' "The End": Wilfred Owen and Leslie Gunston', *N&Q*, 30 (Aug 1983) 325–6.
———, and Onions, John (eds), *Poetry of the Great War: An Anthology* (Macmillan, 1986).
Higham, S. Stagoll (ed.), *Regimental Roll of Honour and War Record of the Artists' Rifles*, 3rd edn (Howlett, 1922).
*Housman, A. E., *A Shropshire Lad* (Grant Richards, 1915).
Hydra: see Appendic C.
*Joergens, Olwen A., *The Woman and the Sage, and Other Poems*, Little Books of Georgian Verse (Erskine Macdonald, Apr 1916).
*Keats, John, *Complete Works*, ed. H. Buxton Forman, 5 vols (Glasgow: Gowans & Gray, 1900–1).
*Keeble, Frederick, assisted by M. C. Rayner, *Practical Plant Physiology* (Bell, 1911). [Owen knew Miss Rayner, and probably Professor Keeble, at Reading in 1912.]
Kermode, Frank, *Romantic Image* (Routledge, 1957).
Keynes, Geoffrey, *A Bibliography of Siegfried Sassoon* (Hart-Davis, 1962).
Lane, Arthur E., *An Adequate Response: The War Poetry of Wilfred Owen and Siegfried Sassoon* (Detroit: Wayne State University Press, 1972).
Lang, Andrew: see *Theocritus, Bion and Moschus*.
*Larronde, Carlos (compiler), *Anthologie des écrivains français morts pour la Patrie*, 4 vols (Paris: Larousse, 1916).

*————, *Le Livre d'Heures* (Paris, 1913).
Léger, Albine: *see* Appendix A 2.
*Locke, J. W., *The Morals of Marcus Ordeyne* (Bodley Head, 1905).
MacCurdy, John T., *War Neuroses*, with a preface by W. H. R. Rivers (Cambridge University Press, 1918).
MacDonald, Stephen, *Not About Heroes: The Friendship of Siegfried Sassoon and Wilfred Owen*, play (Faber, 1983).
*Magnus, Laurie, *Introduction to Poetry* (Murray's School Library, 1902).
*Marsh, Edward (compiler), *Georgian Poetry 1916–1917* (Poetry Bookshop, November 1917).
Masefield, John, *The Everlasting Mercy* (Sidgwick & Jackson, 1911).
Masson, David I., 'Wilfred Owen's Free Phonetic Patterns: Their Style and Function', *Journal of Aesthetics and Art Criticism*, 13 (Mar 1955) 360–9.
Miyoshi, Masao, *The Divided Self: A Perspective on the Literature of the Victorians* (New York University Press and London University Press, 1969).
*Monro, Harold, *Before Dawn: Poems and Impressions* (Constable, 1911).
*————, *Children of Love* (Poetry Bookshop, 1914).
*————, *Strange Meetings* (Poetry Bookshop, 1917).
*Morris, Sir Lewis, *The Epic of Hades* (first published, 1877).
Murry, John Middleton, 'The Condition of English Poetry' (review), *Athenaeum* (5 Dec 1919) 1283–5.
————, 'The Poet of the War', *Nation and Athenaeum*, 28 (19 Feb 1921) 705–7.
*Nichols, Robert, *Ardours and Endurances* (Chatto & Windus, 1917).
Nordau, Max, *Degeneration*, tr. from the German (Heinemann, 1895).
O'Riordan, Conal, 'One More Fortunate', in *Martial Medley: Fact and Fiction* (Scholartis Press, 1931). [Contains a reminiscence of Owen.]
Orrmont, Arthur, *Requiem for War: The Life of Wilfred Owen* (New York: Four Winds Press, 1972).
Owen, Harold, *Journey from Obscurity*, 3 vols (Oxford University Press, 1963–5). *See also* Appendix A 7.
————, *Aftermath* (Oxford University Press, 1970).
*Oxenham, John, *The Vision Splendid: Some Verse for the Time and the Times to Come* (Methuen, Mar 1917).
Pearson, John, *Façades: Edith, Osbert, and Sacheverell Sitwell* (Macmillan, 1978).
Pound, Reginald, *The Lost Generation* (Constable, 1964).
Praz, Mario, *The Romantic Agony* (Oxford University Press, 1933; reissued, 1970).
*Renan, Ernest, *Souvenirs d'enfance et de jeunesse* (Paris: Nelson, n.d.).
Rivers, W. C., 'Mr Yeats Analyses his Soul', *Cambridge Magazine*, 7 (19 Jan 1918) 315–17.
Rivers, W. H. R., *Instinct and the Unconscious: A Contribution to a Biological Theory of the Psycho-neuroses* (Cambridge University Press, 1920).
————, *Conflict and Dream* (Kegan Paul, 1923).
Ross, Robert: *see* Appendix A 5.
Ross, Robert H., *The Georgian Revolt: Rise and Fall of a Poetic Ideal 1910–1922* (Faber, 1967).
*Rossetti, W. M., *Life and Writings of John Keats*, Great Writers (Walter Scott, n.d.).
Royal Academy Pictures (being the Royal Academy Supplement to *The Magazine of Art*), annual volumes (1888–1915).
Russell, Bertrand, *Justice in War-Time* (Chicago and London: Open Court, 1916).
————, *Principles of Social Reconstruction* (Allen & Unwin, 1916).

Rutherford, Andrew, *The Literature of War: Five Studies in Heroic Virtue* (Macmillan, 1978).

*Sassoon, Siegfried, *The Daffodil Murderer* by Saul Kain (John Richmond, 1913).

*———, *The Old Huntsman, and Other Poems* (Heinemann, May 1917).

*———, *Counter-Attack, and Other Poems* (Heinemann, June 1918).

———, *Sherston's Progress* (Faber, 1936).

———, *Siegfried's Journey 1916–1920* (Faber, 1945). [Ch. vi describes Owen.]

———, *Collected Poems 1908–1956* (Faber, 1961).

———, *Diaries 1915–1918*, ed. Rupert Hart-Davis (Faber, 1983).

———, *The War Poems*, ed. Rupert Hart-Davis (Faber, 1983).

Scott Moncrieff, C. K.: *see* Appendix A 6.

Seymour-Smith, Martin, *Robert Graves: His Life and Works* (Hutchinson, 1982).

*Shelley, P. B., *Complete Poetical Works*, ed. T. Hutchinson (Oxford University Press, 1912).

*Sherard, Robert H., *The Real Oscar Wilde* (T. Werner Laurie, n.d.).

*———, *Oscar Wilde: The Story of an Unhappy Friendship* (Greening, 1909 edn).

Silkin, Jon, *Out of Battle: The Poetry of the Great War* (Oxford University Press, 1972).

———, 'Owen: Elegist, Satirist or Neither; A Reply to Dominic Hibberd', *Stand*, 21, no. 3 (Spring 1980) 33–6.

Sinfield, Mark, 'Wilfred Owen's "Mental Cases": Source and Structure', *N&Q*, 29 (Aug 1982) 339–41.

*Sitwell, Edith (ed.), *Wheels 1917: A Second Cycle* (Oxford: Blackwell, 1917).

———,(ed.), *Wheels 1919: Fourth Cycle* (Oxford: Blackwell, 1919). [Dedicated to Owen, contains seven of his poems.]

———, *Selected Letters*, ed. John Lehmann and Derek Parker (Macmillan, 1970). [Contains ten letters to Mrs Owen, 1919–21.]

Sitwell, Osbert, *Argonaut and Juggernaut* (Chatto & Windus, 1919). [Includes war poems].

———, *Laughter in the Next Room* (Macmillan, 1949).

———, *Noble Essences or Courteous Revelations* (Macmillan, 1950). [Ch. iv is about Owen.]

*Sitwell, Sacheverell, *The People's Palace* (Oxford: Blackwell, 1918).

(*)Sorley, Charles Hamilton, *Marlborough, and Other Poems* (Cambridge University Press, 1916).

Stallworthy, Jon, 'W. B. Yeats and Wilfred Owen', *Critical Quarterly*, 11 (Autumn 1969) 199–214.

———, 'Wilfred Owen', Chatterton Lecture on an English Poet, repr. from *Proceedings of the British Academy*, 56 (Oxford University Press, 1970).

———, *Wilfred Owen: A Biography* (Oxford University Press and Chatto & Windus, 1974).

Steiner, George, *In Bluebeard's Castle: Some Notes towards the Re-definition of Culture* (Faber, 1971).

Stephan, Philip, *Paul Verlaine and the Decadence 1882–90* (Manchester: Manchester University Press, 1974).

*Swinburne, A. C., *Poems and Ballads: First Series*, Golden Pine edn (Heinemann, 1917).

*Symonds, John Addington, *Shelley*, English Men of Letters (Macmillan, 1909 edn).

Tailhade, Laurent: *see* Appendix A 3.

* *Theocritus, Bion and Moschus*, tr. Andrew Lang (Macmillan, 1906 edn).

Thorpe, Michael, *Siegfried Sassoon: A Critical Study* (Leiden: Leiden Universitaire Pers; London: Oxford University Press, 1966). [Reprints *The Daffodil Murderer.*]

Tsuzuki, Chushichi, *Edward Carpenter, 1844–1929: Prophet of Human Fellowship* (Cambridge University Press, 1980).

*Vachell, H. A., *The Hill: A Romance of Friendship* (Murray, 1905).

Walsh, T. J. (compiler), *A Tribute to Wilfred Owen* (Birkenhead: Birkenhead Institute, 1964).

Welland, Dennis S. R., 'Half-rhyme in Wilfred Owen: Its Derivation and Use', *RES*, 1 (July 1950) 226–41.

———, 'Wilfred Owen: The Man and his Poetry', unpublished PhD thesis (University of Nottingham, 1951).

———, 'Wilfred Owen's Manuscripts', two articles, *Times Literary Supplement*, 15 and 22 June 1956.

———, 'Sassoon on Owen', *Times Literary Supplement*, 31 May 1974.

———, *Wilfred Owen: A Critical Study* (Chatto & Windus, 1960; repr. with a postscript, 1978).

*Wells, H. G., *The Passionate Friends* (Macmillan, 1913).

*———, *The Wife of Sir Isaac Harman* (Macmillan, 1914).

———, *The World Set Free: A Story of Mankind* (Macmillan, 1914).

*———, *What is Coming? A Forecast of Things after the War* (Cassell, 1916).

(*)———, *God the Invisible King* (Cassell, May 1917).

White, Gertrude M., *Wilfred Owen*, Twayne's English Authors (New York: Twayne, 1969).

*Wilde, Oscar, *De Profundis*, ed. Robert Ross (Methuen, 1905).

*———, *Poems* (Methuen, June 1916).

———, *Works*, ed. G. F. Maine (Collins, 1948).

General Index

Index of Owen's Poems

Index of poems and fragments quoted or referred to in the text. For a note on possibly unfamiliar titles, see p. 208.

The first book to examine the full
development of Owen's poetic voice, this
critical biography by Dominic Hibberd
reveals Owen as a far more complex figure
than had previously been seen, as not so
much an unworldly idealist or a stolid
soldier–poet, but rather as a fugitive
dreamer from Edwardian society who
emerged from his solitude to share in the
agony and speak the dying words of his
damned generation.

Dominic Hibberd has taught at Manchester
Grammar School, Northwestern University,
and the Universities of Exeter and Keele.
He is the editor of *Wilfred Owen: War
Poems and Others*, *Poetry of the First World
War: A Casebook* and (with John Onions)
Poetry of the Great War: An Anthology.